Hard Questions? Real Answers!

Hard Questions?
Real Answers!

Biblically-based solutions for challenging questions of life and faith

Phil Shaw & Greg Palmer

The Christadelphian
404 Shaftmoor Lane, Hall Green, Birmingham B28 8SZ, UK

2021

First published 2021

© 2021 The Christadelphian Magazine and Publishing Association

ISBN 978 0 85189 446 1 (print edition)
ISBN 978 0 85189 447 8 (electronic edition)

Printed and bound in the UK by
Halstan & Co. Limited

Contents

Foreword

A FATHER of a young son, who had symptoms that match what we know as epilepsy, came to Jesus searching for a miracle. He had tried many things; probably he had tried everything he could, and so far nothing had worked. When Jesus told him all things are possible for believers, he responded with a memorable answer, "Lord, I believe; help my unbelief!" Perhaps what he meant was: 'I know that I should believe and I would like to, but I'm struggling; I have doubts and I need your help.'

Sometimes we find ourselves in a similar situation. Since we can't understand completely the mind or the operation of God, and often have inadequate answers, it can lead us to question the reliability of the Bible or even the reality of God. Perhaps we have heard conflicting or puzzling answers from a variety of sources and this only serves to deepen our doubt.

Many are obsessed with destroying the credibility of God and His word. While this is not a recent phenomenon, modern technology and access have multiplied its impact. The attacks on scripture and believers' faith can be challenging to combat either in our interactions with others or in settling the inner voice of doubt that seems to arise unbidden when we least desire it. The Pharisees, Sadducees and Herodians all took turns at asking these challenging and tempting questions of Jesus.

Jesus was caused to reflect on one occasion that such questions came from people who were "deceived, because you don't know the scriptures or the power of God" (Matthew 22:29, NET).

Statements in the Bible and circumstances of life are not always straightforward and we are often challenged to understand them. We may feel that these challenges distance us from God, or He becomes less relevant. We have devoted quite some time to answering these types of question also.

Along the way we have rediscovered a universal truth; it is much easier to ask difficult questions than it is to answer them! We do not suggest that the answers provided to the questions posed, are comprehensive, the only, or necessarily the best way of addressing the issues contained within. Our purpose has been to provide simple, yet credible solutions so that faith might be supported and thinking realigned to the divine mind. Some of these questions are among the most challenging spiritual questions in human experience. We hope to have provided the reader with a framework to consider them along with others that may arise.

We have grouped the questions into categories for the sake of presenting a simple structure. We have also tried to present a balance, and answer questions on a variety of subjects. Some of the questions might seem simple and yet have over the years been an ongoing source of debate and discontent; other questions are complex and are for that reason sometimes avoided. Some answers are short and straightforward, others are detailed and complex. Not everybody will agree on all of the answers. We have presented thoughts and principles for consideration and trust the individual's conscience to help them decide for themselves. It may be tempting to overlook the first two chapters that present foundation principles concerning God, humanity and divine revelation and move straight to the answers. We submit to the reader that the early sections underpin many of the answers and while they may seem superfluous, the messages within are critical to appreciating divine arrangements.

We need to remember that God is (for mortal humans) ultimately unfathomable. This is not an excuse designed to sidestep any difficult questions without offering a decent response; it is a reality. Isaiah expressed it this way:

> "Who has measured the Spirit of the LORD, or what man shows him his counsel? Whom did he consult, and who made him understand? Who taught him the path of justice, and taught him knowledge, and showed him the way of understanding?" (Isaiah 40:13,14, NKJV)

Until we are infused with divine nature there will always be doubts, and even then (if the experience of angels teaches us anything) questions.

We trust that the reader can bridge the gaps in our argument and logic with faith. We feel this to be an acceptable basis, for if we shall never be satisfied with anything less than complete and tangible evidence, we shall have at length left no room for faith which is so essential in coming to God and pleasing Him (see Hebrews 11:6). We trust that we have provided sufficient reasons upon which a solid and tangible faith may rest and that this will prove sufficient for the needs of this present life.

This book is not designed to provide answers to refute the *arguments of unbelievers* (though it may well do that), it is intended to strengthen and develop the *faith of believers*. Our purpose is to confirm truth in the mind of the believer.

We have tried to present clear principles to illuminate the enquiring mind and enable a weary doubter to regain their confidence in the unseen hand of God.

Phil Shaw and Greg Palmer
Australia, June 2021

Acknowledgements

Brethren Philip Davidson, Tony Lines, Colin Story and Sister Hayley-Rose Dangerfield by way of critical review helped to shape the unfinished document into the final manuscript. Brother Philip Davidson in his capacity as a medical practitioner with a special interest in mental illness also provided valuable insight into a number of issues. The assistance of these brothers and our sister is gratefully acknowledged.

Chapter 1

Foundation principles about God

"The universe we observe has precisely the properties we should expect if there is, at bottom, no design, no purpose, no evil, no good, nothing but blind, pitiless indifference." (Richard Dawkins, atheist)

"Sir, my concern is not whether God is on our side; my greatest concern is to be on God's side, for God is always right." (Abraham Lincoln, American President)

LET us start by thinking about the foundation truths concerning God and humanity that will have a significant bearing on the matters in question. We say foundation truths, because they support our faith and are clearly revealed in scripture.

Three 'O's and three 'I's

We will in these summary descriptions be considering the character and physical nature of God. It is possible to distil these down (for the purpose of brevity and recollection) to three words beginning with the letter 'O' and three words beginning with the letter 'I'.

Omnipotent

This word has come to us from the Latin *omnipotens* – which means all powerful. While it is only found once in scripture, the alternative English synonym *almighty* occurs nearly sixty times and always with reference to God. In Hebrew it is the word 'Shaddai' that is so associated with God that it forms half of one of the divine titles, *El Shaddai* (Exodus 6:3), usually translated as "God Almighty". We are being told that unlimited power is intrinsic to the nature of God. This is embodied in the words of Job: "The Spirit of God has made me, and the breath of the Almighty gives me life" (Job 33:4). When we come to the New Testament the idea of the *power* of God is assumed, and the focus of the Greek word represents more the *right* of God to rule because he is all powerful.

Bound up in the ideas of omnipotence are the power and sovereignty of God. The amazing Deity not only has the right to do as He pleases but the power to achieve it. God has the power always to do what He thinks or says. For example, God said, "Let there be light: and there was light" (Genesis 1:3, KJV).

Omniscient

This word is drawn from the Latin *omnisciens* meaning all-knowing. While not found in scripture, it is solidly biblical. Perhaps to illustrate the amazing breadth of God's knowledge we might do no better than cite two scriptures:

> "O LORD, you have searched me and known me! You know when I sit down and when I rise up; you discern my thoughts from afar. You search out my path and my lying down and are acquainted with all my ways. Even before a word is on my tongue, behold, O LORD, you know it altogether."
> (Psalm 139:1-4)

Of his Father, Jesus said:

> "Are not five sparrows sold for two pennies? And not one of them is forgotten before God. Why, even the hairs of your head are all numbered." (Luke 12:6,7)

Omnipresent

Again from a Latin word *omnipraesens* meaning everywhere present. The concept of being everywhere builds on the thought of being all knowing and so the Psalm continues:

> "Where shall I go from your Spirit? Or where shall I flee from your presence? If I ascend to heaven, you are there! If I make my bed in Sheol [the grave], you are there! If I take the wings of the morning and dwell in the uttermost parts of the sea, even there your hand shall lead me, and your right hand shall hold me." (Psalm 139:7-10)

Paul taught: "No creature is hidden from his sight, but all are naked and exposed to the eyes of him to whom we must give account" (Hebrews 4:13).

Immortal

In God's case this is underived absolute deathlessness (1 Timothy 6:16). Immortality was not given to God by anybody else but has always been part of Him. The phrase "from everlasting to everlasting" is found three times in the Psalms (90:2; 103:17; 106:48) describing variously the permanence, the mercy and the glory of God. The Apostle Paul writing to the Romans, picked up these thoughts:

> "For his invisible attributes, namely, his eternal power and divine nature, have been clearly perceived, ever since the creation of the world." (Romans 1:20)

Without understanding through experience, we thus realise that eternity defines God, as the prophet said:

> "For thus says the One who is high and lifted up, who inhabits eternity, whose name is Holy: 'I dwell in the high and holy place.'" (Isaiah 57:15)

When we look at the references to God's immortality, we discover that they are almost always associated with other characteristics of God (light, love, faithfulness, etc.) leading us to the conclusion that immortality is more than just deathlessness. In our minds we can associate everything good with the fundamental immortality of God.

Infinite

By this we mean limitless. All of the inherent characteristics of God are not restricted in time, space or extent. The idea applies to God in two ways. First His own powers are limitless: "Great is our Lord, and abundant in power; His understanding is beyond measure" (Psalm 147:5); secondly of the variety and extent of His works: "who does great things and unsearchable, marvellous things without number" (Job 5:9). God created times and seasons as we know them, and has put the very idea of eternity in our human heart – for the purpose that we should seek after it (Ecclesiastes 3:11; Acts 17:26,27).

Invisible

Invisibility does not mean that God has no form and is only a power or disembodied force; it rather means that *we* cannot see Him. Perhaps this is where the seeds of doubt are most easily sown. We might readily accept the previous astonishing features of God if only we could see Him. The Apostle Paul writing to Timothy penned these well known words: "He alone possesses immortality and lives in unapproachable light, whom no human has ever seen or is able to see" (1 Timothy 6:16, NET). We understand that what limits us from approaching or seeing God is our humanity. Flesh and blood cannot be in the presence of God and live. When Moses was shown the glory of God, he was shielded so he would not die. God said:

> "'You cannot see my face, for man shall not see me and live'. And the LORD said, 'Behold, there is a place by me where you shall stand on the rock, and while my glory passes by I will put you in a cleft of the rock, and I will cover you with my hand until I have passed by.'" (Exodus 33:20-22)

On the other hand, angels, said Jesus, "always see the face of my Father who is in heaven" (Matthew 18:10).

The righteousness of God

This is an often misunderstood or minimised concept. In order properly to appreciate God's dealings with us, and to answer the hard questions, we need to comprehend it and accept it. God's character is righteous.

- "For I will proclaim the name of the LORD; ascribe greatness to our God! The Rock, his work is perfect, for all his ways are justice. A God of faithfulness and without iniquity, just and upright is he" (Deuteronomy 32:3,4).

- "Gracious is the LORD, and righteous; our God is merciful" (Psalm 116:5).

God's perfect character can be summed up by two words, "grace" and "truth". Because of who God is, He always does the right thing at the right time for the right reasons. But ... and it is an enormous 'but', right is not defined by us, but by God. It matters not whether a mortal finite human thinks a thing to be right, what really counts is that God does, and that He will do the right thing always.

God's righteousness rests on the previously considered three 'O's and three 'I's. This means that not only is He right, but He will always do the right thing. Not infrequently do we find someone in government wanting to do the right thing but being quite unable to achieve it in practice for any number of reasons. This does not happen to God as Nebuchadnezzar found out, and was caused to exclaim, "none can stay his hand or say to him, 'What have you done?'" (Daniel 4:35).

God's righteousness is hard for us to understand because we are finite humans who cannot think like God or appreciate eternity. Accepting God's righteousness is not about us agreeing with God, but about us accepting that God will always be right whether we agree with Him or not. This is a challenging concept for us to come to terms with. It requires that we set aside our own ideas of what may be right and embrace the divine. Since God is eternal and infinite and we are not, the arbiter of right and wrong must only be God and not us. God's ways are truly much higher than ours. Yet for all that, God wants us to seek Him and use our free will to choose Him. This is the true essence of humility, seeing God for who He is in contrast to ourselves.

Righteousness is not *part* of God's character: it is a descriptor of the *whole* of it. Many have in their mind restricted the operation of the righteousness of God to things concerning the upholding of His holiness. There is no sense in which this need be the case. Such an approach might bring mercy, for example, into conflict with righteousness. In every sphere of God's dealings, including mercy (see Romans 3:25) His righteousness is evident. Mercy and righteousness are not antagonists: mercy is part of God's righteousness.

Accepting the answers to many of the hard questions means accepting the righteousness of God as a fundamental principle. Thus when a matter seems wrong to us, we can be taught to accept that it is right, because God is right. This is the essence of meekness or teachableness, accepting that God is right even when He doesn't make sense to us at the time.

God's sovereignty

This is simply the absolute right of God to rule and make decisions. It is based on all of the above characteristics of God that between them make it apparent that divine rule will be orderly and beneficent. Although not primarily about God Himself, these words of David make this connection quite plain:

"The Rock of Israel has said to me: When one rules justly over men, ruling in the fear of God, he dawns on them like the morning light."   (2 Samuel 23:3,4)

When Christ and God are finally honoured, the twenty-four elders of the vision cast down their crowns in subjection and declare:

"Worthy are you, our Lord and God, to receive glory and honour and power, for you created all things, and by your will they existed and were created."   (Revelation 4:11)

Taking that declaration piece by piece, it means sovereignty belongs to God because He is the great Creator and His deeds are right.

That being the case, we arrive at the conclusion that God not only deserves to reign but that he should do so unchallenged, as Nebuchadnezzar declared:

"Now I, Nebuchadnezzar, praise and extol and honour the King of heaven, for all his works are right and his ways are just; and those who walk in pride he is able to humble."
(Daniel 4:37)

For most of us, it is relatively easy to accept the sovereignty of God in matters that have little bearing upon ourselves. It is more difficult when we are personally involved. When we have a personal interest in a matter it is easy to suggest that if God's decision were different (i.e., more to our liking) then it would be superior. In this context we may start to question God.

The premise is simple. God is sovereign and does as He pleases and it will always be right despite anything we may think. The first characteristic of those who accept God is humility: simply accepting that God is greater than us. God is in heaven and we are on earth.

The reality of God

All of these attributes amount to one amazing being. The God of heaven and earth is so far removed from our experience and understanding that we struggle at times to accept all of these qualities, let alone understand them. The world that rejects God mocks these things as it does the people who believe them. It would be less challenging to accept the amazing, unfathomable Deity if He were universally accepted. The reason for rejection at the most basic level is human pride. We don't wish to yield to another, particularly One who makes demands of us we might rather not meet, so we reject Him. In order for that rejection to be both credible and complete, people feel it necessary to discredit God. So in a multi-faceted approach, the concept, the reality and the word of God are all targeted for sustained attack. Let us be quite clear: the object of human questioning in this way is not critical appraisal in order to make a fair and reasoned determination, but to justify a previously determined stance of rejection.

The by-product of such divine criticism can be that the faith of the believer is besieged by repeated onslaughts that can erode their confidence. Since the realities of the divine being are so far outside of our experience, doubt can readily creep in.

Despite the witness of the natural world about us that teems with examples of order, design and care, we know God principally through His revelation in the Bible. Without the things revealed to us in the Bible, we would be largely ignorant of the attributes, character and purpose of God. Questioning the existence of God, and doubting the credibility of His word amount to the same thing. If we discredit the one then we nullify the other.

The first attack on the existence of God seems always to be that nobody has ever had a reliable and reproducible experience involving God, and those who might have, are long dead. How is one to believe in something we can neither see nor experience? How can we accept the three 'O's and three 'I's when they are beyond us? To accept God requires faith; there is no doubt that this is the case. We cannot at this time *prove* the existence of God unequivocally by observation or interaction – faith must bridge the gap. But it is not blind faith. There is an impressive weight of evidence within and outside of the Bible that strongly suggests faith in God is not misplaced; we shall return to some of this in our final thoughts.

God could reveal Himself regularly and spectacularly to all inhabitants of this earth. In that He chooses not to, is not evidence that He does not exist, but rather reflects His desire for people freely to choose Him in faith. If the sky were lit up with personal daily messages, for example, then we would have no rational option but to accept God whether we wanted to or not. God rather wants us to elect to serve Him of our own free will. This is no cop-out for lack of evidence, for in truth the amazing detail of scripture amounts to the same weight of proof as a visible demonstration.

Chapter 2

Principles about humanity in relation to God

"To surrender to ignorance and call it God has always been premature, and it remains premature today." (Isaac Asimov, author)

"There are two kinds of people: those who say to God, 'Thy will be done,' and those to whom God says, 'All right, then, have it your way.'" (C. S. Lewis, author)

G OD might be magnificent and wonderful but the first thing to note about humans in comparison is contrast. As presently constituted our attributes do not compare to God. The power of God is contrasted with our weakness, His knowledge with our ignorance and so on. This places us in precisely the wrong position to examine the mind and operation of God. There is a sense in which we are so ill equipped to answer the questions that follow that it is scarcely sensible for us to ask them. It is as though a two-year-old was asked to examine and report upon the latest piece of technology. Perplexingly humans believe we have the mental equipment to match God, and in a battle of wits would emerge victorious.

In almost every sphere of modern science, those at the cutting edge of their field are likely to confess, 'we are just beginning to understand' or, 'there is just so much that we do not know'. Sadly this ignorance does not prevent us challenging God.

For those who choose to believe lies, God is able to send them confusing information that seems to confirm their own position. To the Thessalonians Paul wrote:

> "Because they refused to love the truth and so be saved, therefore God sends them a strong delusion, so that they may believe what is false, in order that all may be condemned who did not believe the truth but had pleasure in unrighteousness." (2 Thessalonians 2:10-12)

When we purposefully set our course against God we find that He fixes the course in place, providing us with the flimsy 'evidence' we desire to prove the case to our own satisfaction. To the genuinely enquiring mind God says, "seek and you will find" (Matthew 7:7), but to the unyielding heart of unbelief there is the promise of confusion and continued ignorance.

The nature of our heart

The Hebrew for heart (*leb* or *lebab*) is used very broadly but most often for feeling, will and intellect. Scripture has much to say about human hearts and sadly little of it paints us in a good light. In Jeremiah we read, "The heart is deceitful above all things, and desperately sick; who can understand it?" (Jeremiah 17:9). The answer clearly is, not any of us; but the prophet goes on to say that God does. The human heart questions God and rejects Him because it is most deceitful and incurably sick apart from God's action on it. David said, "Create in me a clean heart, O God, and renew a right spirit within me" (Psalm 51:10).

The challenges of a deceitful and corrupt heart are not restricted to unbelievers. The writer to the Hebrews warns:

> "Take care, brothers, lest there be in any of you an evil, unbelieving heart, leading you to fall away from the living God." (Hebrews 3:12)

All human hearts (emotive thoughts) are suspect when it comes to making fair and reasonable choices about God. So we need to be really careful in trusting our gut feelings or when it comes to making assessments about God.

The reasons for doubt

Once we have believed in God and His word why would doubt set in? Surely the matter would be settled from the beginning and not require reconsideration. Let us be clear, doubt is not the absence of faith. Remember Jesus said to Peter, "O you of little faith, why did you doubt?" (Matthew 14:31). The Lord did not say, 'you of no faith' – evidently doubt and faith co-exist in Peter's mind.

1. God stretches our faith with doubt.

God wants our faith to grow and get stronger and He does this by working our faith. Overcoming human doubt and trusting more in God, our faith goes from faith to more faith: "For in it the righteousness of God is revealed from faith for faith, as it is written, 'The righteous shall live by faith'" (Romans 1:17).

We are drawn to the idea that some doubt is necessary for faith. Think logically for a moment: if you have seen, felt, and witnessed something, there is no doubt – it is real! Faith is superfluous. If there can be no doubt, where is the need for faith? We do not need faith in tangible realities – we need faith in things we can't directly prove or demonstrate beyond any doubt. Faith by definition is the acceptance of something that has not been (and perhaps cannot be) empirically proven.

Doubt does not necessarily mean rejection of God. There are records of faithful men and women who doubted because the matter in question seemed incredible to them. For example, all of the disciples refused to believe in the resurrection until they received irrefutable proof, despite the combined message of scripture and the clear teaching of Jesus designed to prepare them for the event. The disciples were deaf to the message of Jesus concerning his death and resurrection because it was not what they wanted to hear, and resistant to the message of the women who had seen the risen Lord because they thought it was neither likely nor possible.

Abraham is perhaps the foremost example of one who did not doubt the incredible even when his own wife Sarah did, and is therefore upheld as the "father of the faithful". We read of Abraham:

> "In hope he believed against hope, that he should become the father of many nations, as he had been told, 'So shall your offspring be.' He did not weaken in faith when he considered his own body, which was as good as dead (since he was about a hundred years old), or when he considered the barrenness of Sarah's womb. No unbelief made him waver concerning the promise of God, but he grew strong in his faith as he gave glory to God, fully convinced that God was able to do what he had promised." (Romans 4:18-21)

Abraham knew that conception was physically impossible and believed anyway.

Peter, who initially had enough faith to walk on water towards his Lord, doubted and sank when he considered the strength of the wind. As Jesus caught the sinking disciple he asked him why he doubted. Perhaps it was all a matter of perspective and Peter saw big waves and a little Lord? Perhaps the test was just too great for him and his faith at that time? Perhaps he was simply afraid? We will not truly know until we meet him in the resurrection; but this we know, that Jesus was disappointed; not angry, but disappointed. This did not stop Jesus performing a faith-affirming miracle as they entered the boat and calming the wind in an instant, as if to say to Peter, 'there was no need for doubt, I had everything under control'.

2. Fear is a reason why we doubt and lose faith.

"And he [Jesus] said to them, 'Why are you afraid, O you of little faith?' Then he rose and rebuked the winds and the sea, and there was a great calm. And the men marvelled, saying, 'What sort of man is this, that even winds and sea obey him?'" (Matthew 8:26,27)

Fear is a fertile seedbed of doubt even for the faithful. Perhaps the greatest reason for doubt and fear might have been the circumstances that confronted Ananias. Saul of Tarsus had been wreaking havoc among the ecclesias in Judaea and was headed en route for Damascus living and breathing slaughter for the believers. God came to Ananias and asked him to visit Saul. We can imagine the fear with which Ananias responded to this divine commission to minister to Saul. If anybody had reason for misgivings it was Ananias. Christ dismissed his concerns in a sentence, sent him on his way – and he went! It is a testament to his great faith and meekness that he obeyed and did as instructed. Few of us would match his courage.

While almost certainly disappointed with doubts generated by fear, God is prepared to work with us to restore our confidence provided we do not reject Him. Moses, for example, was given two signs, and Gideon received not two or even three but four miraculous assurances that God was with him.

Peter when confronted with the prospect of the first Gentile convert was warned against doubting. It seems the divine mind knew the innate Jewish prejudice against Gentiles and gave him a threefold vision and the command, "Rise and go down and accompany them without hesitation, for I have sent them" (Acts 10:20). We are often possessed of manifold uncertainties and are capable of enormous procrastination when faced with something we never really wanted to do in the first place. God anticipated this and prepared Peter accordingly.

3. *Stubborn doubt.*

There is doubt born of a mind that does not want to believe and purposefully generates uncertainty to justify its position. Such were the Pharisees of Jesus' day. We might ask why did Gideon receive four signs and when the Pharisees asked for just one, yet the Lord rounded on them with a withering rebuke and gave them nothing? The answer perhaps lies in the motive behind the request. Gideon, a believer, was lacking confidence; the Pharisees as confirmed unbelievers (despite the many signs they had already been given) were seeking an excuse or a pretext for hatred and unbelief. Doubt can be a smokescreen for those who have an ulterior motive, some personal reason, a cherished but immoral pastime they are disinclined to give up. If you don't wish to yield to God then raising a myriad of intellectual, moral and physical objections may provide a measure of dishonest comfort. Dishonest – because the real objection lies not in any of the unanswered hard questions about God but has to do with an "evil, unbelieving heart" (Hebrews 3:12).

Doubt may also come from a heavy heart burdened with trials. The circumstances of life can challenge us and make us wonder where God is in all of the things that happen.

With so many records in scripture of men and women who struggled with doubt it is clear that humanity is doubt-prone. Let us be careful that our doubts only arise from inner weakness and not the pride of human strength. The one receives strength and encouragement delivered with compassion and the other condemnation.

Faith and reason

There is no doubt that we are intended by God to think and to form logical judgements about scripture and about spiritual things. Paul advised the Philippians:

"Whatever is true, whatever is honourable, whatever is just, whatever is pure, whatever is lovely, whatever is commendable, if there is any excellence, if there is anything worthy of praise, think about these things." (Philippians 4:8)

The purpose of such thinking is to "understand the way of your [God's] precepts" as expressed by the Psalmist (Psalm 119:27).

Where does reason sit in the life of a believer? Is faith generated by reason? Can we think our way towards faith and so be converted? Faith has its origin in God (see 1 John 5:4) but reason is entirely human. We suggest then that faith must be the primary, and reason a secondary force in the mind of a believer. Reason must be subject to faith, and not faith to reason. That is by no means to suggest that we have an illogical faith, but that in the minds of each of us are concepts we struggle with and things we do not yet understand; if our faith is based solely on reason it can collapse in the face of challenging questions. The wise man wrote:

"I saw all the work of God, that man cannot find out the work that is done under the sun. However much man may toil in seeking, he will not find it out. Even though a wise man claims to know, he cannot find it out." (Ecclesiastes 8:17)

There will always be things beyond our grasp and inevitably there will be times in our life when we cannot make sense of God. What will happen to our faith if it is based solely on reason? We need to develop what we might term 'a biased faith', biased in favour of God. That is a faith that believes the best of God (even when things seem otherwise), based upon what we know of Him. Faith must transcend reason, such that we can confidently affirm, 'I do not know what God is doing or how He is doing it but I trust Him'.

Reason must serve our faith and not the other way around. Should the questions of life, the disappointments and trials be allowed to challenge our faith? No! They certainly challenge our understanding but we must not let them challenge our faith.

Paul says, "faith comes from hearing, and hearing through the word of Christ" (Romans 10:17); and "whatever was written in former days was written for our instruction, that through endurance and through the encouragement of the scriptures we might have hope" (Romans 15:4). The combined weight of Paul's words is that scripture read (or listened to) and heeded is the basis for faith and hope.[1] If we do not hear the word of God then faith is impossible. We need to take time to ponder the word (mind) of God and faith will be the result. If faith comes by hearing, then greater faith should result from greater hearing. However to the Hebrews is added: "The message they heard did not benefit them, because they were not united by faith with those who listened" (Hebrews 4:2). Hearing the word of God is a prerequisite for faith but it does not *automatically* generate faith. It is possible to hear and not develop faith. Earlier Paul wrote to the Romans, "with the heart one believes and is justified" (Romans 10:10). We note that he did not say, 'with the mind one believes and is justified'; that is to suggest that our heart must play a significant role in the development of faith. Conviction happens in the heart.

To the Corinthians Paul wrote:

> "My speech and my message were not in plausible words of wisdom, but in demonstration of the Spirit and of power, so that your faith might not rest in the wisdom of men but in the power of God." (1 Corinthians 2:4,5)

We are coming nearer to understanding the origin of faith: it comes from hearing and it rests on the power of God. These things are quite accessible and yet Paul candidly observes, "not all have faith" (2 Thessalonians 3:2). Where does faith come from? Putting all our thoughts together Jesus said in the

---

1   We note in passing that the ESV uses the alternative rendering "word of Christ" where the KJV has "word of God". There is no disharmony here for the word of God is about Christ and what Christ said, came from God.

explanation of the Parable of the Sower: "As for that in the good soil, they are those who, hearing the word, hold it fast in an honest and good heart" (Luke 8:15). Faith is the result of good and honest hearts hearing the word of God. Human philosophy is neither necessary nor necessarily helpful.

The exercise of human reasoning may in fact be a barrier to faith; Paul observed that, "the world did not know God through wisdom" (1 Corinthians 1:21). We have known some who through the unchecked influence of human reason have lost their faith but never anybody who through faith has lost their reason. Deep thinking about God and His ways is a very helpful thing, but it must always be supportive and minister to our faith rather than direct and control it. Isaiah pleaded on God's behalf, "Come now, let us reason together" (Isaiah 1:18).

In his last address to the nation of Israel Moses said:

> "The secret things belong to the LORD our God, but the things that are revealed belong to us and to our children forever, that we may do all the words of this law."
>
> (Deuteronomy 29:29)

This means that there are some things we shall never know. There are divine secrets that are hidden from us. No amount of human reasoning will unlock them. However, enough has been revealed to us that we can understand and obey. We need to understand clearly the nature of divine revelation; things are not always in plain sight – we may have to seek them out. This is God's way of selecting those who desire to learn of Him. We find Him when we seek. This concept is explained in the words of the wise man: "It is the glory of God to conceal things, but the glory of kings is to search things out" (Proverbs 25:2). This does not mean that we can search out all God's secrets. With finite minds probing the infinite things of God, there are many things we shall never fully understand. If reason cannot comprehend, that is no cause to say that faith should not accept.

How God teaches – the unfolding plan and revelation of God

Because we only occupy such a small point in time relative to God it can be difficult to grasp that we are part of an unfolding plan that God has had from the beginning. This is the amazing story of redemption recorded from Genesis to Revelation. It's sometimes tempting to doubt God's wisdom in the way He has decided to reveal Himself through history. It is apparent that God has decided to reveal His purpose with the earth to us, gradually and progressively. We can see the development and evidence of God's revelation to us as follows:

1. *Creation.* "For what can be known about God is plain to them, because God has shown it to them. For his invisible attributes, namely, his eternal power and divine nature, have been clearly perceived, ever since the creation of the world, in the things that have been made. So they are without excuse" (Romans 1:19,20).

2. *Conscience.* Developed by God giving law: that is, humans knowing right from wrong, good from evil. "For when Gentiles, who do not have the law, by nature do what the law requires, they are a law to themselves, even though they do not have the law. They show that the work of the law is written on their hearts, while their conscience also bears witness, and their conflicting thoughts accuse or even excuse them on that day when, according to my gospel, God judges the secrets of men by Christ Jesus" (Romans 2:14-16).

3. *The nation of Israel.* God revealed Himself through this people and the law He gave them: "[They] are Israelites, and to them belong the adoption, the glory, the covenants, the giving of the law, the worship, and the promises. To them belong the patriarchs, and from their race, according

to the flesh, is the Christ who is over all, God blessed for ever. Amen" (Romans 9:4,5).

4. **Christ.** God revealed Himself through Jesus Christ. "Long ago, at many times and in many ways, God spoke to our fathers by the prophets, but in these last days he has spoken to us by his Son, whom he appointed the heir of all things, through whom also he created the world. He is the radiance of the glory of God and the exact imprint of his nature, and he upholds the universe by the word of his power" (Hebrews 1:1-3).

Conscience to God based on creative revelation lasted approximately the first 2,000 years, the Law given to Israel the next 2,000 years and since then we are in the Christian era. It must be noted that all through the epochs of revelation the three elements of faith, hope and love have always been essential to grasp for salvation.

- **Faith** – believing God at His word and not rejecting God;
- **Hope** – the confident expectation of what God has promised; and
- **Love** – for God and our fellow neighbours.

Many Jews (and some Christians) have misunderstood the place of God's revelation through the Law of Moses and struggled with the transition to Christ. Two extremes have emerged; either people are reluctant to embrace Christ and cling to the Law, or they relegate the Law to a place of unimportance as a historical curiosity.

In order to understand the Law given through Moses to Israel, we need first to appreciate its purpose. It was a divinely arranged code to regulate behaviour and direct the mind towards faith in God. Concerning the regulations of the Law, Paul wrote to the Colossians, "these are a shadow of the things to come, but the substance belongs to Christ" (Colossians 2:17).

The shadow cast by the Law is seen in two ways:

1. A symbolic representation of the relationship between God and man (the present);

2. A foreshadowing of the purpose of God in reconciliation (the future).

Regarding the first of these, Paul declared the purpose of the Law to be, "that every mouth may be stopped, and the whole world may be held accountable to God" (Romans 3:19). Concerning the second, he wrote to the Hebrews, "the law has but a shadow of the good things to come" (Hebrews 10:1). This disqualifies us from thinking that the Law was an end in itself, and makes it clear that there was something better to follow. If we miss this purpose of the Law we are likely either to elevate it to a place it was never intended to occupy, or dismiss it as irrelevant. The Law of Moses was never designed to save. Consider these words of Paul to the Galatians:

> "So then, the law was our guardian until Christ came, in order that we might be justified by faith. But now that faith has come, we are no longer under a guardian, for in Christ Jesus you are all sons of God, through faith."   (Galatians 3:24-26)

These teach us some fundamental things about the purpose of the Law:

- It was intended to bring us to Christ;

- Its primary purpose was only until Christ;

- It was designed to teach faith.

Those who either cling to the requirements of the Law believing that it saves, or who demand that the Law has ongoing enforceable meaning either in addition to, or instead of, faith in Christ, have missed the points Paul made. Writing to the Romans Paul is even more direct. He says:

"But now we are released from the law, having died to that which held us captive, so that we serve in the new way of the Spirit and not in the old way of the written code."

(Romans 7:6)

This doesn't mean that there is no point for believers in Jesus reading and thinking about the Law of Moses; but it rather means we should use the principles in the Law to focus our minds on Jesus.

The Law of Moses was given to Israel and was for Israel; it was never intended to be applied to other nations. The focus of God at that time was with Israel. The features of the Law were fulfilled in Jesus and the focus of God's dealings broadened to include all nations.

The grand principle of God's salvation is faith. The Law was designed to inspire faith, but sadly the people of Israel largely missed that lofty calling and rather descended to the thought that adherence to law saves. Jesus complained to the Pharisees, "you tithe mint and dill and cumin, and have neglected the weightier matters of the law: justice and mercy and faithfulness" (Matthew 23:23). It remains to this day a challenge to see the Law as inspiration to faith in Jesus and not as a legalistic end in itself.

Some of the difficult questions that we shall consider later arise from a misapplication or a misunderstanding of the intended scope of the Law of Moses. While many of the principles behind the Law are enduring, the Law itself was never to be a binding code for all time, nor was it a means to salvation. The Law taught that there are consequences to human behaviour but it did not provide solutions; rather it directed Israel to God's provision in faith.

Free will and consequences

There can be no doubt that man was created with the freedom of choice, and that the misguided exercise of that freedom has resulted in many unpleasant consequences. From the earliest moments of human history this has been clearly the case:

> "And the LORD God commanded the man, saying, 'You may surely eat of every tree of the garden, but of the tree of the knowledge of good and evil you shall not eat, for in the day that you eat of it you shall surely die.'"   (Genesis 2:16,17)

If Adam and Eve were not free to choose, then the passage just quoted is meaningless. They were allowed to choose any tree; but if they choose the forbidden tree, the consequences would be dire. It has ever been the case that choices have consequences; it is almost Newtonian, for every action there is a corresponding consequence.

There is no suggestion in scripture that sin took God by surprise. We can't imagine Him saying in bewilderment, 'Well I didn't think that would happen'. God, knowing as He does the future, must have known the consequences of poor choice. In creating us as beings with free will He must have understood what would eventuate when we abused our divinely given freedom in stubborn rebellion. This silently instructs us how greatly God must have valued the exercise of personal freedom from both the divine and human perspectives and how gratifying it would be when it worked well.

We might observe, almost in passing, that our free will is somewhat different from that of Adam and Eve in the Garden of Eden. When they made their choice there were no predisposing factors like proneness to sin or constraining circumstances which for us limit the absolute freedom of choice.

Parents often give instructions limiting behaviour in order to keep their children safe – which a child may choose to follow or not. In the same way, God has clearly set boundaries limiting behaviour. He told the people of Israel that:

"If you will diligently listen to the voice of the LORD your God, and do that which is right in his eyes, and give ear to his commandments and keep all his statutes, I will put none of the diseases on you that I put on the Egyptians, for I am the LORD, your healer."   (Exodus 15:26)

Whether or not the unpleasant consequences (in this case the diseases of Egypt) were experienced, depended on the response of the people to divine law in the first place.

Parents of very young children who doubt the ability of the child to understand or physically manage circumstances of everyday life take a very 'hands on' approach and try to prevent a child from making harmful choices. Some people feel that God should adopt the same attitude and treat us as children in order to prevent us from making bad choices and suffering unpleasant results in consequence. Essentially this would involve God intervening in our life removing free choice. This may sound better for us, but was not what God chose to do. When God elected to give us free will He did so because obedience freely chosen when we could have disobeyed, love freely offered when we could have withheld it, are infinitely superior virtues that would not have been possible otherwise. While divine intervention sounds good, thinking through the ramifications, it is not as good as it seems. As parents teaching a child to ride a bicycle we allow them to ride on their own, only when they have demonstrated a degree of proficiency to enable them to do it safely; even then we provide rules and boundaries designed to keep them safe. Imagine a child being able to ride a bicycle but never allowed to do so without the guiding hand of a parent running alongside or in the absence or training wheels. In order to have them experience the joy of riding free, a parent must step back. Inherent in this action is the acceptance of the occasional mistakes. Direct parental intervention in the case of a child who can ride well is rare. As the child gets older and more capable, direct parental intervention is usually resented regardless of the motivation. We suggest that this analogy may help us to see how God acts with us. Much of the suffering in our lives and the world is a direct consequence of God allowing us free will and taking a very 'hands off' approach. Without free will there can be no such thing as the "obedience to the faith" (Romans 1:5, KJV).

In the life of Abraham we are only given a handful of occasions where God intervened in the circumstances of everyday life interspersed by years of seeming inactivity. It would appear that God allowed him to make unwise choices in Egypt and Gerar that threatened to derail His purpose with Isaac as the promised seed. Why didn't God intervene? Clearly God acted to rescue Abraham from the situation he had created, why did He not prevent the unwise choice in the first place? The most logically compelling answer is that God wanted Abraham to learn from his mistakes.

There are occasions where God was consulted to confirm a choice before it was acted on (see Judges 20:23; 2 Samuel 2:1; 5:19) and there were occasions where men failed to consult God and met with confusion and disaster (see Joshua 7:7; 1 Chronicles 13:12). However for the most part, God was not personally active in the choices of men and women in scripture. Rather He laid down principles for life and expected that reasonable choices based on divine guidelines would be made.

Among the Gentile nations for years God largely left them to their own devices. This was summarised by Paul when preaching against idolatry; he said, "the times of ignorance God overlooked" (Acts 17:30). In fact, God has intervened in the general affairs of the world in catastrophic widespread judgement causing the death of everybody only twice that we know of: once in Noah's time and once in judgement on Sodom and Gomorrah. We have no information to suggest that any other major natural disaster occurred as the direct result of the intervention of God. Putting together the histories of Jew and Gentile, God has been remarkably 'hands off' for most of our existence, leaving us to follow Him (or not) and to receive the consequences of our choice.

Some people feel that a loving God would, or should, intervene and stop bad things happening on a personal level. Life is not like that. Where it gets difficult for us to process is when other people make poor choices and we are impacted by the consequences. We might ask, 'how is that fair?' A drunk driver hits a mother with a pram and she is killed leaving the baby a disabled orphan: people ask, 'Why did God allow that?' Some would say, 'God should have been involved, He should have stopped it!' What they are mostly suggesting is, that God should have stopped the consequences; seldom would anybody advocate that God should have curtailed the freedom of either the drinker or the mother going for a walk. As noted before, God has subjected this creation to vanity and a certain meaninglessness and sorrow. We should use our free will to seek God and find hope.

The desire to have God intervene positively in our lives is quite strong. The desire not to have God intervene negatively in our lives is even stronger. Many people don't stop to think that those two things cannot co-exist. God can either take a 'hands on' approach, in which case He will curtail free will and prevent us from doing anything silly in order to limit unpleasant consequences; or He can take a more distant role in which we are free to make choices and must accept the consequences that follow.

Are "time and chance" active in the lives of believers in the same way as others, or does God superintend our lives to a much greater extent than those who reject him? It is clear that ultimate deliverance is the happy future of God's people but does that mean exemption from the challenging circumstances of life now? When Paul said, "for those who love God all things work together for good" (Romans 8:28) he meant, that God will see that all things (good and evil as we perceive them) under His wise supervision turn out for the best. This accords with the words of the Psalmist: "Many are the afflictions of the righteous, but the LORD delivers him out of them all" (Psalm 34:19).

The experiences of life, and our understanding of consequences, are necessary in our preparation for eternity because they are to do with our character development. Even Jesus learnt obedience through the suffering he experienced. Why do some seem to endure much and others little? We cannot say. What we can say is that God is shaping us for His kingdom and glory and only He knows what is best. God works with our choices, not against them; He will not compel. It will only be those who desire immortality (and hence godliness) who will be made equal unto the angels. Those who do not desire God and His ways will not be dragged kicking and screaming to God's kingdom. All are allowed to make a choice. It is clearly God's desire that we all choose Him, but He will not force us.

Ultimately answerable to God

The natural consequence of choice is accountability. In the world in which we live, on a natural and spiritual level we are obliged to take responsibility for our actions. This harmonises with the message of Paul to the Corinthian believers:

> "We must all appear before the judgment seat of Christ, so that each one may receive what is due for what he has done in the body, whether good or evil."   (2 Corinthians 5:10)

God will not hold those accountable who have lived and died in ignorance of Him. Those in ignorance of God are not different from the animals in death – they simply perish (Psalm 49:20). They are not tortured or punished; their lot is simply to cease:

"Their love and their hate and their envy have already perished, and forever they have no more share in all that is done under the sun." (Ecclesiastes 9:6)

The judgement of which Paul wrote, is for those who are enlightened, who know what God expects and are therefore especially accountable.

What must be acknowledged (at least in the writings of Paul if not elsewhere) is the number of times that reference to the judgement is omitted entirely when writing to believers. Paul often moves straight from resurrection to reward, for example:

"The dead in Christ will rise first. Then we who are alive, who are left, will be caught up together with them in the clouds to meet the Lord in the air, and so we will always be with the Lord." (1 Thessalonians 4:16,17)

Paul was not confused. He did not teach one thing to one group of believers and a different thing to another. The reason for the frequent omission is the presumption of a favourable judgement for believers. Paul occasionally omits the judgement, not because it doesn't happen at all, but since it is favourable, it doesn't change the outcome for a believer.

Since believers in Jesus Christ love their Lord, trust him and arrange their lives with his return in view, the presumption of Paul is a reasonable thing. The confidence of Paul is instructive:

"I have fought the good fight, I have finished the race, I have kept the faith. Henceforth there is laid up for me the crown of righteousness, which the Lord, the righteous judge, will award to me on that day, and not only to me but also to all who have loved his appearing." (2 Timothy 4:7,8)

For all those who like Paul "have loved his appearing" an award of the imperishable crown of righteousness *will* be made. In what does Paul's confidence rest? Doubtless it comes from the very purpose of the sacrifice of Christ; our Lord died to save us not to condemn us. Will Christ who died because of our sins, reject us on account of sin? The very idea is absurd! Sin forgiven has been dealt with and will not be used against us. Only the wicked will be rejected because of their sins.

"The Lord knows those who are his" (2 Timothy 2:19) – he does not need a process to reveal them to him. Likewise the Lord is clear about those he doesn't know and it is for this reason that they will be sent from his presence (Luke 13:27). What function does the judgement serve? The judgement will reveal to all what is at this time known only to God and Christ – who are truly God's people and who are not. Jesus will not be making a choice then; he will be revealing to all the choice we have made now. The judgement is not spoken of in terms that indicate a lengthy process; rather it is described as being "as a shepherd separates the sheep from the goats" (Matthew 25:32). One does not imagine a shepherd needing to take time over each animal as if he was unsure; it is not deciding so much as sorting.

Some might say, what of the passage that says, "I tell you, on the day of judgement people will give account for every careless word they speak, for by your words you will be justified, and by your words you will be condemned" (Matthew 12:36,37)? This does not mean that the decision will be deferred until judgement day and based on our explanation of hastily spoken words – but that the decision revealed then, will have been framed by what we have said and done now. A careless word – one uttered without thinking, reveals what is truly in our heart. We might choose our words carefully so as to convey a certain impression but our heart is often revealed in the word uttered without thought.

Scripture reveals those who seek to argue their case with the Judge are destined for disappointment (Matthew 7:22,23). The decision will have already been made and is simply awaiting pronouncement. Any explanation will be for our benefit alone.

Some may be amazed at the grace of God and will be assured of their inclusion; others may be surprised at their rejection and will be reminded of their neglect of Christ (see Matthew 25:35-46).

With those foundational principles concerning God and our relationship to Him in place we now move to consider specific questions. We can take these principles concerning the nature of God and man with us as we consider the answers to the hard questions that follow. We trust that the answers in the pages that follow may encourage the faint-hearted and convince those with a wavering faith of the certainty of the unseen hand of God that is mighty to save us.

Chapter 3

Questions about God

"Isn't it enough to see that a garden is beautiful without having to believe that there are fairies at the bottom of it too?" (Douglas Adams, author)

"God is ever before my eyes. I realise His omnipotence and I fear His anger; but I also recognise His compassion, and His tenderness towards His creatures." (W. A. Mozart, composer)

Why did an omnipotent God take six days to create everything, and why did He require rest on the seventh day?

The question hints at the idea that God might not really be as powerful as we have presented him to be. Concerning the creation of Adam, Eve and marriage, Malachi asks, why did God make one man and one woman and then unite them to be one? The answer is helpful in our investigation, "what was the one God seeking? Godly offspring" (Malachi 2:15). God clearly had a purpose (a godly seed) in creating Eve from Adam and arranging their union. God could have created Eve in the same way as Adam but did not. While the divine method might seem curious to us, it was done intentionally to serve His purpose. It is clear that God was doing more than merely creating; He was teaching lessons about life as well as providing the best circumstances for His purpose to succeed. God did not run out of energy at the end of each day and so could only accomplish a certain amount and no more. Isaiah dismisses the very idea when he wrote, "The LORD is the everlasting God, the Creator of the ends of the earth. He does not faint or grow weary" (Isaiah 40:28).

So the six days, and the seventh have significance to the greater purpose of God. At the end of that creative week we read:

> "By the seventh day God finished the work that he had been doing, and he ceased on the seventh day all the work that he had been doing." (Genesis 2:2, NET)

Here the Hebrew word translated in many versions as "rested" is more helpfully rendered as "ceased". It simply means God stopped creating. He didn't stop working *per se*, as Jesus reminded the Pharisees: "My Father is always at his work to this very day" (John 5:17, NIV). If God actually rested (i.e., had not continued to do what needs to be done in order to maintain life) one might imagine everything would have perished.

The writer to the Hebrews makes a comparison between the Sabbath and the rest to come, the millennial kingdom of God (Hebrews 4:1-11). The days of creation are symbolic of longer periods (1,000 years each) in the purpose of God with the earth, as we know it. The process of creation was purposefully arranged to show us these lessons and to leave us in anticipation of a joyful Sabbath in the future.

The re-creation of the bodies, minds and memories of countless thousands in the resurrection is said to occur "in a moment, in the twinkling of an eye" (1 Corinthians 15:52). Had God not desired to teach the lessons embedded in the Genesis record, one imagines the original creation might have been similarly instantaneous.

If God is all knowing, why did He make humans? Surely He knew that many of us would end up dying and that He would eventually have to send Jesus to his death to fix things?

If God knows the end from the beginning, then human failure and sin should have been anticipated from the outset. It is then argued that to create mankind knowing they would fail is a foolish enterprise and from there that God is either unsound or lacking in foreknowledge.

We might first note that nowhere is Jesus described as an afterthought. To the contrary there are passages that describe him as being integral to God's plan, such as, "This was according to the eternal purpose that he has realised in Christ Jesus our Lord" (Ephesians 3:11). The failure of mankind in the Garden in Eden did not take God by surprise. He had already factored it into His plans. We might ask why then did He not improve upon creation from the beginning? Why commence with a flawed model?

It would have been perfectly possible for God to make only divine beings when He set out to fashion the earth as we know it. The Psalmist tells us in the context of God making the earth, "he makes his messengers winds, his ministers a flaming fire" (Psalm 104:4). Clearly God was capable of making us as angels, yet did not. He made a deliberate choice to create humans. Why?

We know that angels are "mighty ones" and "do his word, obeying the voice of his word" and are "ministers, who do his will" (Psalm 103:20,21). It simply would not do, to have immortal powerful agents of God capable of choosing against God, so they aren't able to! Angels as they are constituted, do not have a choice to serve God – they do and they must – and they enjoy it! While this, as the Psalm suggests, means they do God's pleasure, their service is automatic and instinctive. In that God chose what we might describe as the 'inferior' option (capable of choice) to populate the earth it is presumably because if (and when) they choose of their own free will to serve Him, it would be tremendously gratifying in a way that could not be said if He had created us as angels.

While it is true that countless millions have rejected God, many thousands have not. In the magnificence of the divine plan for this earth (that always included Christ), salvation to man and immense pleasure to God are the two crowning achievements that would not have been realised had God chosen a different model. When God at length grants immortality to those who desire it (Romans 2:7) and they become "equal to the angels" (Luke 20:36) the joy that this gives to the redeemed and the Redeemer will demonstrate once and for all that the creation of mankind was not an experiment in futility but a master plan of the masterful God. The declaration will then be made in genuine thankfulness:

> "Worthy are you, our Lord and God, to receive glory and honour and power, for you created all things, and by your will they existed and were created." (Revelation 4:11)

How do you reconcile the foreknowledge of God and divine pre-determination with human free will?

By divine foreknowledge we mean the ability of God precisely to know the future. This is something that God claims to be capable of, for example:

> "I am God, and there is no other; I am God, and there is none like me, declaring the end from the beginning and from ancient times things not yet done, saying, 'My counsel shall stand, and I will accomplish all my purpose.'" (Isaiah 46:9,10)

That this is within God's ability to do is supported by numerous prophecies that have come true with unerring accuracy.

Pre-determination is about God making a choice that affects the future of either a person or an entire nation, even before they are in existence. Such divine choices can impact us negatively by excluding us, or positively by including us. God's pre-determination in a positive sense is explained by Paul, "those whom he foreknew he also predestined to be conformed to the image of his Son" (Romans 8:29). In a negative sense, Paul wrote of Esau and Jacob:

> "Though they were not yet born and had done nothing either good or bad – in order that God's purpose of election might continue, not because of works but because of him who calls – she was told, 'The older will serve the younger.'"
>
> (Romans 9:11,12)

Human free will is simply the ability of people to make choices about their behaviour and beliefs without being forced into any course of action against their wishes by somebody else. When Joshua spoke to Israel and asked them to, "Choose this day whom you will serve" (Joshua 24:15) it was clear this was a real exercise of free will: they had a choice.

The concern for many is this: supposing that God, knowing the future, can see that we will disobey His laws; since God's foreknowledge is absolute, then it is pre-determined that we will disobey God's law. Doesn't this remove free will? Furthermore, since God is liable to punish us for disobedience, how is that fair since it was God who determined our future?

Happily, we have an example in scripture to help unravel the matter. The example concerns the Pharaoh of ancient Egypt.[1] God revealed to Moses that Pharaoh would not let Israel go and that He would punish Pharaoh for not letting Israel go (Exodus

---

1   This example will be used in this answer and the next two.

3:19,20). Added to this thought God said that He would harden Pharaoh's heart. It may seem on the surface of things that Pharaoh got a raw deal. Commenting on this incident Paul wrote to the Romans, "You will say to me then, 'Why does he still find fault? For who can resist his will?'" (Romans 9:19). The question anticipated by Paul suggests that we might think that Pharaoh had no choice. We will return to the question of God hardening Pharaoh's heart later, but for the moment let us focus on God's knowledge.

The issue is this: did God's foreknowledge affect the outcome, or was it just advance knowledge of what outcome Pharaoh would choose? The question really arises because we as humans can only know the future with certainty if we fiddle with the circumstances to rig an outcome, in the way a conjurer might do. The suggestion is, that God interferes with our choice in a way that is unfair.

We might explain it in this way. A parent knows their child well enough to be a reasonable judge of what they might choose in a given situation. With some success we can determine what the child will freely choose, without influencing that choice. Now, suppose we previously wrote down what we believed the outcome of a choice would be, and we were proved correct; nobody would suggest that our success in predicting the outcome in anyway forced the child into making the choice we anticipated. If we are to guess correctly (and for us it will always be a guess) then we need to know our child well. The better we know our child the more likely our prediction will be accurate. Imagine if we could see inside our child's mind and knew absolutely everything about them and precisely how they thought. We might get the prediction correct all the time. This is perhaps a window into the operation of the foreknowledge of God.

Time moves in only one direction for us – forwards. For us to witness something occur, means that it has already happened. While stopping short of declaring God capable of time travel (but why not?), we might simply remark that God is not bound by time as we are and can alter time (see Isaiah 38:8, for example). Quite how it works for God we cannot be certain (and we are not told) but it is clearly not the same as for us. Physicists might argue passionately for one theory or for another, but it is generally accepted that there is probably a fourth dimension (space / time) that can be altered in such a way as to facilitate time travel. If anybody knows about this and can do it, surely God could. This may provide an explanation for how He knows the future so accurately – perhaps He has already seen it?

Putting all these pieces together, it is clear that God knows the future accurately. But this does not mean that He thereby takes away our free will, merely that He knows what direction our free will is going to take and can use it to His advantage in outworking His purpose. Peter, knowing that God was in control and had foreseen the death of Jesus, still laid the blame firmly at the feet of the Jews when he said, "this Jesus, delivered up according to the definite plan and foreknowledge of God, you crucified and killed" (Acts 2:22). The foreknowledge and plan of God did not mitigate Jewish culpability at all. It was not God's fault but theirs.

How was hardening Pharaoh's heart reasonable?

This question suggests that God treated Pharaoh unreasonably in forcing his hand to refuse Israel permission to leave and then punishing him and Egypt for choices he was never free to make.

We might first note that Pharaoh made a personal and deliberate choice against God and denied the request to let Israel go, before God did anything at all. We note that God "hardened" Pharaoh's heart, He did not direct it. The hardening of Pharaoh's heart was not against Pharaoh's wishes but quite in keeping with his previously revealed intention. In this matter it was Pharaoh not God who made the choice. This explanation accords with the primary meaning of the Hebrew word translated "hardened" – to become stronger. Pharaoh's heart was already set on a course, God simply made it stronger and fixed the direction in place. God did not set Pharaoh on a course he had no mind to pursue.

Secondly it is instructive to consider the circumstances in which the heart of Pharaoh was hardened. Initially it was by allowing, or facilitating the Egyptian magicians to mimic the miracle of a rod becoming a snake (Exodus 7:11-13), so Pharaoh felt that the miracle of Aaron's rod becoming a snake was something he could replicate and was not therefore a divine miracle. Here we notice that Pharaoh was given an excuse to reject the power of God and he willingly took it.

On the occasion of the first plague when the Egyptian magicians replicated the miracle, Pharaoh again hardened his heart (Exodus 7:22). At the end of the second plague (8:15), Pharaoh, seeing that the frogs had lessened, saw no reason to keep his word and hardened his heart. During the third plague, despite there being no respite and his servants correctly identified the hand of God (verse 19), Pharaoh elected to harden his heart. At the end of the fourth plague when Moses removed the flies (verses 31,32), again Pharaoh elected to harden his own heart. At the end of the fifth plague, despite realising that not a single beast in Israel's camp had died and the plague must have been heaven-sent, Pharaoh hardened his heart (9:7). After the plague of boils it is recorded that "the LORD hardened the heart of Pharaoh" (verse 12). After the plague of hail Pharaoh hardened his own heart even further than God had done (verse 34). After the plague of locusts (10:20), the plague of darkness (verse 27) and after the death of the firstborn (14:8), God hardened Pharaoh's heart and fixed the outcome.

God did nothing that Pharaoh was not prepared to do and had done previously himself. As the rejection of the works of God mounted, so God became more against Pharaoh until in the end there was no going back. Pharaoh had deliberately chosen to reject God to the extent that the divine hand cemented him into this path. As was discussed in the previous answer, God knew the direction Pharaoh would take and He used it to suit His own divine purpose. Pharaoh chose to close his mind to the operation and will of God before ever God acted in response. Of the eleven times where the heart of Pharaoh was hardened, six of them were entirely his own choice. It cannot be credibly suggested that what God did was against the wishes of Pharaoh. Quite to the contrary, Pharaoh made his own bed and chose to sleep in it, well before God intervened. Circumstances proved that God's use of Pharaoh was entirely reasonable.

The question remains, *how* did God harden Pharaoh's heart? Perhaps the answer lies in the connection of ideas presented in scripture. For example in Exodus 10 we read, "Not a single locust was left in all the country of Egypt. But the LORD hardened Pharaoh's heart" (verses 19,20). It would seem that God, knowing how Pharaoh would respond, manipulated circumstances to cause him to respond in the way God had determined. Thus the action of God might well be less on the heart of Pharaoh and more on the circumstances that would influence Pharaoh's choice.

This suggestion is in keeping with the record in Daniel 10 where an angel confides that the Prince of Persia who "withstood me twenty-one days" frustrated him. How might a mere man withstand an angel for three weeks? The only answer that serves reason is that the angel was manipulating circumstances (rather than the man) and had yet to find the right strings to pull. This interpretation is supported by the vision in 1 Kings 22:19-22. When Rehoboam made the choice to reject the delegation that came to ask him to ease the burden of taxation, there were divine movements unseen and unrecorded that no doubt provided impetus for him to make his choice in the way God intended, for we read:

"It was a turn of affairs brought about by the LORD that he might fulfill his word, which the LORD spoke by Ahijah the Shilonite to Jeroboam the son of Nebat." (1 Kings 12:15)

How God did it we are not told, but clearly Rehoboam retained his choice for it was he alone who rejected the counsel of the elders in favour of the ill-fated advice of his peers.

How is divine choice fair?

Is it right for God to choose what the destiny of a person might be? Again we might use Pharaoh as an example. God said to Pharaoh, "But for this purpose I have raised you up, to show you my power, so that my name may be proclaimed in all the earth" (Exodus 9:16). We might ask, how is it fair for God to arrange Pharaoh for the express purpose of failure? That being the case he never had a chance.

The answer is in two parts. First as we have already noted, Pharaoh had a choice and he made it. Secondly, God as the sovereign creator has the right to do exactly as He pleases. God is described in scripture as a potter and us as the clay. The metaphor is particularly appropriate because we are essentially constituted from the soil and return to it at death. In considering the Pharaoh question Paul wrote:

"But who are you, O man, to answer back to God? Will what is moulded say to its moulder, 'Why have you made me like this?' Has the potter no right over the clay, to make out of the same lump one vessel for honourable use and another for dishonourable use?" (Romans 9:20,21)

Imagine if clay could talk and one pot complained to the potter that it was fashioned into a bedpan and would rather have been a teapot. A bedpan seemed distasteful and a teapot much more satisfactory. The point being made by Paul is, what right does a pot have, to say to the potter, 'why have you made me for this purpose'? God has absolute discretion in achieving His purpose and can choose as He wishes. In any case, Pharaoh by his repeated recalcitrance confirmed the validity of God's choice.

Since God knows the end from the beginning, His choice is impeccable. God does not force us down a particular course, we do that ourselves. He merely uses the knowledge of what we will choose to do and the sort of person we will become to pre-plan arrangements. This allowed God to say (with perfect reasonableness) of Jacob and Esau before they were born, "The older will serve the younger. As it is written, Jacob I loved, but Esau I hated" (Romans 9:12,13). God knowing the sort of person each would prove to be made a choice before the characters were known to any man, and time proved His choice to be sound. God did not force Esau to reject Him or for that matter coerce Jacob to love Him: they each made their own choice – God merely knew what it would be and so made His choice ... in advance. This is the right of a sovereign God.

Is God unfair in His treatment of us?

Yes! Everyday He graciously loads us with blessings we have no right to expect and mercifully withholds punishment that our sins demand (see Psalm 103:1-11). Since this divine unfairness is entirely favourable to us, nobody seems to mind. You are unlikely ever to hear the complaint, 'God is unfairly generous and large-hearted'. However, this is precisely the case. Were we to be treated as our sins warrant we would be destroyed, and if we only received blessings we deserved then we would almost never get anything. The fact of the matter is – God absolutely does not treat us fairly and we should be forever thankful.

The answer just given in all probability did not answer the question as it might have been intended. Read the other way, the question might suggest that God treats us harshly. Having already considered that God does not treat us as we deserve but deals with us altogether more kindly than that, it is almost pointless to explore the possibility; however, for the sake of completeness, we will.

Let us first look at the simplest of divine blessings – rain and sunshine. We read, "For he makes his sun rise on the evil and on the good, and sends rain on the just and on the unjust" (Matthew 5:45). Far from being unfair in the distribution of these blessings they are freely offered to all whether they are pleasing to God or not. Humans tend to think that we deserve blessings, that we have a right to them – we don't! What about punishment? Jeremiah asked, "Why should a living man complain, a man, about the punishment of his sins?" (Lamentations 3:39) Since the wages of sin is death (Romans 6:23), a living man clearly has not been punished as his sins deserve and therefore has no reason for complaint. Not only so but the mercy of God is available to all who seek Him. Paul explained to the Romans that it was the desire of God to "have mercy on all" (Romans 11:32).

The person who asks this question of God is possibly thinking less on a communal scale and more about their personal circumstances. The question then becomes, 'Is God unfair in His treatment of *me*?' While a generic answer may not suffice for everybody, an individual answer is not possible. What we will briefly do, is look at the circumstances of one man and see how God treated him and whether he thought God was reasonable and fair or not. The man is Job. At the beginning of the book, Job suffered some horrendous trials that were either sent by God, or allowed by God. Almost everything he had was lost (see Job 1:1–2:8). When his wife suggested that they might as well curse God and die, Job responded with a rhetorical question, "Shall we receive good from God, and shall we not receive evil?" (Job 2:10). Job realised that God works in our life through all circumstances, blessing and misfortune. Through the record of the book of

Job. God was at work in the life of Job and his friends to make them more like Him. By the time this process had finished we read, "And the LORD blessed the latter days of Job more than his beginning" (Job 42:12). Commenting on Job's life, James later wrote:

> "You have heard of the steadfastness of Job, and you have seen the purpose of the Lord, how the Lord is compassionate and merciful."   (James 5:11)

If on reflection, not even Job with all of his trials got a raw deal from God, then surely none of us has reason to complain.

Chapter 4

Questions about the Bible

"To be fair, much of the Bible is not systematically evil but just plain weird, as you would expect of a chaotically cobbled-together anthology of disjointed documents, composed, revised, translated, distorted and 'improved' by hundreds of anonymous authors, editors and copyists, unknown to us and mostly unknown to each other, spanning nine centuries." (Richard Dawkins, atheist)

"There are more sure marks of authenticity in the Bible than in any profane history ... I have a fundamental belief in the Bible as the word of God, written by those who were inspired. I study the Bible daily." (Isaac Newton, scientist)

Is the entire Bible inspired?

At a conference at University College London on 'Evolution and Religion' in the 1950s, the theologian who gave the opening address cast doubt on the early chapters of Genesis and concluded that they were myths and legends. A young man in the audience questioned him whether if Genesis was mythical, shouldn't we consider other parts of scripture mythical also. The famous evolutionary biologist and atheist J. B. S Haldane responded:

"The Bible claims from beginning to end to be the inspired, infallible word of God. Either this claim is true, or it is false. There is no halfway position. If it is false (as I believe) then there is no foundation for Christianity at all. If it is true (as this young man believes) then Christians are obliged to accept all the Bible. There just isn't any logical alternative." (cited in *God's Truth*, by Alan Hayward, pages 110,111)

When Paul wrote, "all scripture is breathed out by God" (2 Timothy 3:16) does that mean that we are literally intended to accept it in its entirety? In a word, the answer is "yes". The foundation of our faith depends on scripture being correct. Either we have followed "cleverly devised myths" or the testimony of men who "spoke from God as they were carried along by the Holy Spirit" (2 Peter 1:16,21). There is no middle ground.

We cannot, we must not ignore or reject passages of scripture that are personally challenging or uncomfortable. We either accept the Bible as the word of God or we reject it. The suggestion that to harmonise scripture with modern thought (scientific or social) we might omit or reduce the force of parts of the text has no sound basis.

Commonly it is the Old Testament that suffers from the dismissive approach. A cursory reading of the Gospels will suffice to inform us that Jesus believed the Old Testament narrative. The Gospels abound with quotes from the Old Testament both concerning Jesus and citations made by Jesus. Consider the following list of events and people recorded in the Old Testament that Jesus endorsed in his teaching:

- Creation of Adam and Eve (Matthew 19:4,5).

- Murder of Abel by Cain (Luke 11:51).

- Noah and the flood (Matthew 24:37).

- The destruction of Sodom (Luke 17:29-32).

- Abraham and foreshadows of Jesus (John 8:56).
- Moses and the burning bush (Mark 12:26).
- Manna from heaven (John 6:31-51).
- Moses and the brazen serpent (John 3:14).
- David and the sacred bread (Mark 2:25).
- Solomon and the Queen of Sheba (Matthew 12:42).
- Elijah and the widow of Zarephath (Luke 4:26).
- Elisha and the healing of Naaman (Luke 4:27).
- Jonah and the great fish (Matthew 12:39-41).

If Jesus believed in the inspiration of all scripture there is no reason for us to reject any of it.

Why sixty-six books in the Bible and how did we get them?

The word 'canon' referring to the accepted and accredited scriptures, comes originally from a Greek word *kanon* and is similar in meaning to the Hebrew word *kaneh* that means an accepted measure or measuring instrument. This suggests that the writings needed to conform to a standard before being accepted as scripture, and that there was some sort of process to assess the writings.

Originally only the first five books were accepted as the word of God. These were grouped together and known collectively as "Moses" (after the principal author, 2 Corinthians 3:15), "the book of the law" (2 Kings 22:8,11) or "the book of the covenant" (2 Kings 23:2). By the time Jesus walked the earth the historical and poetical books (known as "the writings") and prophets had been added, and the Hebrew scriptures (as we know them) were established and accepted as the word of God by the Jewish people. Jesus referred to "the Law of Moses and the Prophets and the Psalms" and called them "the scriptures" (Luke 24:44,45). Numerous references to the Law, Psalms and prophets by Jesus leaves us in no doubt that he regarded them as the word of God. A reference to the "second Psalm" in Acts 13:33 further gives us to understand that there was order and structure (though not necessarily always the same order that we have today) to the collected scriptures.

In the times after the exile, Jewish records suggest that Nehemiah was the one who collected the entire writings together and supervised what was included and what was not. This is recorded in the Maccabees:

> "The same things are reported in the records and in the memoirs of Nehemiah, and also that he founded a library and collected the books about the kings and prophets, and the writings of David."   (2 Maccabees 2:13, NRSV)

We thus have thirty-nine Old Testament books by the time of Jesus. Interestingly, the books of the Maccabees did not themselves make it to the accepted canon of Old Testament scripture leaving the authenticity of the story in doubt.

The scriptures had been translated into Greek a few hundred years before Jesus and the resulting Septuagint translation (so named because there were approximately seventy scholars involved) was in routine use in Jesus' day. In our times it is common to call the Hebrew scriptures, the Old Testament. This name is first referenced by Paul who concerning the blindness of the Jews wrote, "for until this day remaineth the same vail untaken away in the reading of the old testament" (2 Corinthians 3:14, KJV). While modern versions almost always use the word "covenant", the term "Old Testament" for the Jewish scriptures, has stuck.

After Malachi, God did not speak through a prophet for about 400 years until John the Baptist. Jesus made it clear that

John marked a new era when he said, "For all the Prophets and the Law prophesied until John" (Matthew 11:13). Jesus promised:

> "When the Spirit of truth comes, he will guide you into all the truth, for he will not speak on his own authority, but whatever he hears he will speak, and he will declare to you the things that are to come." (John 16:13)

So it was in fulfilment of Jesus' words that the Christian era had a new set of inspired writings and these are commonly known as the "New Testament". All of the books that are accepted in the New Testament canon were written before AD 120 when the Holy Spirit was known to be operating among believers.

Peter at least had an understanding that the writings of Paul were scripture when he wrote:

> "Our beloved brother Paul also wrote to you according to the wisdom given him, as he does in all his letters when he speaks in them of these matters. There are some things in them that are hard to understand, which the ignorant and unstable twist to their own destruction, as they do the other scriptures." (2 Peter 3:15,16)

Paul on his part writes with apostolic authority and claims to be inspired by the Lord. This is clearly suggested by the exception in the first letter to Corinth where he makes it clear that the instruction concerning unbelieving partners is a personal recommendation and not an instruction from Christ, "To the rest I say (I, not the Lord)" (1 Corinthians 7:12). This exception proves the rule that his letters carried Christ's endorsement. There is no doubt that the first century ecclesia accepted the word of the apostles as binding whether written or oral.

Paul cites either from Luke 10:7 or Matthew 10:10 in the first letter to Timothy and refers to it as scripture, "For the scripture says ... 'The labourer deserves his wages'" (1 Timothy 5:18). Polycarp of Smyrna writing in approximately AD 108 to the believers at Philippi makes it clear that the four Gospels, 1 Peter, the Pastoral Epistles, Hebrews and at least some of Paul's letters were read and accepted.[1] For example Polycarp wrote, "it is said in these scriptures, Be ye angry and sin not, and let not the sun set on your wrath".[2] Polycarp has clearly cited from Ephesians 4:26 and regards it as scripture.

The earliest list we have of New Testament scriptures is known as the Muratorian canon (named after Muratori who discovered it in 1740) and it contains all of the books we currently endorse with the exception of Hebrews, James and 2 Peter. The Muratorian canon is believed to have been written in Rome towards the end of the second century. However, it was not until AD 367 that we have historical evidence of a list that is identical to our modern Bible.

Without there being any established rules to which we may refer, there were some basic principles that appear to have underpinned decisions concerning a book's claim to be a genuine part of the New Testament scripture. These were:

- Had the book been written or endorsed by an apostle?

- Had the book been widely accepted as genuine by the church?

Any writings that failed this test were excluded. Hebrews took quite some time to be accepted universally because the eastern Church accepted Paul as the author (and therefore accepted Hebrews as scripture) whereas the western Church remained unconvinced that Paul was the author. Non-apostolic authorship was a significant hurdle to acceptance.

The resultant canon of New Testament scripture contains twenty-seven books. We can safely dismiss the notion that the Church of the fourth century (by then corrupt) was instrumental

---

1   See *The early Church from the beginnings to 461*, W. H. C. Frend, page 42.

2   Polycarp's letter to the Philippians, 12:1, translated by J. B. Lightfoot.

in establishing the canon, rather it merely endorsed what had been accepted for several centuries. In a scholarly essay Steven Voorwinde concluded:

> "We can be absolutely certain and not just 'practically' certain about the status of the canon, but our certainty does not depend upon our study of historical data, but it comes from our faith in the sovereignty and providence of God."[3]

This means that God personally saw to it that New Testament scripture was preserved and genuine.

Doesn't the textual inaccuracy of the modern Bible mean it is unreliable?

Presented as it usually is – a rhetorical question – this is rather more a statement than a question. It is supposed that the text of the Bible is inaccurate; so much so that it cannot be relied upon to represent anything like truth. The statement suggests that the original texts have been so corrupted over the years that what we have now is an unreliable shadow of its former self. Those who support such a view advance that even if the text once expressed the mind and purpose of God, it now is suspect and should be discarded.

The uncovering of what are known as the Dead Sea Scrolls in 1947 has revealed texts covering every Old Testament book except Esther. Archaeological and historical evidence points to the scrolls having been written in the first or second century BC. Without detailing the evidence (there are many fine works that do so), we might simply report that there is no evidence that the textual accuracy of the Hebrew scriptures is questionable to any appreciable extent. Brother Derek Banyard records:

3   *The formation of the New Testament Canon.*

"The value of all this to us must be that the scholars found no substantial differences between these ancient scrolls and the manuscripts from which our own Bible today has been translated." **4**

This is in no small way due to the fastidious efforts of Jewish scribes down through the ages who copied the texts meticulously.

It must be conceded that things are not as certain for the Greek scriptures. It was largely the Western Catholic and Eastern Orthodox churches who had the resources and the skills in translation that preserved the Greek scriptures for us. Unfortunately there was often more reverence for the Church than for the word of God and the Jewish fastidiousness was at times lacking in their efforts. As a result there can be some minor variations between the various copies handed down over the years. This occasionally results in some verses being omitted from some modern versions or some minor differences in wording of a character not seen in the Old Testament texts. A Bible reader will often find that a well-published Bible (with translational notes) is quite transparent regarding these minor differences. One such obvious case is 1 John 5:7 where the KJV reads, "For there are three that bear record in heaven, the Father, the Word, and the Holy Ghost: and these three are one". It is now accepted by almost every authority that much of this verse was added in the fifth century and thereafter in Latin versions only. The disputed words were first found in Greek in the Complutensian Version published in 1522. A modern version such as the ESV reads, "For there are three that testify: the Spirit and the water and the blood; and these three agree".

We submit that these minor textual differences do not materially affect the reliability of the message or its ability to make us "wise for salvation through faith in Christ Jesus"

---

4 *God's Living Word*, page 164.

(2 Timothy 3:16). We cannot logically suggest that God would demand faith in scripture and then allow the same scripture to be so compromised that faith is impossible. There has been so much investigation into these minor discrepancies that it is clear that the Biblical critics would have made an exceedingly loud noise had anything of significance been uncovered. While the New Testament text is in some minor points uncertain, the major thrust and teaching is clearly accurate and reliable.

In summary, there is no evidence that the modern scriptures are not exactly what they purport to be, the word and mind of God.

The Bible contains so many contradictions, how can it be right?

This can be an unsettling consideration for a person who has not thought about it previously. On the face of it, the question seems legitimate – the Bible *does* contain contradictions. There are two principal types of contradiction in scripture:

1. The intended contradiction. For example, "God is love" and "God is a consuming fire".

2. The translational conundrum. For example, different descriptions, words or numbers used for the same event.

In relation to the first of these, readers are directed to an excellent work by Brother Len Richardson. A quote from the book will set us on the correct path from the outset.

"There are in the Bible a great many apparent contradictions which are clearly designed to challenge men to think out the meaning. We shall never arrive at Truth by setting one statement against another or by barricading our minds behind one concept to the exclusion of all others. Many of the inspired writers of scripture delighted in the use of paradoxes to present their message, and unless we take this into account we may never arrive at the proper balance." [5]

We shall not be attempting to reproduce Brother Richardson's efforts. We will examine just a few contradictions in later sections. It is the second source of contradiction that we will examine more closely at this time.

Why do translational conundrums even exist? We have probably all heard the phrase 'lost in translation'. This makes it clear that conveying a message from one person to another (even in the same language) is not always straightforward. Problems in translation are well known. At which point some might say, 'Since you have no idea what should be what, why bother at all?' This would be a significant blunder. The straightforward message of the Bible in fundamental terms is uncompromised by challenges of a translational nature. The nature and purpose of God with this earth are clearly evident in translations in many different languages.

There are different types of translation of scripture. Some of them, usually the more paraphrased ones, take intentional liberties with the text to suit the purposes of the translation and may not be relied upon for textual accuracy to the same extent as the more literal translations. Contradictions in the paraphrased versions are to be anticipated. Some modern dynamic versions of the Bible such as *The Message* or *The Living Bible* should not be relied upon fully to represent the original meaning.

In Biblical Hebrew there are just over 8,500 words and in Biblical Greek just under 6,000; however, in English in the seventeenth century when the KJV was written there were more than 60,000 words and now there are more than 150,000. This makes it easy to see that many Hebrew or Greek words get translated in multiple different ways and that the translation may

---

5   *Balancing the Book – a study of biblical paradoxes*, page 1.

have accidentally contributed to a conundrum. For example, the Hebrew word *elep* might mean an ox, a prince, a captain, a family or (most commonly) the number 1,000. A translator might not have understood the intent of the text well enough to choose the most appropriate meaning in English. In Micah 5:2 the KJV reads of Bethlehem, "though thou be little among the thousands of Judah"; this has been amended in more modern versions to reflect a different meaning of *elep* and the word "families" or "clans" is used instead of "thousands". We suggest that the answer to the discrepancy presented between the counts in Numbers 25:9 and 1 Corinthians 10:8, might have a similar explanation. This type of translational problem is relatively rare and does not affect the integrity of the message *per se*.

Sometimes the translation is lost in a cultural or geo-political void. We cannot expect ancient writers would understand modern culture and circumstances any more than we easily comprehend ancient society. Implements, practices and cultural norms that have long since disappeared may present as tremendous challenges to modern translation. It is easy to see how, despite the best of intentions, the meaning is at times obscured or contradictory.

Since few of us understand Biblical Hebrew and Greek well enough to read the Bible in its original form, we rely on translations. Where there are contradictions we need to go back to the original languages (with the assistance of Biblical language tools) and personally seek to resolve them. In around eighty years of combined investigation, the authors have not found any translational contradiction that was not able to be satisfactorily resolved in this way.

Variation in a story may be evidence of authenticity. Eyewitnesses to an event will seldom give exactly the same testimony and may differ on important details. Courts of law are wary of witness testimonies that are identical in every respect as it suggests collusion. We submit that the minor variation in the Gospel records suggests that the witness is genuine without being fabricated. Rather than reject the Bible on account of apparent inconsistency, the reader is encouraged to "search out a matter" (Proverbs 25:2). We are confident those who search in this way will discover for themselves that the scriptures are reliable. Searching out the meaning of a previously uncertain or completely obscure passage of scripture can be very fulfilling and bring tremendous joy.

Why is there no explanation of the origin of angels?

There are many things the Bible does not reveal. This question is really suggesting that God ought to have known that we would want to know such things and that either He didn't foresee our questions, in which case His omniscience is suspect, or they have been left out because the answers are embarrassing, which calls in question His omnipotence. We need to remember the purpose of scripture is not to give us answers to everything – our human brains could not comprehend or retain the information in any case. God has though His divine power "granted to us all things that pertain to life and godliness" (2 Peter 1:3) and revealed them to us in His word. If we are not told, it is because we have no need to know. That the information given is selective we may infer from a study of history. There is so much that could have been recorded and was not. The Apostle John offers this explanation near the conclusion of his Gospel:

> "Now Jesus did many other signs in the presence of the disciples, which are not written in this book; but these are written so that you may believe that Jesus is the Christ, the Son of God, and that by believing you may have life in his name." (John 20:30,31)

The angels are included in the list of things created by God that should therefore praise Him, "For he commanded and they were created" (Psalm 148:5). There is some evidence that angels may once have been mortal (Revelation 19:10; 22:9) but where and when that was (if it indeed was the case) we do not know. Possibly the statement, "Behold, the man has become like one of us in knowing good and evil" (Genesis 3:22) reflects that angels may once have been subject to conditions as we are now and learned the difference between good and evil by experience as we do. What we do know, is that angels are empowered by the spirit of God and are His ministers working to further the divine purpose with the world and us (Psalm 103:20,21; Hebrews 1:7,14).

The Proverbs record, "It is the glory of God to conceal things, but the glory of kings is to search things out" (Proverbs 25:2). While we can search many things out in this life, perhaps it will not be until we are "kings" that we will have the ability and access to complete that task. We can look forward to a myriad of years in which to learn the answers with a mind capable of processing the information.

Why are there no modern prophets?

In the final words of the book of Revelation dictated to John by the angel of the Lord we read:

> "I warn everyone who hears the words of the prophecy of this book: if anyone adds anything to them, God will add to that person the plagues described in this book." (Revelation 22:18)

This clearly gives us to understand that the work of prophets had now ceased and the final prophecy (Revelation) had been given. While the words may specifically refer to the book of Revelation, extending the principle more broadly seems appropriate. The prophecy of Revelation covers all the time between when Jesus gave it and the culmination of God's purpose. There is no requirement for us to know more – we have what we need. The answer may simply be, there are no modern prophets because He has already given us all the messages we need.

This question might suggest that since God does not give us any open visions today, He is unfair; or that if there are no modern prophets, then in all probability there were no ancient ones either, and the claims on behalf of scripture are false.

Jesus addressed the first question in the parable of the rich man and Lazarus. The rich man having missed out on the reward wanted somehow to get a message to his family to ensure they did not miss out. The response was, they have Moses and the Prophets (Old Testament scriptures), let them read them. The rich man replied that if a resurrected messenger visited them then that would be sufficient to provoke repentance. Jesus said, "If they do not hear Moses and the Prophets, neither will they be convinced if someone should rise from the dead" (Luke 16:19-31). The message of the parable is that scripture itself is of such magnificent and sufficient character that it renders subsequent prophetic revelation and miracle superfluous. Simply put, if we have scripture, we have all we need to develop a faith pleasing to God.

The question might also hint at the lack of credibility of the scripture. If we had a modern prophet surely this would settle the matter and demonstrate the truth of God. It is a small leap to conclude that the reason for the absence of modern prophets is that the phenomenon of prophets is false. While there are no current prophets, the message of the ancient prophets is very current and being fulfilled as we speak. There is no absence of divine activity, merely no further revelation. The validity of a prophet rested on the fulfilment of his prophecies (Deuteronomy 18:21,22) and whether they spoke according to previous "teaching and testimony" (Isaiah 8:20). By that measure the prophets of scripture are thoroughly vindicated.

On a side note, in modern times, those who set themselves up (or who are put forward by others) as prophets are almost universally questionable in either teaching, practice or prophetical fulfilment and by those measures are exposed as fraudulent. Since Apostolic times the completed scriptures, the ultimate gift of the Holy Spirit, have provided all we need.

Why does the Bible discourage critical thought?

We read in the Proverbs, "The simple believes everything, but the prudent gives thought to his steps" (Proverbs 14:15). The advice of Paul to Timothy was, "Think over what I say, for the Lord will give you understanding in everything" (2 Timothy 2:7). These two quotes alone give us to understand that God intends us to use our brain critically. Logic demands that if we were not intended to think, then a more basic brain would have sufficed.

If "critical thought" means delving into the purpose of God and the responsibilities of man as revealed in the Bible, then we have every encouragement to indulge it. However, if it means pointless speculation of hypothetical questions or matters significantly beyond the revelation of God, these are dismissed as "foolish, ignorant controversies" (2 Timothy 2:23) and, "irreverent babble and contradictions of what is falsely called knowledge" (1 Timothy 6:20). God knowing our constitution perfectly, realises that such things because they are not of faith and love, will only "breed quarrels" rather than build us up.

We are to use our mind to decide whether a thing is in keeping with the revealed mind of God or not. Isaiah wrote:

> "To the teaching and to the testimony! If they will not speak according to this word, it is because they have no dawn [KJV, light]."
> (Isaiah 8:20)

The Berean believers took this to heart and were commended because "they received the word with all eagerness, examining the scriptures daily to see if these things were so" (Acts 17:11). The Apostle John encouraged his readers to "test the spirits to see whether they are from God, for many false prophets have gone out into the world" (1 John 4:1).

Paul wrote:

> "The unbeliever does not receive the things of the Spirit of God, for they are foolishness to him. And he cannot understand them, because they are spiritually discerned. The one who is spiritual discerns all things, yet he himself is understood by no one." (1 Corinthians 2:14,15, NET)

He was not suggesting that critical thinking is replaced by spirituality, but that spirituality opens the mind to divine possibility and thereby aids critical thought.

While the Bible encourages critical thought concerning the things of God it rightly discourages thoughts critical *of* God. The one leads us to ask, seek and find, resulting in peace and joy, and the other will leave us impoverished of sense and bewildered. On one hand we are encouraged:

> "Whatever is true, whatever is honourable, whatever is just, whatever is pure, whatever is lovely, whatever is commendable, if there is any excellence, if there is anything worthy of praise, think about these things." (Philippians 4:8)

On the other hand we are warned: "Who are you, O man, to answer back to God?" (Romans 9:20).

We may use our mind for critical thought but take care that we are not like those of whom Paul warned Timothy: "always learning and never able to arrive at a knowledge of the truth" (2 Timothy 3:7); or have "itching ears" and "accumulate for themselves teachers to suit their own passions" (2 Timothy 4:3).

Chapter 5

Questions about Israel

"Now just behold these miserable, blind, and senseless people ... their blindness and arrogance are as solid as an iron mountain ... Therefore the blind Jews are truly stupid fools ..." (Martin Luther, theologian)

"Some people like the Jews, and some do not. But no thoughtful man can deny the fact that they are, beyond any question, the most formidable and most remarkable race which has appeared in the world." (Winston Churchill, British Prime Minister)

How was it fair that God chose Israel and not any other nation?

The basis for the choice of the nation of Israel was explained by Moses:

"You are a people holy to the LORD your God. The LORD your God has chosen you to be a people for his treasured possession, out of all the peoples who are on the face of the earth. It was not because you were more in number than any other people that the LORD set his love on you and chose you, for you were the fewest of all peoples, but it is because the LORD loves you and is keeping the oath that he swore to your fathers." (Deuteronomy 7:6-8)

To explore this further we need to go back to the ancestor of the Jewish people, Jacob. God made a promise to Jacob:

"'No longer shall your name be called Jacob, but Israel shall be your name.' So he called his name Israel. And God said to him, 'I am God Almighty: be fruitful and multiply. A nation and a company of nations shall come from you, and kings shall come from your own body. The land that I gave to Abraham and Isaac I will give to you, and I will give the land to your offspring after you.'" (Genesis 35:10-12)

From this we see that both the nation and the land of Israel were the subject of promises to the ancestral patriarchs of the Jewish race. God will always keep the promise that He made even though Israel has proved nationally unworthy of such elevated status. On the eve of their inheritance in the promised land God made it clear that it was:

"Not because of your righteousness or the uprightness of your heart are you going in to possess their land, but because of the wickedness of these nations the LORD your God is driving them out from before you, and that he may confirm the word that the LORD swore to your fathers, to Abraham, to Isaac, and to Jacob." (Deuteronomy 9:5)

Israel are God's people because of the promises made to their ancestors. It is God's sovereign right to make promises to whomever He wishes.

"When the Most High gave to the nations their inheritance, when he divided mankind, he fixed the borders of the peoples according to the number of the sons of God [KJV, Israel]. But the LORD's portion is his people, Jacob his allotted heritage." (Deuteronomy 32:8,9)

We are clearly given to understand that God, knowing in advance, made provision for Israel before they were even in existence. The reference in Deuteronomy 32 takes us back to the narrative in Genesis 10 where the nations were divided and given territory. The Apostle Paul commented on this to the Athenians when he said:

> "He made from one man every nation of mankind to live on all the face of the earth, having determined allotted periods and the boundaries of their dwelling place." (Acts 17:26)

God knew from the beginning that Israel would be His people and arranged affairs accordingly.

Having said all that, it does not mean that only descendants of Abraham can be saved. When the Gospel was preached to Abraham there was always the intention that God would justify all other nations through faith (see Galatians 3:8,9) and that Israel would serve as the nucleus of God's operations with all nations. It was always the case (and still is) that Gentiles are welcome to embrace the hope of Israel by believing the promises to the patriarchs.

Are Israel still God's people despite being spiritually lacking?

When the apostles lived, not only were the Jews morally corrupt but they were the sworn enemies of Christ. In that context Paul wrote to the Romans:

> "As regards the gospel, they are enemies for your sake. But as regards election, they are beloved for the sake of their forefathers. For the gifts and the calling of God are irrevocable." (Romans 11:28,29)

God still loved them despite their conduct, because His promises to Abraham Isaac and Jacob are never to be broken. Even today the Jews nationally are as spiritually lacking as then but the purpose of God is unchanged.

The question is effectively asked and answered by Paul:

"Of Israel he says, 'All day long I have held out my hands to a disobedient and contrary people.' I ask, then, has God rejected his people? By no means!"   (Romans 10:21–11:1)

The divine intention is to restore Israel spiritually as well as nationally as said the prophet:

"They shall not defile themselves any more with their idols and their detestable things, or with any of their transgressions. But I will save them from all the backslidings in which they have sinned, and will cleanse them; and they shall be my people, and I will be their God."   (Ezekiel 37:23)

God has not replaced Israel with Christian believers; He has included Gentile Christians in His family. Just as the Gentiles have gained from Israel's disobedience, they will again profit from their restoration. Paul asks:

"If their [Israel's] trespass means riches for the world, and if their failure means riches for the Gentiles, how much more will their full inclusion mean! ... if their rejection means the reconciliation of the world, what will their acceptance mean but life from the dead?"   (Romans 11:12,15)

Wasn't the regathering of Israel a self-fulfilling prophecy?

It has been said that the restoration of the Jewish people to national status with their ancient homeland is one of the greatest signs of the work of God in modern times. But what if it wasn't God at all? What if those who had the power to make it happen knowing what had been prophesied worked (independently of

God) to achieve it by their own means? If that were the case the miracle of modern Israel is much less a miracle and considerably more an ordinary event.

Can we say that the restoration of Israel only happened because those who believed it, made it happen? and that in the absence of those with influence believing that it would occur, there would be no nation of Israel today?

During the nineteenth and early twentieth centuries, there was a groundswell of activity towards Jewish nationhood and homeland in both British politics and Jewish communities. Both of these groups knew their scriptures well, knew that God had predicted a national revival of the Jews and believed their efforts at restoration were in keeping with divine will. The beliefs of those who were involved in the restoration definitely affected their actions. Did this make it a self-fulfilling prophecy?

Many of the most ardent and influential Zionists were not religious and many of the most religious were not influential. In any case their influence was not substantial enough to affect enough players on the world scene to support their cause. In addition there were some very significant global forces that did not support Jewish nationalism at all. The Zionists were such small players on the global scene that their influence was negligible.

What of the British? Nobody could suggest that in the late nineteenth and early twentieth centuries the British were international minnows, but even they could not readily influence the world community to go in a direction it did not want.

Neither the Zionists nor the religious British politicians had the power and influence to bring about the restoration of Israel by their own efforts. Even after World War Two when world sympathy for the Jewish people reached a peak never seen before, and not repeated since, the UN vote to establish a Jewish State had only thirty-three out of fifty-seven in favour (thirteen against, ten abstentions and one absent). In the vote that created a Jewish state, the Jews were unable to vote and the UK was an abstention. Thus, when things came to a head neither can be said to have contributed to a self-fulfilling prophecy. Conversely, France who had consistently publicly opposed Jewish statehood, voted in favour of the motion in order to secure US favour. The suggestion that those thirty-three nations who voted in the nation of Israel, all did so because they believed they were fulfilling the word of God, is clearly ludicrous. The final decision on Jewish restoration was less influenced by those with a religious or secular belief in its necessity, than it was by a myriad of other factors.

The regathering of Jews after nearly two millennia of dispersion and the re-establishment of a Jewish nation was a very unlikely thing. No amount of self-belief could achieve it. Attempts to explain it away as a self-fulfilling prophecy forget that events that are the subjects of self-fulfilling prophecies must of necessity be within the ability of those involved to accomplish. Jewish restoration was entirely beyond any of its supporters' individual or collective efforts to achieve. It remains the most compelling evidence of the power and existence of God as the prophet recorded: "You shall live, and I will place you in your own land. Then you shall know that I am the LORD; I have spoken, and I will do it" (Ezekiel 37:14). Mark Twain once famously wrote:

> "The Egyptian, the Babylonian, and the Persian rose, filled the planet with sound and splendour, then faded to dream-stuff and passed away; the Greek and the Roman followed, and made a vast noise, and they are gone; other peoples have sprung up and held their torch high for a time, but it burned out, and they sit in twilight now, or have vanished. The Jew saw them all, beat them all, and is now what he always was, exhibiting no decadence, no infirmities of age, no weakening of his parts, no slowing of his energies, no dulling of his alert

and aggressive mind. All things are mortal but the Jew; all other forces pass, but he remains. What is the secret of his immortality?"[1]

We know the secret of Jewish longevity – the promises of an immortal God.

Where was God during the Holocaust?

During the reign of Nazism in the 1930s through to the end of World War Two, some twelve million people perished as a result of what was known as the "Final Solution" [to the problem of undesirables]. Approximately half of these were Jews. The word 'holocaust', meaning utter destruction, has come to be synonymous with what happened to the Jewish people at the hands of the Nazis. Perhaps the Holocaust was the continuation of a divine punishment, but a more compelling answer as to why the Holocaust was necessary from a divine perspective, was that it hunted the Jews out of Europe and paved the way for the world who largely did not have sympathy for the Jews to decide to create a Jewish state. But why a Holocaust of such intensity?

> "The answer is that God allowed evil men free rein for a period of time to convince His people that there was no future for them in Europe and that they should return to their own land. The event to bring this about had to be terrible; it had to be widespread and it had to exceed previous persecutions which they had endured and then shrugged off as the price to pay for maintaining a separate identity in a foreign land. It had to be sufficiently intense to make the Jews realise that they would never be assimilated into the nations in which they lived."[2]

---

1   *Harper's Magazine*, September 1899.

2   *The Sign of his Coming*, Sid Levett and Geoff Henstock, page 53.

What if God knew that to make the nations of the world freely vote to establish the state of Israel required the Holocaust? Perhaps there was no other way to set up the Jewish state? Is the re-establishment of Israel, so vital to the divine purpose, a sufficient moral cause for God to allow such horror? Not being in possession of all the facts nor having adequate intellectual equipment to process them if we did, we cannot answer these questions with certainty, but it seems likely that the answer to all of them is "Yes". If that is the case, from a divine perspective the Holocaust was not just morally defensible but necessary.

Does this make God responsible for the Holocaust? No! God did not wind Hitler up and let him go. The culprits were the Nazis under the leadership of Hitler, together with all those complicit Germans and members of other European nations who acted as instruments of the Nazi regime. This was human nature at its worst – doing what awful things history has shown humanity is capable of. Despite that God allowed this and used it to further His purpose. He would have been disgusted by the depths of human depravity. In the past God used the Assyrian and Babylonian nations to punish His people, and then pronounced judgement upon them for their own wickedness. For example:

> "Woe to, Assyria, the rod of my anger; the staff in their hands is my fury! Against a godless nation I send him, and against the people of my wrath I command him, to take spoil and seize plunder, and to tread them down like the mire of the streets. But he does not so intend, and his heart does not so think; but it is in his heart to destroy." (Isaiah 10:5-7)

This makes it clear that God at times uses evil men for a specific purpose while not condoning their evil actions.

Ultimately, we just need to trust that a loving and omnipotent God made the right choice in allowing Hitler's Nazis free rein. When we are immortal we shall doubtless comprehend this with clarity. There is another time of dreadful death and destruction yet to come upon the earth. It will be necessary to shock people into acknowledging their need for the kingdom of God and the rulership of Jesus Christ.

Chapter 6

Questions about science

"To an honest judge, the alleged marriage between religion and science is a shallow, empty, spin-doctored sham." (Richard Dawkins, atheist)

"This most beautiful system of the sun, planets and comets, could only proceed from the counsel and dominion of an intelligent and powerful Being ... This Being governs all things, not as the soul of the world, but as Lord over all; and on account of His dominion He is wont to be called Lord God or Universal Ruler." (Isaac Newton, scientist)

Is faith blind to the facts?

This question suggests that there are scientific facts that contradict the Bible which are ignored by Bible believers. It suggests that faith in scripture is either dishonest or blind, or both.

Let us be very clear: there are no scientific facts of which we are aware that are embarrassing to faith in God. Critics of the Bible have been searching for these for so long now that it seems safe to suggest that there will never be any embarrassing discoveries for the believer. It has actually been the other way around.

Rather than being unsupported by science, there are numerous suggestions from what we know that make belief in God credible. The theoretical physicist Freeman Dyson once said, "The more I examine the universe and study the details of its architecture, the more evidence I find that the universe in some sense must have known we were coming" (cited by Bill Bryson in *A Short History of Nearly Everything*). While this falls well short of admitting a deity with a purpose, it suggests the evidence at least points in this direction.

Bible believers do not need to produce scientific evidence for how something occurred, though often that evidence is available. They merely need to establish there is no scientific evidence that precludes the events of the Bible from happening.

The relevant facts for a Bible believer are:

- The Bible is consistent with the laws that govern the natural world.
- Bible history is consistent with archaeology.
- Bible prophecy is consistent with secular history.

This gives Bible readers confidence that they are not following "cleverly devised myths" (2 Peter 1:16) but things that are true and reliable. The Bible still requires faith (and God has designed it to be so) and this proves too large a hurdle for some, but there are no scientific reasons for rejecting the Bible.

What is truth?

This question was asked of Jesus, in a spirit of sarcastic despair by Pilate during one of the trials he presided over. Pilate had been so bullied, hoodwinked and cajoled by the Jewish version of truth that he was now thoroughly sceptical as to whether anybody could ascertain what the truth was in relation to Jesus.

A fact is an observable or demonstrably correct thing. However a fact may be used to support a conclusion that is not true and therefore not truth. In a court of law a false conviction or acquittal occasionally occurs. These would always be supported by facts that may of themselves be true but not tell the whole story and therefore not be truth. For a thing to be true it needs to be factually correct and honest in intention while not omitting any details. That is why the courts ask for evidence to be, 'truth, the whole truth and nothing but the truth'. Facts may be skewed or misinterpreted but truth can never be; it is complete and correct. Truth is the ultimate correct conclusion.

Science seeks to discover and reveal facts. It seldom purports to know truth. Since human scientific endeavour first began, many things that were accepted as truth (e.g., a flat earth) have with greater knowledge been completely overturned. This has led many scientists to be wary (quite rightly) of presenting data or conclusions as truth. The facts of today may be discarded tomorrow. The Bible does not principally concern itself with facts, it claims to reveal truth: that is things that are always true. Mostly these are things about God and His purpose.

Each of us needs personally to decide whether the Bible is truth. Sadly many people have made that assessment (and dismissed scripture as a fable) without ever having read it! The honourable approach would be to conduct a thorough and proper investigation with an open mind and then draw conclusions based on the evidence. Science will never prove the Bible true. Science supports the conclusion that the Bible is true, but the ultimate acceptance of truth rests with the individual and their preparedness to accept God. God describes Himself as the "God of faithfulness" (Deuteronomy 32:4), that is, the ultimate reality and faithful to His promises.

Doesn't modern science contradict the Bible?

Our premise is there is no reason why science should contradict the Bible. Modern scientists might, but science *per se*, does not. We must also realise from the outset that science and the Bible are about different things and do not often intersect. When scientists restrict themselves to established scientific method and thereby are true to science they will not contradict the Bible message.

Scientific method may be defined as "principles and procedures for the systematic pursuit of knowledge involving the recognition and formulation of a problem, the collection of data through observation and experiment, and the formulation and testing of hypotheses" (Merriam Webster).

The process may be elaborated as below:

1. Make observations.
2. Conduct research.
3. Form a hypothesis.
4. Test the hypothesis.
5. Record results.
6. Draw conclusions.
7. Repeat to test the conclusions.

At the end of the process when the hypothesis has been established it becomes an accepted scientific fact. This does not mean that the accepted facts of today don't get discarded tomorrow. Scientific method can improve and conclusions of yesterday might be discarded when more information is to hand. Scientific fact is not the same as truth.

The area in which science most seems to challenge the Bible relates to the origin of the earth and life as we know it. The Theory (actually theories, plural) of Organic Macro-evolution (to give evolution its proper name) espoused by many scientists suggests that the Biblical record of creation is false. However we might note from the outset that the concept of evolution falls outside the realm of accepted scientific method as set out above. Macro-evolution is neither observable, nor can all the relevant data be gathered, and no experiment can be devised to demonstrate it or reproduce it. It may well be argued that the "problem identified" that first prompted the theories of evolution was human dissatisfaction with the God of the Bible. Charles Darwin said as much in private letters to his friends. David Hume writing some fifty years before Darwin said, "I have no explanation for complex biological design. All I know is that God isn't a good explanation, so we must wait and hope that somebody comes up with a better one" (cited by Richard Dawkins in *The Blind Watchmaker*). One suspects that the reason why God was assessed to be a poor explanation is most likely connected to a desire to not be accountable to God. For the many scientists who accept God, creation makes beautiful sense.

Organic Micro-evolution, that is, change within species definitely occurs and we can observe it today. This is how we get all dog species from wolves for example. It is an enormous leap of faith to extrapolate that to Organic Macro-evolution and suggest that all things evolved. Micro-evolution is an observable reality and a very different thing (despite sounding very similar) from Macro-evolution. The one says in effect, 'I can jump a long way', the other supposes that therefore I could, and in fact have, jumped to the moon. The one does not naturally follow the other and is (literally and logically) a big leap.

Evolution, despite what some scientists might say, is predominantly an attempt to explain life without God rather than a scientific piecing together of facts pointing towards a credible conclusion. Evolution is now such an accepted phenomenon that most modern scientists are ignorant of its gaping holes and the lack of good science. Evolutionists appeal to science for support and assume they have it. An explanation excluding God is so pleasing to the humanist psyche, the lack of scientific method and the utter implausibility of the concept of 'complexity from simplicity' (in flagrant breach of scientific law) are gullibly swallowed by the community at large without complaint. In the way already discussed previously, it is not beyond the scope and means of God to send "a strong delusion" to those who have previously made up their mind against Him.

The scientific community prides itself on accuracy of data and conclusions. A noted researcher Dr William McBride who brought the dangers of thalidomide for unborn children to the world's attention, was later treated as a pariah for falsifying evidence against another drug, Debendox. Dr McBride was so certain that Debendox was suspect that when the evidence did not support it, he tampered with the results to make it look like it did. In doing so he lost all credibility and was rejected entirely by the scientific community. What would drive a person to falsify evidence in this way? The logical answer can only be a lack of evidence combined with a pre-existing conclusion. Various scientists at times have been similarly so determined to support evolution that they have deliberately fabricated evidence – the Piltdown Man hoax for example. If there was evidence that supported evolution, why would any scientist perpetrate a hoax? The clear answer is they would not.

Some of the 'evidence' advanced in favour of evolution might also be used to support creation; the conclusion reached depending on the point of view of the observer. Comparative anatomy is an example of this. Similarity in form and function may as equally suggest a common designer as a common ancestor. Evolution, despite many claims in favour of it, does not have an agreed mechanism that has been proven, has not passed the test of science and is not universally accepted by scientists. The definitions of the word 'unscientific' are:

1. Not in accordance with scientific principles or methodology;

2. Lacking knowledge of or interest in science (Dictionary. com).

Evolution may legitimately be described as unscientific because it fails the first definition. Thus while evolution and the Bible are clearly in conflict, it does not follow that science and the Bible must therefore be at odds.

Let us be clear – by the above definition, scripture is also unscientific. This does not mean that it must be contrary to science, or that the Bible is wrong, merely that the Bible and science are fundamentally about different things. The Bible is principally concerned to show us *why* God did things, what His purpose is, and asks us to believe God. Science on the other hand is primarily concerned with observing *how* things happen with a view to improving outcomes for man and has almost nothing to do with faith. Science is about fact, and the Bible about truth. Those two things while sounding similar do not often share the same space. That does not mean that scripture and science need be at odds with each other. Readers who desire more are directed to books written for the purpose, such as *Bible and Science* by John C. Bilello.

The writers know of no scientific fact that contradicts the message of the Bible. To be fair, this is in no small part because they do not share many common subjects. When the Bible speaks of subjects now understood by modern science there is harmony and not conflict. The ancient record of the wind patterns and the water cycle in Ecclesiastes 1, while lacking scientific detail, is in complete harmony with what we now know occurs; and we might add, considerably advanced knowledge for the times in which it was written. For almost every matter recorded in scripture that is relevant to science there are notable scientists who can demonstrate that the Bible and science are in agreement – Biblical quarantine laws are a good example of this.

Are evolution and creation compatible?

Having stated in the previous answer that evolution and creation are in conflict, one might imagine the question to have already been answered. There are some who wish to fuse creation with the theories of evolution. The resultant theories have various names, Theistic Evolution (TE), God Directed Evolution (GDE) and Evolutionary Creationism (EC). The names and the details may vary but the intention is the same – to harmonise the Bible record with evolutionary theory.

The various mergers of evolution and creation propose that God with His divine power and initial concept started the process, and essentially left things to evolve themselves over millions of years, while offering limited guidance along the way. We submit from the outset that this endeavour is misguided because evolutionary theory primarily excludes God, and was formed in large part to eliminate the need for God. Those who accept evolution (in a non-theistic sense) reject such an endeavour as do those who accept the Bible record. The entire approach seems to be an utterly unnecessary attempt to legitimise the Bible scientifically, quite forgetting that science and the Bible do not consider common subjects and that neither evolution nor the Bible (as discussed briefly above) are in the realm of science.

Theistic Evolution in rejecting the literal reading of Genesis 1-3 inevitably bends out of shape such fundamental concepts as the origin of marriage, sin, forgiveness and death, ultimately twisting Bible meaning and thereby taking those who embrace it away from the truth of scripture and denying the hope of salvation. Theistic Evolution as a theory is therefore fundamentally flawed. Evolution essentially maintains that there was no design and no purpose, that life was a happy accident. The Bible maintains there was both design, Designer and purpose. The two ideas are mutually exclusive. Theistic evolution offers parts of each concept but is in harmony with neither. Brother Michael Storey succinctly wrote, "The theories of Evolution and Theistic evolution, in all their various forms subvert our faith in God".[1]

Some believers are really interested in the past and natural history and are searching to find answers for 'scientific discoveries' that would seem to complement their faith. We just need to bear in mind that human history as we know it from Adam and Eve is around 6,000 years old. We simply are not told by God and therefore do not know what was on the earth before that. It is pointless to speculate to the point of developing new theories when our focus should be on the present and future.

What about the age of the earth?

Science estimates the age of the earth (by radiometric dating) to be 4.54 ± 0.05 billion years.[2] The Bible states, "in six days the LORD made heaven and earth, the sea, and all that is in them" (Exodus 20:11). We can quite easily count forwards from Genesis 1 using genealogies and Bible timelines and arrive at a figure of approximately 6,000 years. This appears to make the Biblical age of the earth approximately 0.075% of the actual age. At this point scientists exclaim triumphantly, 'The Bible is clearly wrong' and use this as evidence to reject the whole. Can we reconcile the two?

The phrase "in six days the LORD made heaven and earth" (Exodus 20:11) does not demand that everything had

---

1   *The God we Worship*, page 3.

2   *Age of the Earth*, U.S. Geological Survey, 1997.

no existence before the first day. The Hebrew word translated "made", means "to do or make, in the broadest sense and widest application" (*Strong's Concordance*) and has more than fifty different applications in the Bible that include the idea of creating but also of appointing, of furnishing and bringing forth. Textually we are not required to limit the word to the idea of initial creation. If we read Exodus 20:11 as a summary of the work of creation in arranging the celestial and terrestrial bodies and creating life on earth, it sits easily after the prologue of Genesis 1:1 that states, "In the beginning, God created the heavens and the earth". Brother David Levin makes the point that "Structurally, chronologically and conceptually verses 1 and 2 form a separate unit that precedes the first day". [3] Thus verse 1 and 2 of Genesis chapter 1 describe the situation before the six days of Biblical creation commenced. In the beginning (whenever that was) everything came into existence. The prologue in Genesis is describing the beginning of the universe not the work of creation upon earth subsequently detailed from Genesis 1:3.

What happened in the period between the beginning and when God ordered arrangements for our benefit and created life on earth is unknown. While we might dearly love to know, God has not revealed it to us. We can surmise that there may have been previous creations upon the earth but this is not provable. If there were previous creations (and we think this likely) it might explain some of the apparently ancient fossils, dinosaurs, the origin of angels and other events that don't fit well with our current 6,000 year history of life. While science seeks to unravel the mysteries of the entire history of the earth, the Bible is only concerned with comparatively recent events.

In summary, it seems that God created the universe a very long time ago but created life on earth as we know it today

---

3   *The Creation Text – Studies in early Genesis*, page 7.

about 6,000 years ago. There need be no conflict between the Bible and science concerning the age of the earth.

If God created the earth, why is there so much imperfection?

The reality of life on earth as we know it is less than perfect. All natural life is plagued by disease, death, and subject to adverse events from weather and all sorts of other phenomena outside of our control. The atheist looks at this and wonders, could a powerful loving God have made this? Wouldn't an omnipotent God have done a better job? The believer looks at the world with all its intricate parts and marvels at the God who created it. Which view is correct?

The first question to answer is this: is what we currently see around us the end point that God intended in the first place? The answer is clearly no! Paul writing to the Romans declared, "the creation itself will be set free from its bondage to corruption and obtain the freedom of the glory of the children of God" (Romans 8:21). Currently we are "in bondage to corruption" and have not yet arrived at the climax intended by God. We might then logically ask, did God create everything subject to disease and frustration in the first place? The answer again from Paul is that "the creation was subjected to futility ... because of him [God] who subjected it, in hope" (Romans 8:20). The earth as originally created was described as "very good" (Genesis 1:31). As a result of sin God made some fundamental changes and declared:

> "Cursed is the ground because of you; in pain you shall eat of it all the days of your life; thorns and thistles it shall bring forth for you; and you shall eat the plants of the field. By the sweat of your face you shall eat bread, till you return to the ground, for out of it you were taken; for you are dust, and to dust you shall return."
> (Genesis 3:17-19)

On another level we may well argue that God is using the world as we see it now with all of its problems, and that suffering and hopelessness are the very things that God chose to use to bring many sons to glory.

Because we were not there, and scripture has little comment, we cannot know with certainty what things were like before the curse of corruption was pronounced, but they were significantly better than at present. While it is tempting to say that God brought the curse (which is true at one level), the cause lies firmly at the feet of man; God said "because of you". To blame God for our present bondage is a bit like an inmate blaming the judge for his imprisonment. If the judge were to act unreasonably and with no regard for consequences and justice, the criminal would be at liberty; if justice were upheld then the sentence is only the fault of the criminal.

The second point to be made is that God does not intend to leave the world in the present imperfect state. We are clearly told that the earth will be transformed and again be like the paradise that was Eden. Isaiah in chapter 35 paints a beautiful picture of a restored earth. John recorded for us, "there will no longer be any curse, and the throne of God and the Lamb will be in the city. His servants will worship him" (Revelation 22:3). In words that we cited earlier from Romans 8 we are told that when God condemned creation to corruption He did so "in hope". While this present life is not all we might wish it to be, the divine intention is that we might not be content with the present and hope for the future. Many choose not to embrace the hope of Eden restored and elect rather to ignore God and live this present life as they wish. Unhappily this only ensures that they will not be selected by God to share His transformed earth.

Some might say, why has God taken so long before intervening? Surely a loving God would have acted way sooner than now? These questions forget that time is not the same for God as for us, or that His purpose in waiting is to ensure the maximum participation in His wonderful future (see 2 Peter 3:8-13).

If there was a worldwide flood, and animals were only saved by the ark, how do we get the biodiversity and geographical dispersion that we see today?

We might note that entire books have been written on this subject. Clearly such a detailed consideration is entirely beyond our scope. We will however attempt to summarise the material and endeavour to show by logic that the Bible and science are not in disagreement. Let us take this question in several parts for separate examination.

Let us first consider a worldwide flood. If there was a worldwide flood, there should presumably be evidence in keeping with that. We would expect to see:

- Water covering the entire earth at some point.

- Geologic formations able to be laid down and changed quickly (as in Mount St. Helens eruption in 1980).

- Widespread anthropological evidence of flood stories in diverse communities.

Suffice to say that there is evidence of all of these things. Incidentally the idea of a local flood is excluded scientifically as well as Biblically. Water finds its own level and could not sit "above the mountains, covering them fifteen cubits deep" (Genesis 7:20) unless it were global. God declared that, "the waters shall never again become a flood to destroy all flesh" (Genesis 9:15). There have been many local floods since Noah's time – this would invalidate the promise of God. The idea of a global flood is scientifically and Biblically credible.

Biodiversity is readily explained by Micro-evolution that was discussed previously. Noah needed only to take one pair of wolves from which all the dog species now extant could descend. It is anticipated that as few as about 8,000 species may have been involved. In any case the dimensions of the ark were sufficiently large (approximately 137 × 23 × 14m with three stories) to house the animals we now have. Considering the human population, we would expect to see all people closely related and evidence of a single progenitor. Modern genetics has confirmed this.

Land bridges – connecting strips of land that are known to have existed in the past, readily explain the movement of animals. In 1991 a platypus fossil was found in South America suggesting that Australia's unique animals may not necessarily be unique. It may seem unlikely to us that animals travelled vast distances, but it is certainly not impossible. Evolution itself relies upon this concept so it must be conceded by evolutionists that this could have happened.

For natural science to disprove the flood it needs to demonstrate that it was not possible – science has not been able to do this. Not having evidence in favour is quite different from having evidence against.

Has science made God obsolete?

Perhaps some scientists would like to think so, but the answer is emphatically no! Science does not even have all the answers to questions that are within its arena of interest let alone all the other deeper questions of life. Why are we here? Science does not know. What is our destiny? Science cannot say. Is there purpose to life, and if so, what is it? Science has no idea! Some scientists might like to think answers to questions like these are likely to be revealed in time as they gain greater insights into the physical nature of things – this seems very unlikely.

However, all these questions are answered straightforwardly in the Bible. There is no reason to dismiss the Bible just because it does not answer the 'how' questions. We submit that answers to most of the 'how' questions would be beyond the capacity of mortal man's contemplation. Clever scientists, with difficulty unravel *what* has been done, *how* things were done is seldom able to be determined, and *why* things were done is utterly beyond them. The Bible with elegant simplicity explains why we are here, "you created all things, and by your will they existed and were created" (Revelation 4:11); the destiny of man is revealed to be, "evildoers shall be cut off, but those who wait for the LORD shall inherit the land" (Psalm 37:9); the purpose of life simply stated that, "all the earth shall be filled with the glory of the LORD" (Numbers 14:21). We don't need to understand it (and just as well!) we merely need to believe it. There will come a time when invested with divine nature we will be able to comprehend the work of God, but that time is not yet.

While science offers no answers to the biggest questions of life, the Bible answers them all. Biblical answers are not so complex that they require multiple qualifications to be understood, they are plain to the ordinary person. Only the Bible has real answers to the big questions of life, and only the Bible can be trusted. There is no danger of science providing either answers or hope. Sadly some people have gullibly placed their faith in the hands of science in the hope that cryogenic preservation will enable advanced science to re-create them at some later date. There is only one hope for life beyond death, poetically stated in Psalm 49:15, "God will ransom my soul [life] from the power of Sheol [the grave]".

Science offers no hope but the Bible does. There is a time coming when full knowledge will supersede current Biblical revelation as the Apostle Paul said: "Now I know in part; then I shall know fully" (1 Corinthians 13:12), but that knowledge will come from God Himself and not from the wisdom of man.

Can you really believe in miracles?

This question is not concerned with what we might call serendipitous miracles, such as an out of control vehicle colliding with a baby's pram and the child miraculously not being hurt. We are talking about intentional suspensions of natural law by supernatural means such as occurred in the battle against the Amorites in Joshua 10:13. Such miraculous events usually defy scientific explanation and demand a supernatural cause. Miraculous events are quite common in scripture and the means by which they are accomplished is always attributed to the power of God.

In a conversation with Nicodemus, Jesus likened the power of God to the wind. He said, "The wind blows where it wishes, and you hear its sound, but you do not know where it comes from or where it goes" (John 3:8). We all accept that wind is a real thing, despite it being utterly intangible. The spirit or power of God is often described in scripture as the "breath of God" not necessarily because it *is* divine breath, but because we may thereby understand it.

Such miraculous suspension of natural law as was seen in Biblical times is not witnessed today. This does not mean that God never was active, merely that there is currently no open evidence of the work of God. Throughout Biblical history there were times when visible evidence of God was absent, for example in the early life of Samuel: "the word of the LORD was rare in those days; there was no frequent vision" (1 Samuel 3:1). Because there have been no clear miracles in which natural law was suspended in modern times, some people suggest that the records of what happened must be myth. Today, walking on water is only accomplished by illusion or by trickery. Science cannot explain it or support it and so it is dismissed. We would normally have imagined that both Peter and Jesus would have sunk. Scientists mostly dismiss the idea because it contradicts the concept that only less dense things can float in any liquid. For the record of walking on water to be true, it demands supernatural power. Modern science cannot explain miracles such as walking on water, has no evidence or record, so it readily dismisses the miraculous as fairy tale.

It is often asked, 'If God could do it then, why doesn't He do it now?' the inference being that if He doesn't do miracles now then He couldn't in the past. If God performed a modern miracle, such as the sun and moon remaining motionless then surely everybody would be obliged to believe? Perhaps, though not necessarily. If the experience of Pharaoh counts for anything, many of those would begrudgingly believe. God wants willing obedience and faith, not reluctant compulsion. Such a demonstration would replace faith with sight and deny God the pleasure of having us trust Him without requiring absolute tangible proof.

We accept that humans can interrupt natural laws – for example a hand catching a falling apple from a tree is an intervention, which has altered the course of the law of gravity. It is not difficult to conceive that God can act similarly but in a cosmic way that we are too small to see.

Seeing life and the wonders of creation as a miracle and something which is ultimately inexplicable is what leads us to worship God who is greater than us: "O LORD how manifold are your works, in wisdom you have made them all. The earth is full of your creatures" (Psalm 104:24).

There are miracles of an entirely different character that we have seen that support the veracity of God. The modern state of Israel is a notable example. We submit that a study of modern Jewish history is credible testimony to the amazing character of Bible prophecy and the hand of God. Israel is a modern miracle. Each tiny step might be explicable in an everyday sense, but the whole story so utterly incredible as to demand the finger of God.

When we consider the make-up of the Bible, we realise that it contains only about two per cent miracles by volume of words. The rest is history and prophecy. This has always been a powerful argument for the veracity of the scripture in that we see God revealing Himself primarily through prophetic control in human history – in particular the miracle of the history of the people and nation of Israel.

Chapter 7

Questions about religion – in principle

"No man ever believes that the Bible means what it says: He is always convinced that it says what he means." (George Bernard Shaw, playwright)

"A thorough knowledge of the Bible is worth more than a college education." (Theodore Roosevelt, American President)

If you are sincere and loving, does it matter what you believe?

There are records in scripture of men who were sincere in their belief but were either misguided or lacking, and required instruction or redirection. The following list found in the Acts of the Apostles contains five premier examples of this:

1. The Ethiopian Eunuch (Acts 8).
2. Saul of Tarsus (Acts 9).
3. Cornelius the Centurion (Acts 10,11).
4. Apollos (Acts 18).
5. Disciples of John (Acts 19).

All of these men had a strong faith in God that inspired their actions: the Eunuch to be a pilgrim, Saul – a persecutor, Cornelius – a philanthropist, Apollos – a teacher, and the disciples of John – firm followers. Perhaps we might readily accept that Saul was astray, but scripture reveals that all of these men were not headed in a right direction and required instruction in the true Gospel. In each of the cases they were lacking in the true knowledge of Jesus and that needed to change. Even the devotion, prayers and good works of Cornelius were insufficient; he needed to heed the "message by which you will be saved, you and all your household" (Acts 11:14).

If a certain destination is important, the path we choose is critical. The saying, 'all roads lead to Rome' may have worked in the Roman Empire because the Romans built the roads and pretty much all roads did lead to Rome. In spiritual matters however, there are only two roads: the wide road leading to destruction and the narrow road leading to life. If we are on the wrong road we will reach the wrong destination regardless of how sincerely we believe we are on the right road.

What we believe influences the way we go and the choices we make. If our beliefs about God and salvation are wrong then this will be reflected in how we live. How we live helps frame the verdict of Christ when he judges us. If we leave the teaching of Jesus and the apostles and absorb human elements into our faith then this places our salvation in jeopardy. It is a frightening thought that if we reject Jesus' teaching then he may reject us. Let us be as sure as we can that we are following that which is right.

The scriptures state that God's word is the only truth revealing what we must believe that will result in our eternal salvation. Unless we believe the truth of scripture we are not eligible for immortality. Paul longed for a time when he would receive:

"The crown of righteousness, which the Lord, the righteous judge, will award to me on that day, and not only to me but also to all who have loved his appearing."   (2 Timothy 4:8)

The Catholic Church for example, teaches quite differently: that we currently possess immortality and that the kingdom of God is already here and consists only of the Church. Surely the failure to believe this hope of Paul places us at considerable eternal risk.

Consider the following plain scriptures:

- "To the teaching and to the testimony! If they will not speak according to this word, it is because they have no dawn" (Isaiah 8:20).

- "Go into all the world and proclaim the gospel to the whole creation. Whoever believes and is baptized will be saved, but whoever does not believe will be condemned" (Mark 16:15,16).

- "Whoever believes in him [the Son of Man] may have eternal life" (John 3:15).

- "Whoever believes in the Son has eternal life; whoever does not obey the Son shall not see life" (John 3:36).

- "The hour is coming, and is now here, when the true worshippers will worship the Father in spirit and truth, for the Father is seeking such people to worship him" (John 4:23).

- "This Jesus is the stone that was rejected by you, the builders, which has become the cornerstone. And there is salvation in no one else, for there is no other name under heaven given among men by which we must be saved" (Acts 4:11,12).

- "Blessed are those who wash their robes, so that they may have the right to the tree of life and that they may enter the city by the gates. Outside are the dogs and sorcerers and the sexually immoral and murderers and idolaters, and everyone who loves and practises falsehood" (Revelation 22:14,15).

Surely the combined message is that belief in the true Gospel revealed in the scriptures is critical for salvation and any other path will not bring life. Notice carefully that the Bible does not merely teach that we need to know the truth, but to believe it, love it and live it.

So yes, it does matter what we believe.

There are so many religions, how can you be sure yours is true?

This question has two major considerations: first, of all the religions in the world, can we be confident that Christianity is the path of choice and secondly of the varieties of Christianity, can we be sure that Christadelphian teaching presents the best option?

The question to be asked of any religion is how might a person verify the information? Most religions have either sacred writings or an oral tradition handed down for generations. Oral tradition cannot be measured or tested and is therefore simply a matter of blind faith. We may reasonably dismiss these because they have no tangible foundation. Holy writings, on the other hand, can be tested. Of the sacred writings, none can compare with the Bible in terms of internal and external historical accuracy. Quite simply, the evidence in favour of scripture eclipses all other sacred writings and sets it in a class alone. This leaves us with Judaeo-Christian religions as the only serious contenders for the faith of choice.

Judaism rejects Jesus as the Messiah and consequently the entire New Testament record. The Jewish scriptures comprise only the first part of the Bible, the Old Testament. There is no significant difference between the quality of internal and external evidence supporting the New Testament and that supporting the Old Testament. This means that the Bible (in its entirety) may be accepted as the word of God. Thus the Jewish rejection of the New Testament is unfounded. This leaves us only with the Christian religions as serious contenders for the religion of choice because they accept the Bible as a whole.

Or do they? There are a variety of positions among Christianity with respect to the Bible. Some give lip service to the Old Testament but essentially dismiss it as out-dated and superseded. Some accept most of the Bible but dismiss some parts of it. Some accept all of scripture but don't value it as highly as church tradition or law, while others accept the entire Bible as the only authority. The notion of *Sola Scriptura* (the Bible only) must be the preferred option as it is not dependent on human thinking for truth. We have now narrowed down our quest for the true church to those who accept all of scripture as the only authority for life and faith.

However, this does not narrow down our search sufficiently, for among those faiths that accept only the Bible as an authority there is still quite some variation. Not only do we need to accept the Bible as a whole, we need to accept what the Bible teaches and reject what it rejects. Every Christian community claims a belief in Jesus with the fundamental acceptance that he died for our sins, but that does not make them all the same. While it is not our purpose to conduct an analysis of each point of teaching, it is not a difficult task to determine right from wrong. To begin with, we can summarily dismiss the major wrong teachings that have crept into Christianity largely under the influence of pagan thought.

1. The immortality of the soul.
2. The Trinity and the pre-existence of Jesus.

3. A supernatural Devil responsible for sin.

4. The substitutionary death of Jesus.

These major wrong teachings concern the nature of God and man and the ultimate destiny of man. There has been much discussion and much ink spilled over these doctrines and we will not add to it here. Suffice to say that they are all fundamentally astray from Bible teaching and have their origins in ideas borrowed largely from Egyptian, Babylonian, Greek and Roman philosophy.[1] These are not minor acceptable differences, but fundamentally divergent ideas. Any Christian community that believes any of these is not truly following the teaching of Jesus and therefore by definition not truly Christian. Eliminating just these four wrong teachings makes our list of contenders very small.

We can further refine our list with the addition of just four fundamental teachings of scripture:

1. Baptism consequent upon intelligent belief in the Gospel.

2. The hope of Israel.

3. The resurrection to immortality.

4. The kingdom of God on earth.

Again these are not optional, nice to have, thoughts – they are critical elements of the Gospel. The consequences of believing false ideas and / or failing to accept truth will be to lose the way and eventually to act contrary to God's will. This will be seen in actions that are manifestly different from Bible teaching.

We are left with Christadelphians (and possibly a very few others) as being the best representatives of Bible teaching. With a discussion of only eight critical doctrines we can identify truth from error. This is not to suggest that *only* these teachings are

---

1   The reader is directed to an excellent survey by Laurence Lepherd entitled *Losing the way* for further information on how these false teachings crept into the early church.

important, but rather demonstrates that understanding saving truth is not as complex as it might at first appear. Thus while individual elements are commonly represented across a variety of Christian churches, Christadelphian teaching as a whole is virtually unique.

Religion means binding again to God. Thus, true religion must take us nearer to God, to His purpose and to His salvation. We must take the Berean approach – search the scriptures daily to see if the teachings match the Bible. We are confident that in this way Christadelphian faith will be seen to be true. If there are other communities or individuals who accept the truths of scripture and reject error, then they too embrace saving faith.

So many smart people believe in doctrines you say are wrong. Can you really be right?

The previous answer by force of its logic demands that most of those who declare themselves to be Christian do not believe what Jesus taught. Among them are some outstanding scholars of language and scripture. We have in our mind some of the excellent teachers of the twentieth century church, men of towering intellect with a commanding grasp of scripture. Could such as these be wrong, and if so, how?

We submit that the approach often taken with respect to subjects is to accept the (essentially Catholic) doctrines of orthodox Christianity and to appeal to the Bible for support. We suggest that this approach is fundamentally flawed. Any church or teacher ought to be guided by the Bible and not approach the Bible with a preformed mould into which passages of scripture may be pressed. It matters not that the reader is genuine: if the approach is biased then the outcome can hardly fail to be astray from the true intent of the passage. It is as if the Bible is read through a prism of church dogma and is therefore re-focused to appear as orthodox thought expects. By elevating church thought above scripture, the voice of God is muffled and becomes unclear.

If the scriptures are given the respect they deserve, they will be allowed to inform us, and not the other way around. We must be continually vigilant and read scripture for ourselves with unveiled eyes and hear scripture with unbiased ears or we could easily find ourselves accepting unsound expositions with similar prejudice.

The Christadelphian faith does not have a monopoly on genuineness, on Bible study or on capable teachers. What we do have is an absence of church hierarchy and tradition, an absolute respect for the authority of God's word and a personal desire to acquaint ourselves with it. These features combine to ensure that while our members are just ordinary people and untrained in any seminary, our beliefs can be tested and seen to be essentially the same as the apostles and Jesus taught.

The Gospel is simple and the simple embrace it. This is the clear message of Paul to the Corinthians:

> "Not many of you were wise according to worldly standards, not many were powerful, not many were of noble birth. But God chose what is foolish in the world to shame the wise; God chose what is weak in the world to shame the strong; God chose what is low and despised in the world, even things that are not, to bring to nothing things that are, so that no human being might boast in the presence of God."
>
> (1 Corinthians 1:26-29)

Being learned is not necessarily an advantage in understanding the Gospel and may be an impediment. Jesus said:

> "I thank you, Father, Lord of heaven and earth, that you have hidden these things from the wise and understanding and revealed them to little children; yes, Father, for such was your gracious will." (Matthew 11:25)

Is open fellowship acceptable?

Early in the Acts of the Apostles we read:

> "So those who received his word were baptized, and there were added that day about three thousand souls. And they devoted themselves to the apostles' teaching and the fellowship, to the breaking of bread and the prayers. And awe came upon every soul, and many wonders and signs were being done through the apostles. And all who believed were together and had all things in common." (Acts 2:41-44)

Note the order: they received the word, were baptized, devoted themselves to the apostles' teaching – then they shared fellowship on that common basis.

Open fellowship describes purposeful (rather than unwitting) individual or collective fellowship with those who do not share common beliefs. Collectively it is the practice of ecclesias welcoming those of different faiths to the Lord's table and breaking bread with them; individually it is the practice of those brothers and sisters who break bread with us visiting other churches and sharing the symbols of Christ with them. Historically these things have not been part of the accepted practice of our faith. Our brotherhood, like the early believers, has traditionally held that correct teaching and practice must underscore fellowship. In the last few decades some ecclesias and brothers and sisters have practised open fellowship. Is it simply a question of moving with the ecumenical times or is there reason and wisdom in the traditional approach?

The Apostle Paul made it clear that:

> "What pagans sacrifice they offer to demons and not to God. I do not want you to be participants with demons. You cannot drink the cup of the Lord and the cup of demons. You cannot partake of the table of the Lord and the table of demons." (1 Corinthians 10:20,21)

Paul made it clear that the idolatrous worship of the pagans had nothing in common with the table of the Lord and there was to be no fellowship between the two. Does this extend to those who believe in Jesus but differ as to the particulars?

The Passover feast is especially typical of the memorial meeting. This is made clear in the words:

> "Christ, our Passover lamb, has been sacrificed. Let us therefore celebrate the festival, not with the old leaven, the leaven of malice and evil, but with the unleavened bread of sincerity and truth." (1 Corinthians 5:7,8)

When Israel were commanded to keep the feast of the Passover they were explicitly instructed:

> "This is the statute of the Passover: no foreigner shall eat of it, but every slave that is bought for money may eat of it after you have circumcised him. No foreigner or hired worker may eat of it ... If a stranger shall sojourn with you and would keep the Passover to the LORD, let all his males be circumcised. Then he may come near and keep it; he shall be as a native of the land. But no uncircumcised person shall eat of it." (Exodus 12:43-45,48)

The modern parallel to circumcision is baptism as confirmed by the Apostle Paul to the Colossians:

> "In him also you were circumcised with a circumcision made without hands, by putting off the body of the flesh, by the circumcision of Christ, having been buried with him in baptism." (Colossians 2:11,12)

Given that the shadow (the Passover) is based on the real thing (the breaking of bread) we are drawn to ask, why the prohibition on strangers eating the Passover? Clearly it must have been based on the restriction of those not in covenant relationship with Christ sharing the breaking of bread.

It may be argued, other Christians worship God and Jesus as we do, surely the differences are cosmetic? When the Samaritans (who later showed their true colours) came to Zerubbabel and said, "Let us build with you, for we worship your God as you do" (Ezra 4:2) it may have seemed heavy-handed of Joshua and Zerubbabel to send them away with the words, "You have nothing to do with us in building a house to our God" (verse 3). The crux of the matter was the teaching. Zerubbabel realised as Jesus was later to declare that the Samaritans, "worship what you do not know" (John 4:22). They might seem like peripheral matters but to Joshua and Zerubbabel they were crucial. Brother Harry Tennant once wrote of this very question:

> "The issues are central and not marginal. They lie at the very heart of everything which all of us confess to hold dear. They concern the Lord our God, His Son the Lord Jesus Christ and the atonement by which we are cleansed from our sins."[2]

Our beliefs are distinctive and different from others. This was discussed at length two questions previously. Almost all other Christian communities will differ on at least one of the four basic wrong teachings that deny saving truth. Most of them accept, if not demand all four. Seldom will any other church accept all of the four positive truths. The Apostle Paul rhetorically asked the Corinthians, "what fellowship has light with darkness?" (2 Corinthians 6:14). We believe other concepts about God, Christ and the atonement are as different from truth as light is from darkness. The Apostle John is characteristically direct, as well as being black and white. He wrote:

> "Many deceivers have gone out into the world, those who do not confess the coming of Jesus Christ in the flesh. Such a one is the deceiver and the antichrist ... Everyone who goes on ahead and does not abide in the teaching of Christ, does not have God. Whoever abides in the teaching has both the

---

2   *The Christadelphian*, Volume 121 (1984), page 366.

Father and the Son. If anyone comes to you and does not bring this teaching, do not receive him into your house or give him any greeting, for whoever greets him takes part in his wicked works." (2 John verses 7,9,10)

Some might say, to refuse participation to a visitor to this aspect of our worship might be offensive and would turn them away. We would respond that a carefully prepared and graciously offered explanation by a sensitive brother or sister should satisfy a genuine person. Rather than be put off, they are likely to yearn for greater fellowship. A person to whom truth does not matter might thereby be discouraged, but a genuine seeker should be encouraged. To offer full fellowship on any basis other than a proper sharing of the covenant of Christ cheapens the fellowship and dishonours Christ.

Wrong teachings about the Father, Son and salvation disqualify one from the sharing that characterises the family of God. To share with them as we would with each other suggests that we accept their teaching. Open fellowship cannot be endorsed. It is a form of dishonesty to our brothers and sisters and to Christ.

"Either we believe that the faith we confessed at baptism and have sought to live out in our lives is true to scripture and to God, or we do not. For those of us who do so believe, and all of us should in honesty do so, surrender or compromise will be disastrous to *our* faith. The meaning would have gone out of life." [3]

Why are so many wars caused by religion?

Many significant wars have not been fought in the cause of religion; most of the major wars of the twentieth century were

---

3   Harry Tennant, *ibid*.

not. The idea that most of the wars of history have been caused by religion is demonstrably false. The vast majority of wars have been conducted in the pursuit of profits or power, or waged for territory or tribal supremacy, even if religion has been caught up in those pursuits. But there is a very real sense in which religion can moderate those forces. David Hart notes that:

> "Religious conviction often provides the sole compelling reason for refusing to kill ... or for seeking peace ... the truth is that religion and irreligion are cultural variables but killing is a human constant." [4]

Millions were killed at the hands of Mao, Stalin and Pol Pot. To say their murderous totalitarianism had nothing to do with their atheism is completely to misunderstand them and the ideologies on which their actions rested.

However the sad reality is that some wars *have* been fought in the cause of religion. The atheist looks at this unhappy fact and declares that we would all be better off without religion. The mistake the atheist makes is to lump all religions together, the false with the true and reject them *en masse* without appreciating the major differences that exist between them. Since it is utterly unreasonable to hold Christianity accountable for the wars of other religions, such as Islam, we will confine our discussion to wars in the name of Christ.

We have previously narrowed down true Christianity to those who believe the Gospel as defined in scripture. Christ is neither represented by nor is responsible for the actions of a counterfeit church. It may give the cause of Christ considerable bad press that many evil things have been done in his name but we must realise that these are motivated by flesh and not spirit. Not all who call Jesus "Lord" belong to him, as he sadly reflected: "Why do you call me 'Lord, Lord,' and not do what I tell you?" (Luke 6:46)

---

4   *Atheist Delusions: The Christian Revolution and Its Fashionable Enemies.*

Since Jesus there have been no wars fought in the cause of the truth of the Gospel because nobody who believes the real message of Jesus would ever be involved in a war! True believers submit to persecution rather than fight against it. Jesus declared quite plainly, "Love your enemies and pray for those who persecute you" (Matthew 5:44) and later to Peter, "all who take the sword will perish by the sword" (Matthew 26:52). In the last 2,000 years, many wars have indeed been fought in God's name but none of them by anybody who believed and practised truth. We would even go so far as to say we could use the desire for sanctioned violence or the willingness to participate in war to help discern between truth and error. Human pride rather than the truth of God lies behind wars fought in the name of Christ.

If a man declares he is on God's side but his actions (in going to war) clearly demonstrate that he is not, it is unreasonable to use his actions as evidence against God. It is not logically sound to demand that God ought to be responsible for man's disobedience.

What should be a Christian's attitude to war?

Since the origin of our community this has been an important discussion. The name "Christadelphian" was coined to provide the societies of the Brethren denominational identity for the purpose of conscientious objection to military service during the American Civil War. Our objection to war and military service has been traditionally based upon a number of principles:

- We are not to resist evil (Matthew 5:39,44).
- We are not to kill (Romans 13:9; James 2:11).
- We are strangers and pilgrims (Hebrews 11:13; John 17:14-18).
- Our allegiance is to Christ (Colossians 3:24).

- To obey the government except when it conflicts with the laws of God (Acts 5:29; Romans 13:1-7).

Participation in and support for war will see us contradicting these principles. The true Christian perspective at this time is to shun violence and avoid war. That is not to say that true Christians never sin and are never violent. They ought never to be – but sadly we frequently fail to match the example of Christ. We may not excuse our failure citing human nature as the cause, but we must strive to follow Jesus more perfectly. Having learned the principle of non-resistance from Christ the message of the apostles was that we should be, "not violent but gentle, not quarrelsome" (1 Timothy 3:3). This is equally important on the personal as well as the broader level.

Underpinning our attitude to war is the question of our relationship to the State. Believers must see themselves as citizens of the kingdom of God who happen to be residents (usually with the status of citizens because of birth) of whichever country they are in. The questions surrounding whether a cause is just, whether a war is necessary, whether defence against a hostile aggressor is justified, all become superfluous for the believer. None of these causes are ours. When (and only when) Christ commands us to fight for him, will it be permissible to do so.

Jesus said to Pilate:

"My kingdom is not of this world. If my kingdom were of this world, my servants would have been fighting, that I might not be delivered over to the Jews. But my kingdom is not from the world." (John 18:36)

There will come a time when Jesus returns to set up his kingdom that his servants will fight, but that is not now. Anybody participating in war in the current arrangement of things is not fighting for Christ or for his cause, despite what they might say. Christ and modern politics do not mix.

Christians have adopted the ideas of Greek philosophers and moulded them into what is called 'Just War Theory'. This specifies conditions in which it is believed to be acceptable for Christians to engage in conflict. We might simply note that it is not Biblical and may therefore be dismissed.

Don't Christadelphians merely 'cherry pick' the Bible?

Let us be quite clear, we do not have licence and may not apply scripture as we see fit, accepting one principle and rejecting another. We must accept all of what God teaches us whether we like it or not.

This does not mean that we are subject to (and must keep) all the regulations of the Law of Moses. Humanists are quick to point out we have no right to hold scripture sacred if we eat bacon or prawns for example. True it is that a modern Christian does not often keep these and other regulations of the law though they may if they choose, but in so doing they have not 'cherry picked' rules to follow and set aside others.

Since Jesus came and fulfilled the law, the ordinances and provisions it contained have been set aside. This is clearly shown in Hebrews where we read of the new arrangement:

"In speaking of a new covenant, he makes the first one obsolete. And what is becoming obsolete and growing old is ready to vanish away." (Hebrews 8:13)

Speaking of the old arrangement the writer goes on to say:

"According to this arrangement, gifts and sacrifices are offered that cannot perfect the conscience of the worshipper, but deal only with food and drink and various washings, regulations for the body imposed until the time of reformation." (Hebrews 9:9)

Clearly the regulations of the Law of Moses that are of a ceremonial and ritual nature are no longer required. Actually, atheists in pointing out that we don't follow the ritual of the law, have ironically themselves 'cherry picked' scripture and ignored the passages that declare the ritual laws are now obsolete. The ritual laws applied to the nation of Israel and were never intended to be applied to Gentiles in the Christian era.

Laws that concern moral principles however remain in force and are almost always reinforced by Christ or the apostles and given greater impetus. The following message to the Roman believers emphasises this quite clearly:

"Owe no one anything, except to love each other, for the one who loves another has fulfilled the law. For the commandments, 'You shall not commit adultery, You shall not murder, You shall not steal, You shall not covet,' and any other commandment, are summed up in this word: 'You shall love your neighbour as yourself.' Love does no wrong to a neighbour; therefore love is the fulfilling of the law."

(Romans 13:8-10)

When early Christians were asked to, "Abstain from what has been sacrificed to idols, and from blood, and from what has been strangled, and from sexual immorality" (Acts 15:29), the context clearly establishes that all the law did not need to be kept. The dietary recommendations were to keep the peace between Jews and Gentiles as the Jews initially struggled with the concept of universal salvation. The Apostle Paul was later able to write:

"I know and am persuaded in the Lord Jesus that nothing is unclean in itself, but it is unclean for anyone who thinks it unclean."

(Romans 14:14)

The new arrangements under Christ might be less physically exacting but they are more spiritually demanding. We now do not need to be particular with diet and ritual but the command not to commit adultery, for example, has been extended considerably. Jesus said, "I say to you that everyone who looks at a woman with lustful intent has already committed adultery with her in his heart" (Matthew 5:28). Whereas it was a physical impossibility to keep all the provisions of the law, it is much simpler in Christ. However, the difficulty now lies in fulfilling the spirit of the law which none of us can do perfectly.

We might well ask, what was the purpose of the ceremonial and ritual law? Why was Israel given it, and why should we read it?

> "So then, the law was our guardian until Christ came, in order that we might be justified by faith. But now that faith has come, we are no longer under a guardian." (Galatians 3:24,25)

The Jews were intended to see principles about God and Christ in the law and to look forward to him; we who can see the actual image of Jesus use the shadows in the law to provide interesting dimensions to the person and teaching of Christ.

'Cherry picking' parts of the Bible we like, and ignoring those we don't, is clearly "distorting the word of God" (2 Corinthians 4:2, NET) and ought to be rejected. Accepting the arrangements in Christ that have made the regulations of the Old Testament law obsolete is not 'cherry picking' and perfectly acceptable. A believer may choose to follow Old Testament ceremonial and ritual laws and equally they are free to elect not to. "Each must be fully convinced in his own mind" (Romans 14:5).

If they don't exist, why didn't Jesus expose demons and devils as false?

In the times of Jesus, it was common to attribute some types of disease (notably mental illness and other brain diseases) to demon possession. Demon possession was blamed for things for which ancient medicine had no explanation. In the Gospels, we do not find the attribution of demon-induced illnesses evenly distributed across ancient Palestine. Only in the less educated, more Gentile connected and more superstitious areas is it common; illness was not normally attributed to demons in Judea. This suggests that demon possession is more in the minds of the sufferers (and their acquaintances) than in actual reality.

When Jesus healed such people the record of the incident often states that he cast out the devil or the unclean spirit. When Legion was healed of madness the afflicting demons asked Jesus to be allowed to possess the nearby herd of pigs, and upon consent being given, they entered the pigs who went mad and ran down a hill and drowned themselves. Such incidents suggest that demon possession is a real thing.

Which position is correct? In ancient Greek understanding, people believed that a demon was the spirit of a deceased person. In the Pythagorean commentaries we read:

> "The whole air is full of souls. We call them *daemones* and heroes, and it is they who send dreams, signs and illnesses to men; and not only men, but also to sheep and other domestic animals. It is towards these daemones that we direct purifications and apotropaic rites [magic designed to ward off evil spirits], all kinds of divination, the art of reading chance utterances, and so on."

The Greeks believed that much disease was the result of various demons. That other causes of disease were understood is clear for we read:

> "And news of him went out through all Syria; and they took to him all who were ill with different diseases and pains, those having evil spirits and those who were off their heads, and those who had no power of moving." (Matthew 4:24, BBE)

This passage identifies three conditions not attributable to demon possession. Things that had an obvious physical cause were excluded from the idea of demon possession, and only those with no apparent cause (such as epilepsy, mental illness and various infections) were attributed to demon possession. To treat the disease one had to identify the demon involved and then undergo whatever would be likely to rid the person of that demon. Demons could also be rather more benign causing euphoria or prophetic utterances such as those of the oracle of Delphi.

It is certainly true that this idea had infiltrated Jewish thought. Jews also performed exorcisms and Jesus refers to this when he said, "if I cast out demons by Beelzebul, by whom do your sons cast them out?" (Matthew 12:27). It is difficult to underestimate how widespread and socially accepted the idea of demon possession was among Jewish communities in Jesus' day.

Modern medicine does not accept demon possession as a cause of illness and has entirely different treatments based on understanding the pathophysiological causes. That the ancient remedies did not work is evident from the testimony of those who came to Jesus. The fact that modern treatments are often very successful should cast doubt upon the ancient belief.

It has been suggested that since God tasks particular angels with creating evil (compare the destroying angel in the final plague on Egypt) that it was a similar phenomenon at work in the days of Jesus. This would explain why Jesus was so successful in curing those who were afflicted but does not explain why modern medicine is. Presumably if angels were tasked by God to create evil in the ancient world, they would still be at it today and modern treatment should be ineffective. The theory of angels acting as God's agents to do evil in the lives of men and women in ancient times seems unsupportable.

Since the Bible does not teach an immortal soul, the Greek concept of demons cannot be correct. Consequently, nobody in the Gospels was possessed by a demon; they (and others) merely thought they were. This leaves us with the knowledge that Jesus healed an actual disease rather than cast out a demon. People were simply suffering from disease and Jesus by the power of God healed them.

Jesus may have been acknowledging the personification of sin as the ultimate cause of evil. We are well acquainted with the idea that the devil is used in scripture as a personification of sin. When an intangible object is personified it becomes more real. God wants sin and the effects of sin to be keenly felt, to be very real in our consciousness. He wants us to see them as undesirable interlopers. That sin is an unwanted intruder into our lives is clear from the words of Paul, "Now if I do what I do not want, it is no longer I who do it, but sin that dwells within me" (Romans 7:20). Paul speaks of sin as a separate entity tangibly residing within us when we know from James chapter 1, it is simply our own lust. If it is reasonable to personify sin, it is by no means bizarre to personify disease. In a very real sense all of the diseases and afflictions are caused by the curse introduced in the Garden in Eden and ultimately the result of sin.

What Jesus did, and what people thought he did, were not the same things. Even when the record speaks of Jesus casting out demons he was simply healing people. If demon possession was either simply illness or illness personified, why not just say, 'it was not a demon, the man was sick and I healed him'? The question is further complicated on some occasions when Jesus apparently has conversations with the devils. If a demon were not a real thing, why would Jesus interact with it as though it was? Whatever the demon was, Jesus effectively dismissed it as nothing compared to the power of God. In that sense it really didn't matter what the problem was – the focus was entirely on the solution.

Modern paediatricians will cheerfully accommodate the ignorance and false beliefs of a child (rather than confront them) because there is no reason not to and it will make no difference anyway. A child with severe cramping abdominal pain might complain of 'crocodiles in my tummy'. There is no harm in co-operating with this assessment of the illness and using it in the cure. The child might be told, 'I have got some medicine to send the crocodiles away'. Everybody but the child knows what is going on and nobody is hurt in the process. That the doctor does not inform the child of the correct aetiology of the disease does not mean that they agree with them; they are merely accommodating them for the purpose of calmly and gently taking control of the situation. In time the child will grow and learn, but that need not happen on the day. We submit that this is what Jesus did – accommodating the superstitious beliefs trusting that by gaining confidence in Jesus the people would then learn from him and in time dismiss their superstition as childish.

The man who came to Jesus searching for a miracle, had a son whom he believed was possessed by a spirit. Said the father, "it seizes him, it throws him down, and he foams and grinds his teeth and becomes rigid" (Mark 9:18). Such symptoms are completely consistent with (and explained by) epilepsy. However, the father believed it was a devil, and by his own admission struggled to believe Jesus. What was most important for the father? To be corrected regarding his wrong (though widely accepted) notion of a demon, or to have his son healed and he himself brought to trust in Jesus? Clearly the man was not yet a disciple of Jesus and was steeped in pagan superstition, yet by healing his son and thereby establishing credibility, it was likely the man might become a follower and leave superstition behind. Rather than acceptance of a pagan concept, the healing might have provided a gateway to better understanding. Seldom are converts made through confrontation. Had Jesus dismissed the prevailing opinion and practice, the opportunity to convert the father would probably have evaporated. By accommodating their ideas and showing (by healing) that he had the power of God, there was a greater chance of them believing Jesus and abandoning superstition to serve only the living God. Conversely, when the Apostle Paul in Lystra tried both healing and dismissing pagan superstition at the same time, it precipitated discontent and in the aftermath, he was stoned even though he had performed a notable miracle (Acts 14:8-19).

What about the pigs in the healing of Legion? Mark records:

> "The unclean spirits came out and entered the pigs; and the herd, numbering about two thousand, rushed down the steep bank into the sea and drowned in the sea." (Mark 5:13)

How can we suggest that Jesus was accommodating a concept when the reality seemed quite different? Precisely how Jesus sent the pigs mad, we cannot say – it must have been by the power of God; but we are confident answering why. The man called Legion really believed he was possessed by multiple demons; for him this was the explanation for his severe bouts of psychotic behaviour. Legion not only needed to be healed, but he needed to know that he was healed. The description of the symptoms suggests that there were sane moments that punctuated his madness. Had Jesus healed him without a demonstration of the fact, he might well have thought, 'I have felt sane at times but the madness has always returned; how long will it be this time before I am again tormented?' He needed some assurance that the demons he believed were in him were gone. Presumably the power of God drove the pigs down the hill and provided Legion with visual confirmation that his madness was gone.

We submit that the ignorance and superstition that led people to believe that illness resulted from demon possession was not challenged by Jesus in the interests of having them believe him and learning a better way. The story of Legion suggests that this was successful for he became a preacher of Jesus.

Are Christadelphians a cult?

The idea of a cult is today almost universally insulting. Merriam-Webster's Dictionary defines a cult as "a small religious group that is not part of a larger and more accepted religion and that has beliefs regarded by many people as extreme or dangerous". While the Christadelphian faith certainly fits the first part of the definition we would reject that we are either extreme or dangerous. Complementing the above definition there are essentially four accepted principles that a religious group might have before it would be considered a cult. These are:

- Divergence (teachings that are different from mainstream Christianity).

- Exclusiveness (membership seen as critical for salvation).

- Secretive (certain practices and ideas are only available to the initiated few).

- Authoritarian (a human leader who expects total loyalty and unquestioning obedience).

We need to remember that Christianity was viewed as a cult when it first began. The Jews described the Apostle Paul to Felix in terms that made it clear what they felt about Christians:

"We have found this man a plague, one which stirs up riots among all the Jews throughout the world and is a ringleader of the sect of the Nazarenes."   (Acts 24:5)

When Paul came to Rome he was interviewed by the Jews who said, "We desire to hear from you what your views are, for with regard to this sect we know that everywhere it is spoken against"

(Acts 28:22). Clearly, being a minority and being different is not always a bad thing.

Divergence

The Christadelphian community accepts (even rejoices in) the fact we have divergent beliefs from mainstream Christianity. We feel that we have returned to the roots of Christianity and as in the case of the first ecclesia this has caused the established religious communities (who then as now reject the teaching and practice of Jesus) to view us as a dangerous cult.

Exclusiveness

We do not assert that we are the only ones who have the truth, merely that what we believe *is* truth. It may sound similar but there is an important difference: one is exclusive and the other is not. We believe anybody (Christadelphian or not) who believes the truths of scripture can be saved. While we restrict full fellowship (sharing the bread and wine) to fellow Christadelphians in a similar way to other churches, we would maintain that this does not make us more exclusive than any of them. Our community in common with others has views regarding marriage outside of the faith and preserving the teaching and practice of our faith in line with scripture. This may be viewed by some as undesirable exclusiveness; however we believe we follow scriptural teaching and practice when extending or withdrawing fellowship (see 1 Corinthians 5:11; 2 John verses 10,11).

Secretive and authoritarian

There is no secrecy but rather transparency and openness, and no person at the head of our faith. While it is true that there have at times arisen from within the Christadelphian community (as in other churches) splinter groups that may have had some tendencies to either exclusiveness, secrecy or human leadership, they are the exception that proves the rule. Such extreme views are neither shared, nor accepted by the Christadelphian community *per se*. Other than size and lack of acceptance by other churches, the only point of identity as a cult, is that Christadelphian beliefs differ from traditional views.

The Roman Catholic Church, while possessing accepted mainstream beliefs and being quite large, without doubt has the final three points of identity as a cult. The first words of the Athanasian Creed are:

> "Whosoever will be saved, before all things it is necessary that he hold the Catholic Faith. Which Faith except everyone do keep whole and undefiled, without doubt he shall perish everlastingly."

It is common knowledge that within the Catholic Church there are accepted secret organisations such as the Jesuits. The head of the Catholic Church is a man (the Pope) who demands allegiance and has through the ages been a party to killing those who dissent. One could cogently argue that the Roman Catholic faith has more to identify it as a cult than the Christadelphian faith.

Because the Christadelphian community is relatively small, comparatively recent and differs from mainstream Christianity in many of its beliefs, the established churches choose (unfairly we suggest) to dismiss us as a cult. The American screenwriter and film producer Robert Altman once drily observed that a cult was simply, "not enough people to make a minority". We feel that the Christadelphian faith has been unfairly labelled as a cult primarily because we are small. We simply appeal again to the Berean spirit to make a choice based upon (and only upon) scripture.

It must be acknowledged that there are inherent dangers in seeing our community as having the truth of the Gospel when many others do not. This can lead to a feeling of being superior (when we clearly are not), a sense of being above the law (when we should be subject to it), a fear of contamination leading to aloofness (how then shall we preach?) and a sense that our community traditions place us on the path to salvation (when they clearly do not). We need to guard against these ideas and realise that we have been grafted into the hope of Israel and while we might stand fast through faith we must not become proud (see Romans 11:20-22).

Is it right that all unbelievers will die?

It is right that we all die! We are mortal – it is our nature. We all die because it is the result of sin. "All have sinned and fall short of the glory of God" (Romans 3:23). The crux of the question really concerns the reality and finality of death. It is asking whether death is the absolute end for unbelievers and whether they have no hope.

The Bible teaches plainly that without God there is nothing beyond death and no consciousness in death. There is no teaching in scripture that leads us to believe that people will live on in some spiritual sense. [5]

All of us are at the end of this life destined for the oblivion of the grave. Sadly, unbelievers will have "no more share in all that is done under the sun" (Ecclesiastes 9:6). The critical element is belief. If we are without it then we are without hope. Those who die without Christ do not have a worse death than any others – they simply die and stay dead. There is no further punishment, but neither is there any reward. If this seems unfair, we must remember that is a consequence of a choice not to believe or seek for God. Jesus has promised:

"Ask, and it will be given to you; seek, and you will find; knock, and it will be opened to you. For everyone who asks

---

5   For a discussion of texts that have been used to support immortal souls the reader is referred to excellent books such as *Wrested Scriptures* by Ron Abel, *A look at those difficult passages* by Harry Whittaker, and *Puzzling Passages* by John Hellawell.

receives, and the one who seeks finds, and to the one who knocks it will be opened." (Matthew 7:7,8)

We surely would not suggest that God ought to compromise His principles and grant life to those who neglect Him, dismiss Him or hate Him.

Only believers in God have a hope of returning from the grave. There will be some believers who are alive when Jesus returns and only these of all people who have ever lived (assuming they are judged worthy) will not die. Speaking of the last day Jesus said of these people, "everyone who lives and believes in me shall never die". Speaking of those who have already died he said, "Whoever believes in me, though he die, yet shall he live" (John 11:25,26). The hope of the Bible for those who have died is to return from the grave, to be resurrected and then changed into immortal beings. The hope for those living when Jesus returns is to be changed. Sadly, those without God have no hope (see Ephesians 2:12; 1 Thessalonians 4:13).

Isn't Christianity just a psychological crutch?

David wrote, "the LORD was my support" (Psalm 18:18) The Hebrew word translated "support" means a staff or a crutch. The hope of believers makes them more resilient, more joyful and stronger than other people. In a very real sense, we are supported psychologically by being believers in Christ. Christianity *is* a psychological crutch and claims to be the only true rock of support. However, the question supposes that there is nothing of substance behind the feelings of support, that the psychological benefits of Christianity are completely intangible and the hope imaginary. At its heart the question suggests that the reward of immortality discussed briefly in the previous answer is not real, that the hope is hopeless. The assumption is that believers in Christ do not face up to the real world and are simply using their faith to make them feel better and avoid the issues of life. In short, is faith credible and sensible or is God merely an imaginary friend?

In order to please God we need (according to Hebrews 11:6) to believe in both the reality of God and the reality of the reward. If there is no reward then faith is pointless. If the hope of eternal life were no hope at all, then Christianity would only be a psychological crutch. However, if the hope is real then the entire life of a follower of Christ is infused with purpose and meaning.

Writing to Titus, Paul stated in the introduction that he was "in hope of eternal life, which God, who never lies, promised before the ages began" (Titus 1:2). God guarantees the promise! To reduce the hope is to discount God entirely. The matter is as simple as, does God exist or not? Believers say, 'He does', and stake their eternal future on the reality of His existence. Atheists declare, 'there is no God', and insist that faith is vain. The atheist, having dismissed God, suggests that believers have an imaginary security blanket as their hope.

Let us consider the matter logically: if believers are wrong about God (and there is not the slightest suggestion that we are) we will eventually die – having gained or lost nothing – because there is nothing to gain or lose in the first place. If atheists are wrong about God they will have lost the gift of eternal life and condemned themselves to eternity in the grave. Which of us can afford to be wrong? Blaise Pascal once famously said, "If you gain, you gain all. If you lose, you lose nothing. Wager then, without hesitation, that He exists". We are by no means believers because it is the safest bet, but when beset with doubt it can be reassuring that at the very least it is a logical option. Atheists are in a lose / lose position; they have robbed the present life of meaning and disqualified themselves from the future. On the other hand Paul assured us that, "godliness is of value in every way, as it holds promise for the present life and also for the life to come" (1 Timothy 4:8). We stake our faith on the resurrection of Jesus Christ. If he has not been raised our faith is futile.

How did Jesus' death take away our sins?

It must be admitted, victory by death seems on the face of it to be a very unlikely mechanism. Paul declared as much writing to the believers in Corinth, "Christ crucified, a stumbling block to Jews and folly to Gentiles" (1 Corinthians 1:23). Human reasoning cannot see how this would work and dismisses it as ridiculous. While clearly Jesus' death was for us, and the scriptures plainly tell us as much (1 Corinthians 15:3), we might first look at what his death achieved for himself.

Jesus was made of the same stuff as us. Though he was the Son of God he was very much a man. This means that he was affected by fleshly desire just as we are, being "one who in every respect has been tempted as we are, yet without sin" (Hebrews 4:15). For Jesus, the battle with sin raged all his life and was only halted at death, "For one who has died has been set free from sin" (Romans 6:7). When Jesus was raised to immortality, he was thereafter entirely free from the temptation to sin. Sin and death had for him been defeated, "We know that Christ, being raised from the dead, will never die again; death no longer has dominion over him" (Romans 6:9). Jesus' death brought release from the battle with sin and his resurrection granted him life eternal and a new nature.

The law of sin and death had been reversed in one man – Jesus. Just as sin and death came into the world through one man (Adam) so sin and death were defeated in one man – Jesus Christ. Sin was defeated because Jesus never sinned, and death was defeated because Jesus was resurrected.

He could not stay in the grave, "because it was not possible for him to be held in its power" (Acts 2:24). Our Lord was promised and given immortality. It is painfully evident both that we deserve to die, and that we will die. How does Christ's victory translate to us? How can we become sinless? How do unrighteous people get transformed into righteous saints? So many hard questions! Happily the answers are quite straightforward.

Our sins are forgiven and righteousness is conferred by God by our understanding of what He has done for us and our belief in the work accomplished by Christ. We get to share the victory by association with Jesus. Through faith in Christ and baptism into him we associate ourselves both with the death of Jesus and with the life he now lives, anticipating that the glory he now has will be something we too experience. For God graciously accepts our faith in Him and accounts us righteous, forgiving us all sin and reserving us a place in His kingdom.

All of this required Jesus to die a violent and unnatural death as a criminal. Jesus did not get old and die as we do; his life was cut short in a voluntary act of sacrificial obedience. In this way he demonstrated in one act both how evil sin is, and how right (or righteous) God was in condemning sin. This demonstration did not merely involve the death of Jesus, but also his life of sinlessness and his resurrection and ascension to glory. Had Jesus deserved to die because of his *own* sins his death would have meant nothing; but since he died for *our* sins his death counts for everything. Had Jesus not been raised, his death would have been a worthless hollow victory and an exercise in futility, but now we are "saved by his life" (Romans 5:10). Through the life, death and resurrection of Jesus we have hope. He now lives to intercede for all believers and will come again to complete God's work of transformation and redemption.

Righteousness "will be counted to us who believe in him who raised from the dead Jesus our Lord, who was delivered up for our trespasses and raised for our justification" (Romans 4:25).

The critical step for us is belief. We need to believe that Jesus:

- Came as a man (1 John 4:2).

- Lived a sinless life (Hebrews 7:26).

- Died in obedience to God (Philippians 2:8).

- Was raised to eternal life (Acts 13:30-37).

- Asks us to share his victory through belief and baptism (Romans 6:8).

These things are folly to the natural man. For many, the idea of a sinless man dying to save us is unbelievable; but, as Paul explained, "it pleased God through the folly of what we preach to save those who believe" (1 Corinthians 1:21). If we believe in Jesus, then forgiveness, righteousness and immortality can be ours.

Aren't you simply following your parents' faith?

If your parents are believers, it is to be hoped that you are following their faith. This will be a great source of comfort and delight to them. However there is nothing simple about it! There are many families who have children who do not share their parents' faith. Wise parents will arrange family circumstances to encourage their children to accept Christ, but this is by no means a foregone conclusion.

If one or both of our parents are in the faith and we grow up exposed to its teaching, it seems sooner or later we will ask questions about faith. It can be a cause for genuine doubt especially when we see our parents not living up to what they preach. It comes down to being fully convinced in our own mind – and this can only come from our own personal discovery and conversion. We must at some time make the faith our own and put our faith in Jesus Christ.

Suggesting that faith *only* runs in families, fails to consider the call of God. The purpose of God with men and women is to bring them into His eternal family; He is always at work calling them to the Gospel. It is the divine method for God to call individuals who He knows will teach their families – for example, Abraham of whom God said:

> "I have chosen him so that he may command his children and his household after him to keep the way of the LORD by doing what is right and just." (Genesis 18:19)

As parents we have a divine command to teach our families the way of God:

> "These words I am commanding you today must be kept in mind, and you must teach them to your children and speak of them as you sit in your house, as you walk along the road, as you lie down, and as you get up." (Deuteronomy 6:6,7)

Preaching may be an easier task if the prospective believer has already been exposed to the Gospel within a family of believers, but ecclesias all over the world have many converts from families who are not Christadelphian. Clearly these are not simply following their parents' faith. Faith in God and Christ is a deeply personal thing. Families can encourage it but are powerless to create it. It is a response to the call of God. A family might be the vehicle that brings God to an individual, but it cannot bring an individual to God – only a personal response to the divine invitation can achieve that.

If baptism is important, why wasn't the 'thief on the cross' baptized?

It is argued that since he was nailed to a cross, there was no way for him to be baptized after his confession and repentance. If he was accepted by Jesus (Luke 23:43) in the absence of baptism, how can we demand it is critical for any of us?

We might first note that nowhere in scripture are we told that the thief who was crucified alongside Jesus was not previously baptized. It is possible (though we have no record of it) that the man had been baptized by John or perhaps by Jesus' disciples. To demand that since there is no *record* of a baptism, there was *no baptism*, is unsound logic. To argue from silence is always questionable. There is no record of the baptism of most of the apostles – that in no way demands that they were not baptized.

The Apostle Paul makes it clear that baptism connects us to the death of Jesus. In symbol we die with him. "Do you not know that all of us who have been baptized into Christ Jesus were baptized into his death?" (Romans 6:3). The spiritual power of baptism for a believer lies in the symbolic connection to the death of Christ. The 'thief on the cross' had a literal connection – he *actually* died with Jesus. We might reasonably argue that he was "baptized with the baptism" with which Jesus was baptized, to use the words of the Lord himself when referring to his death (Mark 10:38). Seen this way, rather than not being baptized at all, his association by way of death was a greater baptism than any of us will ever undertake.

Rather than diminish the importance of baptism, we submit that the record of the repentant thief and the promise of Jesus, "you will be with me in paradise" (Luke 23:43) underlines the truth concerning baptism: "if we have died with Christ, we believe that we will also live with him" (Romans 6:8).

Despite the considerable emphasis on baptism we note that Jesus' ultimate disqualification is lack of belief. Mark 16:16 does *not* say, 'whoever does not believe *and is not baptized* will be condemned'. We might think the added words are implied but they are clearly omitted. While in normal circumstances there is no reason why baptism should not follow belief, there may be extraordinary conditions where baptism is practically unable to follow belief. This leaves us to ask whether in these circumstances belief alone may be sufficient. What if death occurs after belief and repentance but before baptism? Would we demand that the person *must* be excluded from salvation? Perhaps this matches the circumstances of the thief on the cross?

If belief only is deemed acceptable by a loving God in circumstances of extremity, it does not negate the sound teaching that baptism is important for salvation, nor provide any precedent for us to reject baptism in the overwhelming majority of cases.

Chapter 8

Questions about religion – in practice

"Just in terms of allocation of time resources, religion is not very efficient. There's a lot more I could be doing on a Sunday morning." (Bill Gates, businessman)

"It is only when men begin to worship that they begin to grow." (Calvin Coolidge, American President)

Do I have to be a member of an ecclesia?

Having already suggested that anybody who believes the truth of the Gospel will be saved, Christadelphian or not, the question arises, why be a member of a Christadelphian ecclesia? Surely such membership is either ancillary or surplus to salvation. The advent of the COVID-19 pandemic in early 2020 saw global challenges to the way ecclesias operated. Many people have reviewed ecclesial participation in the light of restrictions on gathering and worship, and have wondered whether the concept of ecclesial membership and involvement as we once knew it remains relevant.

We need to remember that the societies of believers initially established by the apostles are not of human origin. God conceived them and Christ instituted them.

Let us consider some important Bible principles about the ecclesia.

1. *Jesus established the ecclesia.* It was to be a public, earthly institution and would mark out, affirm, and oversee those who profess to believe in him as the Son of God (Matthew 16:18,19; 18:15-20). Jesus established the ecclesia to declare publicly those who belong to him in order to give the world a display of the good news about himself (John 17:21,23; see also Ephesians 3:10). Jesus wants the world to know who belongs to him and who doesn't. How is the world to know who belongs to him and who doesn't? They are to see those who identify themselves with his people in the visible, public institution he established for this very purpose. They are to look at the members of his Ecclesia. Jesus intends for his people to be marked out as a visible, public group, which means joining together in local ecclesias.

2. *The ecclesia as a body.* Ecclesial membership is implied in the metaphor of the body of Christ.

   > "The eye cannot say to the hand, 'I have no need of you,' nor again the head to the feet, 'I have no need of you.' On the contrary, the parts of the body that seem to be weaker are indispensable, and on those parts of the body that we think less honourable we bestow the greater honour, and our unpresentable parts are treated with greater modesty, which our more presentable parts do not require. But God has so composed the body, giving greater honour to the part that lacked it, that there may be no division in the body, but that the members may have the same care for one another. If one member suffers, all suffer together; if one member is honoured, all rejoice together."   (1 Corinthians 12:21-26)

There is a unity and organic relationship implied in the imagery of the body. There is something unnatural about a Christian attaching himself to a body of believers and yet not choosing to be a functioning member of that body. We are told that, "Christ is the head of the church, his body" (Ephesians 5:23). Surely we would not wish to distance ourselves from either Christ or his body. There may be times when through isolation, misfortune or illness we are unable to share the blessings of an ecclesia, but this should for most of us be the exception and not the rule.

3. *Appointment of leaders and administrators of groups of believers.* Elders were appointed in every city to shepherd the flock (Titus 1:4). Ecclesial membership is implied in the way the New Testament required elders to care for the flock in their charge. Elders could extend their focus and care for anyone within the limits of their ability. However, it would seem that the Bible gives elders a special responsibility to care for a specific group or community of people.

> "Pay careful attention to yourselves and to all the flock, in which the Holy Spirit has made you overseers, to care for the church of God, which he obtained with his own blood." (Acts 20:28)

These verses do not say elders cannot invest in unbelievers or those who are not yet ecclesial members, but it does make clear that their first responsibility is to a particular flock. How do elders know who their flock is if not through membership?

4. *Discipline / accountability.* Ecclesial membership is implied by the way the ecclesia is supposed to discipline its members. The ecclesia appears to be the final court of appeal in matters relating to membership.

"If your brother sins against you, go and tell him his fault, between you and him alone. If he listens to you, you have gained your brother. But if he does not listen, take one or two others along with you, that every charge may be established by the evidence of two or three witnesses. If he refuses to listen to them, tell it to the church. And if he refuses to listen even to the church, let him be to you as a Gentile and a tax collector." (Matthew 18:15-17)

If there is no such thing as ecclesial membership, how do we define the group of people who will take up this extraordinarily delicate and vital matter of exhorting those who are unrepentant and finally rendering a righteous judgement about their standing in the Christian community? It is hard to believe that anyone who shows up claiming to be a Christian should be a part of this process. "The church" must be a definable group to handle such weighty matters so that we know who the scripture is referring to when it says, "take it to the church".

5. *Excommunication / withdrawal of membership.* The fact that excommunication exists, implies ecclesial membership. Paul indicates this in 1 Corinthians where he deals with the necessity of putting someone out of the ecclesia.

"For what have I to do with judging outsiders? Is it not those inside the church whom you are to judge? God judges those outside. Purge the evil person from among you." (1 Corinthians 5:12,13)

There are two significant implications here: one is that there is an 'in the ecclesia' group and an 'outside the ecclesia' group. Being in the ecclesia is definable. The other implication is that a person can be removed from being 'in the ecclesia'. Such a formal removal would not be possible if there were no such thing as membership. Membership helps to define who is an accountable part of the ecclesial body.

6. *A place of communal memorial and reading, comfort and teaching.* Paul wrote:

> "Command and teach these things. Let no one despise you for your youth, but set the believers an example in speech, in conduct, in love, in faith, in purity. Until I come, devote yourself to the public reading of scripture, to exhortation, to teaching."
>
> (1 Timothy 4:11-13)

Evidently the public place where this was done was the place where the ecclesia met. We may remember Christ by way of bread and wine on our own (and some have no other choice) but there is a scriptural injunction that we should be "not neglecting to meet together, as is the habit of some, but encouraging one another, and all the more as you see the Day drawing near" (Hebrews 10:25).

There is a tendency for some to be nominal members of an ecclesia but never attend. Perhaps they live far away and have not chosen to join a local ecclesia? Perhaps electronic remote methods are preferred? Neither the ecclesia of which they are nominally a member nor any local ecclesias are in a good position to minister to (or to be ministered by) these brothers and sisters. Such a choice has little to commend it. There is little good that others can do for us and even less that we may do for them if we are detached and aloof.

The ancient Amalekites did not pick off those Israelites in the centre of the camp, but those on the fringe. Active membership of an ecclesia, while not absolutely mandatory for salvation, is the most advisable course of action. For most of us there is no good reason (and several bad ones) why we should not be active ecclesial members. The COVID-19 pandemic has reminded us that we may have to come up with creative ways to remain connected, but ecclesial fellowship continues to be a critical concept in the life of a believer.

What is the point of prayer and can it work?

Prayer, at its simplest is conversation with God. It requires faith, as the Hebrews were simply reminded: "Whoever would draw near to God must believe that he exists and that he rewards those who seek him" (Hebrews 11:6). That is, faith in the reality of God and faith that prayer can work.

There has been much discussion about the value of prayer; is it just for our benefit, so we feel comforted or can it change things? We feel it must be both. Prayer unburdens our soul and unleashes assistance from the Almighty to help. There are two caveats to the second part of the last sentence: God will only act in accordance with His purpose for us and He often acts in ways unseen or unnoticed. We can thus mistake what we see and experience for inaction or lack of care. Regarding the first of these we are told:

> "We are certain that if we make any request to him which is right in his eyes, he will give ear to us: and if we are certain that he gives ear to all our requests, we are equally certain that we will get our requests."　　(1 John 5:14,15, BBE)

Regarding the second thought, Jacob was caused to reflect, "Truly, the LORD is in this place and I was not conscious of it". This can make the prayer a challenge for us. Are we prepared to trust God when the answer is not what we had hoped for? Will we continue to believe even though God's timing seems off to us? Shall we doubt the hand of God merely because it is not obvious to us? These are hard questions to ask, but if we have faith we are promised that God will work in our lives.

Some might say, 'I asked God for something and I was ignored'. Perhaps we might feel this most keenly regarding a serious illness of a loved one. We prayed earnestly for recovery, and they died! We must trust that God knows what is best. Paul affirmed, "We know that for those who love God all things work together for good, for those who are called according to his purpose" (Romans 8:28). In any case the death of a believer is merely sleep. Perhaps our mistake in praying for recovery is in presenting God with the desired outcome and giving Him no space to work. Rather we would do better to present the problem. God can work through all the options and select that which He knows is best in the long run.

What we have said so far has focussed on only one aspect of prayer – request. There is another entire consideration of thankfulness. In prayer we can show our appreciation to God, and declare his greatness. God clearly delights to receive praise and worship for the Psalmist records, "Give praise to the LORD; for it is good to make melody to our God; praise is pleasing and beautiful" (Psalm 147:1, BBE).

We are clearly told that, "Even before a word is on my tongue, behold, O LORD, you know it altogether" (Psalm 139:4). This was amplified by Jesus when he said, "your Father knows what you need before you ask him" (Matthew 6:8). Paul picked up the thread of this thought and comforted believers with the thought that:

> "We are not able to make prayer to God in the right way; but the Spirit puts our desires into words which are not in our power to say." (Romans 8:26, BBE)

All that being the case, one might ask why bother at all? If God knows what we need, knows what we are going to say and even accepts the words we can't even manage to say – why pray at all? It would be a dull friendship if we never talked, never asked for help or expressed appreciation for each other. Why should our relationship with God be different?

We submit that prayer has a threefold purpose: to strengthen us, to gladden the Father and to change circumstances. Not every prayer will achieve all three.

Should we pray to Jesus?

Some believe that prayer is only to God. People of many denominations pray to God and Jesus. The Catholic and Orthodox churches pray to God, Jesus and many people long since dead. What is the Biblical position? It is clear that we should honour Jesus (John 5:22,23) – does that include prayer to Jesus?

Jesus when he taught us to pray said, "Pray then like this: Our Father in heaven ..." (Matthew 6:9) We might imagine that if Jesus intended prayer to himself then it would be here in his premier teaching on prayer. It may be argued that while he was on the earth, conversation with Jesus was possible and those who interacted with him talked personally to the Lord – there was no need to encourage or teach it, it just happened. Is that different from prayer and should prayer be made to Jesus now? We must examine the record of scripture closely to explore the question.

In the Old Testament every prayer (with the exception of idolatrous prayer) is offered only to God. In the New Testament the picture is not substantially different but there is less clarity. There are nearly eighty clear references that teach praying to God, most of them in Jesus' name.

One passage in the Gospels has Jesus saying, "If you ask me anything in my name, I will do it" (John 14:14). However the word "me" is disputed and left out of some manuscripts. The early manuscripts tend to omit it, while many of the later ones include it. Among the Bible reading churches, prayer to Jesus was little known before the profusion of English Bibles in the twentieth century. One can't help but feel there might be a connection between the inclusion of the word "me" in John 14:14 and the practice of prayer to Jesus. The other records (of requests in Jesus' name) in John make it clear that such requests are addressed to God.

The bulk of the occasions in New Testament scripture of conversations / prayers to Jesus occur in the Acts of the Apostles. We have listed the relevant passages for consideration:

- "And they prayed and said, 'You, Lord, who know the hearts of all, show which one of these two you have chosen to take the place in this ministry and apostleship from which Judas turned aside ...'" (1:24).

- "And as they were stoning Stephen, he called out, 'Lord Jesus, receive my spirit.' And falling to his knees he cried out with a loud voice, 'Lord, do not hold this sin against them.' And when he had said this, he fell asleep" (7:59,60).

- "And he said, 'Who are you, Lord?' And he said, 'I am Jesus, whom you are persecuting'" (9:5).

- "Now there was a disciple at Damascus named Ananias. The Lord said to him in a vision, 'Ananias.' And he said, 'Here I am, Lord.' And the Lord said to him, 'Rise and go to the street called Straight ...' But Ananias answered, 'Lord, I have heard from many about this man, how much evil he has done to your saints at Jerusalem. And here he has authority from the chief priests to bind all who call on your name.' But the Lord said to him, 'Go ...'" (9:10-15).

- "'And I said, what shall I do, Lord?' And the Lord said to me, 'Rise, and go into Damascus, and there you will be told all that is appointed for you to do'" (20:10).

- "When I had returned to Jerusalem and was praying in the temple, I fell into a trance and saw him saying to me, 'Make haste and get out of Jerusalem quickly, because they will not accept your testimony about me.' And I said, 'Lord, they themselves know that in one synagogue after another I imprisoned and beat those who believed in you. And when the blood of Stephen your witness was being shed, I myself was standing by and approving and watching over the garments of those who killed him.' And he said to me, 'Go, for I will send you far away to the Gentiles'" (22:17-21).

We note that all except the first of these occurs as a result of direct interaction with or as part of a vision from Jesus himself. Such visions and encounters are of such exceptional character (and do not now occur) that they provide no adequate precedent suggesting prayer to Jesus in our times. Regarding the first passage of the replacement of Judas, the record gives no clear evidence as to whether the request was made to Jesus or to God. Commentators are again quite divided and this passage must be regarded as inconclusive evidence for prayer to Jesus.

The few passages from Corinthians to Revelation that have some connection to the idea of conversation / prayer with Jesus are listed below:

- "... three times I pleaded with the Lord about this" (2 Corinthians 12:8,9).

- "I thank him who has given me strength, Christ Jesus our Lord, because he judged me faithful, appointing me to his service" (1 Timothy 1:12).

- "... grow in the grace and knowledge of our Lord and Saviour Jesus Christ. To him be the glory both now and to the day of eternity. Amen" (2 Peter 3:18).

- "Even so, come, Lord Jesus" (Revelation 22:20).

As the list progresses the 'evidence' for prayer to Jesus becomes less compelling and only the first of these might be categorically said to be a prayer. The word "Lord" in that reference is ambiguous: there is nothing in the context or language of the text in 2 Corinthians 12 that demand that the prayer was made to Christ; it could well have been to God and a number of commentators take that view. It is again, inconclusive. We may not demand that the reference in 1 Timothy 1:12 is a prayer – it need not be.

What about the phrase "calling on the name of the Lord"? Doesn't this suggest prayer to Jesus? Again we will list the relevant passages for consideration:

- "Rise and be baptized and wash away your sins, calling on his name" (Acts 22:16).

- "For there is no distinction between Jew and Greek; for the same Lord is Lord of all, bestowing his riches on all who call on him. For 'everyone who calls on the name of the Lord will be saved'" (Romans 10:12,13).

- "To the church of God that is in Corinth, to those sanctified in Christ Jesus, called to be saints together with all those who in every place call upon the name of our Lord Jesus Christ" (1 Corinthians 1:2).

- "Flee youthful passions and pursue righteousness, faith, love, and peace, along with those who call on the Lord from a pure heart" (2 Timothy 2:22).

We suggest that these references have more to do with Christian conversion than with prayer. In any case none of them clearly teach prayer to Jesus.

Throughout scripture, teaching and practice concerning important subjects is always clear. We are not left to wonder about the resurrection or the return of Christ, for example, they are taught explicitly. The only clear Bible teaching and practice concerning prayer would have us pray to God. This leaves us with no clear passage providing evidence that men and women in ordinary prayer addressed their words to Christ.

Can we therefore demand that prayer must only be made to God and that prayer to Jesus is utterly improper and ought never to be made? It might seem on the surface that to ask is to answer. However, language as strong as "utterly improper" and "never", seems unwarranted and without clear scriptural direction. Given the New Testament teaching regarding honouring and worshipping Jesus, we might have expected prayer to Jesus would be explicitly prohibited if it were never intended. This is clearly not the case and some references remain uncertain. While there is no clear teaching in scripture in favour of prayer to Jesus, there is no absolute prohibition either.

Perhaps therefore, in practice this question may be left to the individual conscience. However, we must remember that we have no place exercising our conscience in a way that upsets others. It is likely (given the clear apostolic teaching and practice of prayer to God) that ecclesial prayers offered to Jesus would be uncomfortable and even disturbing for many. Our recommendation would be that those who feel it appropriate to pray to Jesus do so only in *personal and private* prayer. Addressing our *public* prayers to God is in keeping with apostolic practice and will make for ecclesial harmony.

The final word on the matter comes from Brother A. D. Norris who wrote:

> "Praying to Jesus is yielding to a kind of evangelical fashion. It is no abiding part of our heritage from the Lord, the apostles, or the scriptures."[1]

What is the role of Jesus in prayer?

If we don't pray to Jesus, what is he there for? Is Jesus some sort of divine postman relaying messages to God?

---

[1]   *The Person of The Lord Jesus Christ*, page 42.

We will look first at the scriptures concerning *intercession*. It is clear that this was a role taken on by prophets in the Old Testament; Moses pleaded:

> "Please pardon the iniquity of this people, according to the greatness of your steadfast love, just as you have forgiven this people, from Egypt until now." (Numbers 14:19)

Jeremiah clearly was in the habit of interceding for Israel but such was their wickedness God told him not to bother, "Do not pray for this people, or lift up a cry or prayer for them, and do not intercede with me, for I will not hear you" (Jeremiah 7:16). This has now clearly become the role of Jesus and several times we are told that he pleads our cause to God:

- "He bore the sin of many, and makes intercession for the transgressors" (Isaiah 53:12).

- "Who is to condemn? Christ Jesus is the one who died – more than that, who was raised – who is at the right hand of God, who indeed is interceding for us" (Romans 8:34).

- "He is able to save to the uttermost those who draw near to God through him, since he always lives to make intercession for them" (Hebrews 7:25).

How does intercession work?

The man of God (in our case Christ) pleads for us to God and God responds favourably. Jesus as a high priest has been "appointed to act on behalf of men in relation to God" (Hebrews 5:1). The connection between the work of Jesus in his death (as a mediator) and the work of Jesus in heaven (as an intercessor) is clear. Christ is the perfect intercessor as a result of his work on earth. In the same way that Israel was often unaware of the prophets pleading on their behalf, we don't know of the approaches made by Christ to God on our behalf. While the act of intercession presumes that we have sinned and are estranged from God (there would otherwise be no need of an intercessor), if we are so entrenched in sin that God despairs of us as He did with Israel, then no amount of prayer will succeed.

What does it mean to ask in Jesus' name?

Three times John records Jesus saying whatever we ask God in his name we shall receive (John 14:13,14; 15:16; 16:23). Can we ask for something that Jesus never had? Can we ask for something that Jesus would not want us to have? Can we ask for something not within God's will? Clearly not! All these requests could not be genuinely made "in his name". To ask in the name of Jesus is to make a request that our Lord would be happy to put his name to. It must therefore be for something that improves our faith, the faith of others or contributes positively towards God's purpose with us – something in accordance with God's will. This is not just about divine etiquette and proper forms of address; it is far more profound than that. We ask and God hears us for Christ's sake because we are his. It is not that God will only hear a prayer that is postmarked as it were, by Christ, and if we forgot to say "in the name of the Lord Jesus Christ" then God would not listen. Such words as "in the name of the Lord Jesus Christ" carry no magical force, they are neither a mantra nor a talisman but simply a powerful reminder of how our lives and our prayers should be framed around God and His Son. If our lives are not fashioned such that Christ would be honoured, concluding a prayer with the phrase "in Jesus' name" is barely more than an insult to the spirit of grace.

Some might say – how can we know what the will of God is? While we may not be able to be specific, there are clear indications in scripture as to the nature of God's will for us. Consider the list below:

- Deliverance (Galatians 1:4).

- Eternal inheritance (Ephesians 1:11).

- Maturity and completion (Colossians 4:12).
- Holiness (1 Thessalonians 4:1-4).
- Rebirth as children of God through His word (James 1:18).

The will of God is generous and expansive towards us. We can ask for help with anything on that list and be assured of a positive response.

Paul wrote to the Colossians:

"Whatever you do, in word or deed, do everything in the name of the Lord Jesus, giving thanks to God the Father through him." (Colossians 3:17)

This is an acknowledgement that all our lives need to be under the overarching ambit of "the name of the Lord Jesus" and that everything we have, or can ask for, is because of him. Jesus taught, "No one comes to the Father except through me" (John 14:6): this is a truth for our entire life and we reflect on it when we pray. To the Ephesians Paul wrote, "through him [Jesus] we both [Jews and Gentiles] have access in one Spirit to the Father" (Ephesians 2:18).

When we pray, we recognise the close relationship that exists between God and Christ, as John recorded: "No one who denies the Son has the Father. Whoever confesses the Son has the Father also" (1 John 2:23). We might now add in one more passage on the intercession of Christ from Romans 8:

"Likewise the Spirit helps us in our weakness. For we do not know what to pray for as we ought, but the Spirit himself intercedes for us with groanings too deep for words. And he who searches hearts knows what is the mind of the Spirit, because the Spirit intercedes for the saints according to the will of God." (verses 26,27)

Many translators have wrestled over this passage trying to convey the proper message intended by Paul. It remains one of the more difficult passages to interpret. We offer our own paraphrase and we trust that it might help make the passage clear:

> 'In the same way a Christlike spirit helps us to pray. In our weakness we do not know what to pray for, but the spirit mind works with our inner feelings of grief, and Christ who knows our disposition and searches the hearts of his holy ones accepts these feelings and takes them to God on our behalf.'

That is, Christ searches our hearts and takes even the thought that we can only express with sighs and groans, then presents an appeal to God on our behalf. This is intercession at its most magnificent best and is surely one of the deepest blessings we have in Christ. When we cannot even find words to pray, our unexpressed thoughts are scanned by the Lord Jesus and offered to God.

The final thought on the role of Jesus in prayer is that he is now the instrument of God to respond to our prayers. Twice in John 14:13,14 the Lord says, "I will do it"; not 'God will do it' but "I will do it". That Jesus now has the power and the desire to do this is clear for he said, "All authority in heaven and on earth has been given to me ... behold, I am with you always, to the end of the age" (Matthew 18:18-20). Not only does our Lord assist with our requests, he is the agent of God's response.

Do I have to preach?

Yes! Jesus commanded his apostles, "Go into all the world and proclaim the gospel to the whole creation [everybody]" (Mark 16:15). The Apostle Paul had received a personal commission to preach and he felt this obligation very keenly. Paul said, "Woe to me if I do not preach the gospel!" This does not mean we all have to preach in the same way. Some are orators and can share public messages compellingly, some can write well, others can chat with neighbours and friends, and all of us can be an example for good.

Turning this question on its head, we might ask, 'Why wouldn't you want to preach'? If your faith is solid and you are not ashamed of Jesus, then there is every reason to share the good news with everybody. The challenge for us is that preaching in many environments is not well received, the preacher is likely to be mocked and the response can be minimal. This can be quite discouraging. In this context it is easy to ask, 'Do I have to preach'? Peter urged his readers always to be "prepared to make a defence to anyone who asks you for a reason for the hope that is in you" (1 Peter 3:15). You might readily think that it does not make you feel good and those to whom you preach don't seem to want it – then why bother at all? Put yourself in their situation. At the moment every unbeliever is:

> "Separated from Christ, alienated from the commonwealth of Israel and strangers to the covenants of promise, having no hope and without God in the world." (Ephesians 2:12)

If they don't become believers they will stay that way. Paul simply asks, "How are they to believe in him of whom they have never heard? And how are they to hear without someone preaching?" (Romans 10:14) The more we love and appreciate God, the more willing and able we will be to be His messengers of hope.

What should be the form of the bread and wine that are used as emblems of Jesus at the memorial meeting?

Jesus said the bread was his flesh, which he would give for the life of the world. The value of the flesh or body of Jesus lay in service. The word *soma* (body) in the Greek may also be translated 'slave'. So the bread represents his body given in service. We might respectfully say that apart from the service Christ offered, there is no value in his flesh; indeed he himself said the flesh profits nothing, it is the word of God that is spirit and life. As we think then of bread we think of the word, made into flesh, the flesh of Christ. As we think of his body we are reminded of his service.

Some brethren taking the concepts quite literally have stumbled over the words of the KJV in 1 Corinthians 11:24 and either insist that in the distribution of the bread it *must* be broken as though there was some important spiritual significance in the action. Conversely others feel the whole idea of "broken" reminds them that not a bone of Christ was broken and so they feel it should be avoided entirely. In consequence some brethren omit the word in 1 Corinthians 11:24 leaving a hole that would normally be occupied by a verb and making it sound odd and incomplete. Others replace it with the word "given" (as in Luke 22). To avoid controversy some of the wording in our 2002 Hymn Book has been changed. It must be realised that not all manuscripts include the word "broken". Some of the later ones omit it. We think this possibly reflects the unease with the association of ideas. Actually, understood correctly there is no problem in us using it and thinking of it.

The difficulty arises when we equate the ideas of 'body broken' with 'bones broken' (scripture quite clearly tells us that did not occur) and get tangled in a knot not easily unravelled. We might however readily observe that it is perfectly possible to have a broken body without breaking any bones. Furthermore we recall that David spoke of his bones having been broken (Psalm 51:8) and there is every reason to believe that it was purely a spiritual comment and there were in fact no broken bones at all. There is however a better and perfectly rational scriptural explanation that makes sense without needing to either explain the idea of 'body broken' or remove the word "broken". In Biblical Greek the word 'broken' is never used of bones and only of bread and mostly in the context of the tokens of our Lord. We might therefore rearrange the syntax of the verse for our English ears to read, "Take eat, this [bread] which is broken for you is my body". With this simple device all of the difficulty evaporates and we need not even concern ourselves with the breaking of Jesus' body and what that may or may not signify.

Understanding it in this way we can be content whether we adjust the order of the words or not. Turning our attention to the bread itself, because the Passover was not for another twenty-four hours we lean towards the idea that it was not unleavened bread. We might simply observe though, there is not one single credible piece of evidence to be gained either from scripture or from first century history as to precisely what form the bread was that the early believers used in their remembrance. Was it leavened or unleavened? We are simply not told. There are spiritual arguments that favour both sides. We might say that since Christ was one of us, the bread should be leavened, and we could equally argue that since he was sinless it should be unleavened. Scholars of the highest merit differ on this interpretation. We should be careful in that context not to insist on one interpretation to the exclusion of the other.

It occurs to us that since there has never been a man like Jesus (mortal and sinless) we can hardly restrict him to a single symbol. Were we able to have both leavened and unleavened bread together they might between them begin to comprehend in symbol the nature of Christ. We should not debate vigorously and absolutely not fractiously the point. The precise character of the symbol is not the critical element here; if this was critical to our remembrance it would have been clearly detailed. The critical point is to see Christ in the symbol. Paul interprets for the Corinthians the true significance of our keeping of the feast without leaven to refer to our attitude and not our bread. We suggest that the wisest counsel on this point is to defer to the arrangements preferred by the majority, and recognise that they might vary from place to place.

It is likely that what they shared came from one loaf, yet the practicalities of very large memorial services preclude this. Again it does not seem to us to be a point upon which we ought to squabble. When we share the bread together we are reminded that we ought to be doing what Jesus did and "present our bodies a living sacrifice"; it is this thought that should be uppermost.

As the wine is poured out it becomes a symbol of the blood of Jesus poured out which is in turn a symbol of a life given in service. Isaiah said, "he poured out his soul to death" (Isaiah 53:12). Jesus used the idea in reverse in John 6:53-56 where the intention of the Lord is that we eat bread and drink wine but he asked us to eat his flesh and drink his blood.

The Jews recoiling at the literal nature of this missed the point and rejected it completely. The Catholics, on the other hand take it literally and believe that when their priest pronounces that it is the body and blood of the Lord, it magically transforms into the actual body and blood of the Lord in a process unknown to scripture but known to them as transubstantiation.

Since drinking wine equals drinking blood, and blood equals life, Jesus is saying that unless we get the same spirit, desire and emotion for God that he had we will not have life. Together the symbols speak of the embodiment of the word of God and a life of dedicated service. As we take these tokens week by week we are reminded that we are not merely to believe Christ but to imitate and follow him.

The wine reminds us of the multitude in Christ. Each sip of wine does not come from just one grape and since it is blended together, not even just one vine. As we share it together we are reminded that we being many are one in the same way as the bread.

In 1 Corinthians 10:16, Paul styles it "the cup of blessing". The third of the four ceremonial cups the Jews drank from at Passover was called "the cup of blessing". It is hard to conceive that Paul would use this language and be unaware of the significance that it had in connection to the Passover. The Passover was the shared feast of deliverance. Paul says the cup is the sharing of his blood. The message is that we share deliverance through the work of Christ and that we remember it by the tokens provided.

In the same way that there is confusion with the syntax concerning the breaking of the bread, there has been a similar confusion over the expression, "drink ye all of it" in the KJV. There is an amusing story that happened at an ecclesia that used a communal cup. A nervous newly baptized brother misinterpreted the scripture and did precisely what he thought he was told (and to his subsequent embarrassment) drank all of the wine and there was none left for anybody else. By rearranging the words, all such confusion is eliminated; it means, 'drink from it, all of you'. In modern versions the confusion of seventeenth century syntax is avoided.

The point is – this is something that we should all share. We have a common need, there is a common solution and we must all embrace it. Like the bread, we ought not to insist on any special arrangements as if the exact nature of the symbol means something special of itself quite apart from our remembrance of Christ. We suggest that whether we have a communal cup or not is neither here nor there.

After one of the many cyclones that periodically ravage Vanuatu, a brother who lives in utter isolation on an outlying island confided that he had lost all possessions and having no money at all, was obliged to remember Christ with what he had. He elected to use bananas for bread and seawater for wine. This continued for several weeks until we arrived with fresh supplies.

On another island where bread was baked and sold only on Tuesday and Thursday, we discovered with alarm one Sunday morning that rats had got into the cupboard and were munching into the small loaf that had been intended for the meeting. Being simply unable to get any more and not feeling that we would (or even that we should) use something a rat had chewed, we elected to use cracker biscuits instead. Happily, rats appear not to like wine so the rest of the memorial tokens were unchanged.

We are by no means endorsing the use of alternative symbols *per se*, but we would trust that Christ was honourably remembered in the circumstances, and that the solemn reflections conducted as well as could be managed, were, like Hezekiah's Passover of old, graciously accepted by the Lord and our Father in the spirit in which they were offered. Perhaps the precise nature of the tokens is not spelt out in scripture to allow those in similar extremity to participate in solemn remembrance of Christ without hindrance.

There remains the question of the contents of the cup; should it be alcoholic or not? There is little doubt that what was drunk would have been wine of some description but again we are not told.

The reference in 1 Corinthians 11 to some getting drunk at the love feast is suggestive but not conclusive, as it is clear that the excess lay in the associated meal rather than the memorial cup. Some have argued that only wine could match the symbol of life after death. Mere grape juice would go off, but wine matures and ripens with age. In this respect wine does seem a more appropriate symbol and it certainly connects well with the Old Testament references we saw earlier. Christians have traditionally used wine for almost all of the years of record keeping.

However we must use care that we don't absolutely demand something unsupported by scripture merely because it is traditional. No clear New Testament scripture specifies what must be in the cup. The clarity is all about what it represents. The only clues to the contents of the cup are by inference and type, and these we obtain by working back from the shadow, which is a practice not without difficulty.

The better method is to interpret the shadow using the real thing. In this case the real thing is Christ and not wine, and this gives no unmistakable direction as to what the nature of the symbol must be. The types would suggest (but not absolutely demand) the cup contain wine (Job 1:13).

We must also realise that the wine that they had then would bear only generic resemblance to that which we have today. In their book *Divine Vintage: Following the Wine Trail from Genesis to the Modern Age*, Joel Butler and Randall Heskett note that wines in Jesus' day were often infused with honey, dried fruits and spices like pepper and curry. Winemakers also often added tree resins like myrrh, frankincense and terebinth (oak) to preserve the beverage. For all that, modern refinements and fortification such as are now common would have been utterly unknown to the early ecclesia.

To sum up this question, we can see little reason why the contents of our cup of remembrance should not be alcoholic wine and that would seem the most sensible choice in practice, but to descend to argument where scripture provides no absolute guidance seems foolish. As with the bread, perhaps we should follow the practices preferred by the majority and feel constrained only by the bounds of love and mutual submission.

How should we dress for a memorial meeting?

We will answer this in two parts: first, how should we dress *per se*, and secondly are there additional principles when considering the breaking of bread service?

How should we dress? The Bible does not offer regulations binding on Christian believers but principles that are all embracing. How we dress reflects our attitudes to life and godliness. We are not told what the woman wore, but in Proverbs 7:10 there is a story of a woman dressed like a prostitute. Clothes convey an impression either good or bad. The Christian should endeavour to project a good image. The general principles are:

- *Decency (not dressing outrageously).* "Women should adorn themselves in respectable apparel" (1 Timothy 2:9).

- *Modesty (not flaunting our body).* "... with modesty and self-control" (1 Timothy 2:9).

- *Moderation (not flaunting our wealth).* "Not with braided hair and gold or pearls or costly attire, but with what is proper for women who profess godliness" (1 Timothy 2:10).

- *Inner beauty (rather than external beauty).* "Do not let your adorning be external – the braiding of hair and the putting on of gold jewellery, or the clothing you wear – but let your adorning be the hidden person of the heart with the imperishable beauty of a gentle and quiet spirit, which in God's sight is very precious" (1 Peter 3:3,4).

- *Not following worldly fashions.* "Do not love the world or the things in the world" (1 John 2:15). "The grace of God has appeared, bringing salvation for all people, training us to renounce ungodliness and worldly passions, and to live self-controlled, upright, and godly lives in the present age" (Titus 2:12).

The reader will note the passages are predominantly about the dress of women. The principles are the same for men but the need to emphasise and reinforce them not quite as compelling.

The dress of believers should be decent and respectable. We should be noted for our character rather than our appearance.

With this background let us move on to consider the second part of the question – dress for a memorial meeting. Other than an instruction that sisters should cover their heads and brethren should not (see 1 Corinthians 11), there are no scriptures that dictate what we ought to wear. Given the status of Christ and the importance of the memorial gathering the common practice of dressing well has considerable merit but is not mandated in scripture.

Jesus only had the one set of clothes so for him there was no choice to be made. Whether he went to a synagogue or the temple or was simply going about his daily tasks he wore the same clothes. Perhaps the issues arise for us because we have many (different) choices of what we might wear. Nobody ought to suggest that the man of modest means should be in any way excluded or embarrassed. The Gospel is for all people, especially the poor. To shame those "that have not" would almost certainly shame Jesus. For those in modest circumstances (like the Lord) the Old Testament practice of washing and presenting ourselves clean (see Exodus 19:10) has considerable merit. Our outward presentation is to be a reflection of our inner preparation. Having prepared our minds to meet with Christ we would naturally want to look as presentable on the outside as circumstances permit.

Despite the lack of direct teaching concerning dress at the memorial gathering, there are some principles drawn from scripture that may be of assistance.

- *God looks not at outward appearances but at the heart.* This means that we must not judge a person by what they wear. Paul made it clear to the Corinthians that we have no right to shame those brothers and sisters who do not have access to the same levels of luxury that we do. The original idea (1 Corinthians 11:22) was with respect to the quality of food brought to a communal meal. A wealthy family had plenty while a poor family had little. Instead of sharing (which is now a more common practice) each ate their own, with the result that the poor were embarrassed. Flaunting one's wealth is not to be recommended. James particularly warns against selective treatment of the well dressed at gatherings:

> "If a man wearing a gold ring and fine clothing comes into your assembly, and a poor man in shabby clothing also comes in, and if you pay attention to the one who wears the fine clothing and say, 'You sit here in a good place,' while you say to the poor man, 'You stand over there,' or, 'Sit down at my feet,' have you not then made distinctions among yourselves and become judges with evil thoughts?"   (James 2:2-4)

- *Not dressing to be noticed.* We should not be dressing to be fashionable – to be seen as being well dressed. Such a concept would tend to pride and smug self-satisfaction rather than thankful remembrance. We would do well to remember that "this is the one to whom I will look: he who is humble and contrite in spirit and trembles at my word" (Isaiah 66:2).

- *Not insisting on our personal preference.* Concerning matters of a peripheral nature Paul wrote, "Why do you pass judgement on your brother? Or you, why do you despise your brother?" (Romans 14:10). It seems unreasonable to demand of our brother or sister that they see the matter exactly as we do. Not every ecclesia will see things the same way, nor for that matter every brother or sister. When we hold combined gatherings we need to be careful not to give or take offence in this regard. Rather we should esteem our brother better than ourselves – and our Lord highest of all.

Should female believers wear trousers?

It must be said at the outset – this is predominantly a question for modern western nations. It has its basis in a passage from Deuteronomy which reads:

> "A woman must not wear men's clothing, nor should a man dress up in women's clothing, for anyone who does this is offensive to the LORD your God." (Deuteronomy 22:5, NET)

For hundreds of years in western countries, breeches, or trousers have been garments traditionally worn by men and skirts and dresses garments worn by women. While still in place to some degree today, those traditions have changed considerably. However, because of the historical distinction, some interpret the passage to demand that women wearing trousers is contrary to the teaching of scripture.

What is the answer? There is no straightforward approach to this question that suits all cultures, circumstances and time periods. Manners of dress change over time and vary according to culture. Traditionally, Chinese women wear trousers and Middle Eastern men do not. Men in the South Pacific often wear skirts, and Scotsmen occasionally wear kilts. Would scripture promote an ideal that did not suit all circumstances? We suggest not. The people listening to Moses as he spoke the message of Deuteronomy would not have thought, 'this means ladies can't wear trousers'. Moses' audience (male or female) did not wear trousers. The distinction between male and female dress in Old Testament times was more about colour, than style and cut, and whether a veil (female) or turban (male) was worn.

Furthermore, the passage in Deuteronomy is not instruction for clothing *per se* but a condemnation of idolatry. Cross-dressing was common among the Canaanites and was associated with idolatrous worship and indecent behaviour. Concerning Deuteronomy 22:5 we read:

"In the books of the idolaters it is commanded that when a man presents himself before the star of Venus, he should wear the coloured dress of a woman; and when a woman adores the Star of Mars, she shall appear in armour."[2]

Interestingly, we note that what determined female dress was colour rather than style. Clearly the background of the law was idolatrous cross-dressing. We suggest that this law is not so much targeting a style of clothing but the concept of a woman clearly endeavouring (by what she wears) to impersonate a man and vice versa. The behaviour behind the clothing choice is what the law in Deuteronomy was designed to address. Let us be quite clear – intentional cross-dressing with immoral motives is clearly utterly improper.

Are all trousers male garments? Clearly not! A pair of pink floral pants can hardly be considered "men's clothing" merely because they are trousers. In the western world trousers are now considered part of a woman's wardrobe. We must accept that styles change over time – what was once outlandish might now be commonplace and what was once common might now be outlandish. We need not be constrained to feel that acceptable standards for everybody were set in western countries in the Victorian era and ought never to move.

The questions that ought to occupy a Christian woman's mind when purchasing / making clothes and when dressing, are those of modesty and decency (see the previous answer). Modesty is not necessarily related to the type of clothing. Any style of clothing can be immodest. A woman undertaking some activities would find it difficult to be modest wearing a skirt or a dress. There might be some (and this certainly used to be the situation) who would say, 'she should not do the activity in that case'; this is not especially practical in our modern world. It makes sense for women to dress in clothing suited to the activity with an eye on modesty.

---

2   *Manners and Customs of the Bible*, James M. Freeman, page 111.

There are some who would say, 'women wearing trousers is worldly'. Again, this depends on time periods and cultural context. It is difficult to demand that we must (in modern times) resist these styles of garment on that basis. There are modest ladies' trousers, and there are exceedingly immodest trousers that follow worldly fashions. Clearly our clothing choice should not follow immodest fashions.

Putting the arguments together, there does not appear to be Biblical justification for demanding a sister in Christ (in our time and context) only wear skirts and dresses. The underlying principle in Deuteronomy certainly applies today – men should dress in an appropriately masculine fashion and women in an appropriately feminine fashion. We suggest then that the entire matter is a conscience issue. Those who allow women to wear trousers should not mock those who do not, and those who do not must not judge those who do.

What about ecclesial gatherings? Some would say that a woman wearing trousers and jeans for everyday occasions is acceptable, but when they attend an ecclesial gathering they must wear a skirt or a dress; for others it makes no difference. Clearly there are some very strong views both ways. If the members of the local ecclesia have no objection, then it seems unreasonable not to accept modest clothing of any style; however if some (with a weak conscience) would be upset, then we have no business driving our liberated conscience like a mad person through the gathering causing disquiet and upheaval.

Does it matter whether sisters wear head coverings or not?

Some within our community would say, 'yes it matters', others, 'no it doesn't' and still others 'it's a conscience issue'. Is the issue about antiquated dress codes for women or are there spiritual considerations that are important?

Before we commence, note that under the Law of Moses, the priests wore head coverings (see Exodus 29:9). The Jews have continued and extended this custom by requiring all males to wear head coverings during worship. In contrast Paul the preacher of the Gospel of grace taught that a man ought not to cover his head "since he is the image and glory of God" (1 Corinthians 11:7). We might ask ourselves why did God require a distinctive change from the Law of Moses? There is no particular reason given but other passages throw light on the possible reason and what the practice represented. Covering the head in the Old Testament and so under the Law represented humility, shame, servitude and grief (see 2 Samuel 15:30; Esther 6:12; Jeremiah 14:3,4). It is clear that Paul is teaching in Jesus Christ our status has been elevated from that of servants to the Law, to that of sons of God in Christ. In this new status it is inappropriate for a brother in Christ to cover his head (Christ).

The premier text in scripture that speaks about this subject is 1 Corinthians 11:1-16. Before we begin looking at this passage it is worth noting that explicit instructions for head coverings for sisters are only given here so we must take care with our conclusions.

Paul was dealing, in 1 Corinthians 11, with ecclesial practices when brothers and sisters meet together to worship, and it is worth noting that this passage comes in a general context concerned specifically with the breaking of bread (sandwiched between 1 Corinthians 10:15-21, about the emblems, and 11:17-34, where the apostle returns to that theme). When the ecclesia meets together particularly for the breaking of bread and worship it is an important event and the form and function of our gathering is an acted parable of the redemption of the family of God. It has pleased God and our Lord Jesus Christ that we in so doing might more clearly proclaim to each other the work of redemption.

The points made by the apostle for worship are as follows:

- **Verse 1:** Paul's guidelines come from Christ.
- **Verse 2:** He therefore expects us to uphold them.
- **Verse 3:** There is a divine order: God-Christ-man-woman.
- **Verse 4:** Men covering their head dishonour Christ.
- **Verse 5:** Women uncovering their head dishonour Christ.
- **Verse 6:** A head covering is the most practical way for a woman to demonstrate the principle of divine order.
- **Verses 7-12:** It is about divine order and arrangement.
- **Verses 14,15:** Natural arrangements reflect the spiritual.
- **Verse 15:** It is about covering human glory.
- **Verse 16:** Paul recognises no other practice for any ecclesia.

We might summarise the principles in tabular form to make it plain.

Principle used by Paul	Points for men to note	Points for women to note
Headship (verse 3)	Christ is the head of man	Man is the head of woman
Glory (verse 7)	Man is the glory of God	Woman is the glory of man
Order of creation (verse 8)	Man not created from woman	Woman created from man
Purpose of creation (verse 9)	Man not created for woman	Woman created for man

Principle used by Paul	Points for men to note	Points for women to note
The angels (verse 10)	–	She should be covered
A woman's hair is her glory (verse 15)	Feminine styles are degrading	Hair is for beauty
Conclusion	**Head should be uncovered**	**Head should be covered**

Some modern translations of 1 Corinthians 11 offer the word "wife" in some of the verses suggesting that these arrangements are only for married women and reflect the order in marriage only. We might simply note that the Greek is the same in all cases and there is no suggestion within the text that a difference is intended. We are of the opinion that Paul included all sisters in his scope.

Paul's teaching is based on upholding the divine order in the symbol of headship. It is God-Christ-man-woman. How are men covering their head dishonouring Christ and how do women uncovering their head dishonour Christ? When men cover themselves they are symbolically covering Christ and thereby suggesting that they bypass Christ in the divine order. When women uncover themselves they are symbolically suggesting that humanity has no need of the covering of Christ. Either way Christ's position is lessened and he is dishonoured. When the head of a sister is covered, the entire ecclesia (whom she represents) acknowledges that they need the covering provided by Christ.

Verses 7 and 15 teach that the woman is "the glory of man" and that a woman's hair is a "glory to her". So, one of the prime reasons for the head covering of sisters is to cover the glory of humans – both man and woman – which is represented by a woman's hair.

Paul asks, "Is it proper for a woman to pray to God with her head uncovered?" (verse 13, NET). Clearly Paul felt that his arguments led to a conclusion and he expected his readers to arrive at it. The obvious answer Paul expects us to give to the question in verse 13 is, 'No, it is not proper'. The logical flow of his argument breaks down if we arrive at a different conclusion. Sisters ought to cover their heads at the breaking of bread.

Is that a conclusion for all ecclesias and for all time, or just for Corinth at that time? The principles that underpinned Paul's answer are enduring and therefore have relevance for all time. Paul bases his answer on the difference between divine and human glory, it is not about social expectations or equality of the sexes – he has elsewhere made it clear that they have equal status before God (Galatians 3:28). Paul is simply concerned that in worship we ought to preserve the divinely given order.

Verse 10 is a difficult passage and has often been subject to tortured and curious explanations. The NET reads, "For this reason a woman should have a symbol of authority on her head, because of the angels". The symbol of authority is clear enough; the covering symbolises that we are subject to Christ. The difficult words are "because of the angels". What has a head covering to do with angels? We offer two possible suggestions:

1. Elsewhere it is clear that angels are, "ministering spirits sent out to serve for the sake of those who are to inherit salvation" (Hebrews 1:13). Evidently they carry out their duty on behalf of the Lord who reminded the ecclesia at Ephesus that he, "walks among the seven golden lampstands" and knows their works (Revelation 2:1,2). We would not wish the Lord's angelic servants to report back that we cared little for his appointments.

2. It was through Eve's desire to be like the angels that the fall occurred (see Genesis 3:5,6). As a result of the fall, God said to Eve "He [your husband] shall rule over you" (Genesis 3:16). The head covering could point to this event.

It is important to realise that these arrangements give men no licence to impose their will (as opposed to God's) upon sisters, for the men ought to be equally subject to God and Christ.

Paul's conclusion is that a sister not covering her head at the meeting for breaking of bread, is to:

- Dishonour her head (1 Corinthians 11:5) – i.e., her husband and / or Christ.

- Be improper (verse 13).

Clearly the head covering ought not to be an immodest fashion statement. Such would negate the principle of covering human glory. How these principles are adopted in practice will vary with ecclesias. Some discourage unbaptized sisters from having their heads covered, some wear a head covering for almost every meeting, others for the memorial gathering only. We suggest that these are details upon which Christ has not provided clear guidance and might therefore be left to the individual conscience.

Should we wear religious jewellery?

There are many symbolic shapes that have come to represent Christianity. Each has a long history of significance and use. It may be good to research this history, as it can help inform our decision. Many Christians wear these symbols as a demonstration of their faith. Some examples would be the cross, star of David, dove, fish, alpha and omega – even wedding rings may fall into this category if representing a Christian marriage and commitment to it.

Reasons why some people could wear symbolic religious jewellery with a clear conscience might be:

1. God used symbols in the past to remind and teach people principles.

2. It reminds us of our commitment to God and Christ.

3. It is a way for people to notice our faith and to preach.

The cross for example is universally seen as a symbol of Christianity. It could be worn to demonstrate one's commitment to Christ, the depth of human sin, suffering as the path to faith and perfection, the love of God, forgiveness, Jesus dying for sin; the bare cross is seen as a symbol of the resurrection.

Some people because of their conscience would not wear religious jewellery. The Bible forbids use of physical images to represent God or to be used to worship Him:

"You shall not make for yourself a carved image, or any likeness of anything that is in heaven above, or that is in the earth beneath, or that is in the water under the earth."

(Exodus 20:4)

Images dishonour God and Christ for they obscure their glory. Religious items of jewellery are graven or made by the hands of people. Images can also mislead us. They can convey false ideas about God and Christ.

It could be said that the crucifix as used in Catholicism as an aid to prayer, as a physical tool to overpower evil and as a representation of the Trinity is enough to make one wary about wearing one. The Roman Church has a massive culture built around images and physical paraphernalia. A focus on these images and physical things during prayer or worship is really idolatry – as the veneration of the thing inevitably occurs.

Israel fell into worshipping physical representations when they made the golden calf and after that worshipped the brazen serpent. The origin of many symbols, including the cross, can be traced back to pagan symbols of worship and so God commanded Israel not to flirt with these images:

> "But thus shall you deal with them: you shall break down their altars and dash in pieces their pillars and chop down their Asherim and burn their carved images with fire."
>
> (Deuteronomy 7:1-6)

Jeremiah was very direct:

> "Learn not the way of the nations, nor be dismayed at the signs of the heavens because the nations are dismayed at them, for the customs of the peoples are vanity. A tree from the forest is cut down and worked with an axe by the hands of a craftsman. They decorate it with silver and gold; they fasten it with hammer and nails so that it cannot move. Their idols are like scarecrows in a cucumber field, and they cannot speak; they have to be carried, for they cannot walk. Do not be afraid of them, for they cannot do evil, neither is it in them to do good."
>
> (Jeremiah 10:2-5)

As a community we have avoided images as an object of worship or symbol of faith. It has been a hallmark of our ecclesias to focus on the reality of our heavenly Father and Jesus Christ through the revelation of scripture alone. One could ask these questions as a test of spiritual jewellery and idolatry in general. Do we attribute power to it? Is it worshipped for its own sake? Are we consumed by how it makes us look? Does this draw attention to me for the wrong reasons? Does it replace worship from the heart?

A Christian, by definition, professes to be a follower of Christ. We simply note that there is no evidence that Jesus wore jewellery. It is quite unlikely given the circumstances and culture of his upbringing that Jesus would have personally had any things of this nature at all. If the Lord did not need them, why would we? They must then be considered superfluous to salvation. That is, they are simply unnecessary. However, must we consider them forbidden to the follower of Christ?

In Bible times, jewellery (other than rings worn by important men) was principally worn by women. Isaiah lists them as:

> "The finery of the anklets, the headbands, and the crescents; the pendants, the bracelets, and the scarves; the headdresses, the armlets, the sashes, the perfume boxes, and the amulets; the signet rings and nose rings."   (Isaiah 3:18-21)

Sometimes such jewellery was associated with pagan idolatry as recorded by Hosea 2:13. When we get to the New Testament, the Apostles giving direction to the early ecclesia recommended an approach to appearance largely free from adornments. Peter wrote:

> "Do not let your adorning be external – the braiding of hair and the putting on of gold jewellery, or the clothing you wear – but let your adorning be the hidden person of the heart with the imperishable beauty of a gentle and quiet spirit, which in God's sight is very precious."   (1 Peter 3:3,4)

Jewellery should not be the standout feature of a believer. While some forms of religious jewellery are not inappropriate, they are simply unnecessary. What identifies a believer is the inner quality of the heart reflected in a gentle demeanour. We have no need of physical symbols.

Perhaps it is a question of identity. Why are we wearing the item? Does having a piece of jewellery connect us with any who are not true followers of Christ? If so, we have no business having anything to do with it. This probably excludes most religious jewellery and symbols. Would we want to look like those who feel a crucifix is some sort of talisman? Almost certainly not! Something that identifies a believer with the hope of Israel (such as a star of David) might be viewed differently from something that identifies a believer with apostate Christianity.

In our opinion, on balance the evidence is stronger against the wearing of religious jewellery. However, it is a matter of personal conscience. The following passages support not judging, and the strong in faith deferring to the weaker in matters of conscience (1 Corinthians 10:31; Colossian 2:16).

Should we have religious tattoos?

In the first century many believers would have had tattoos, as slaves of the Roman Empire were routinely tattooed as a mark of ownership and discipline. Tattooing or inscribing permanent marks on the body has been part of civilisation from early times. When God set a mark upon Cain to distinguish him – was this a tattoo? Tattoos have become very popular and mainstream in recent times. About one in four people would have tattoos in the US and Australia. Some of the reasons why people would get tattoos today are for beautification, artistic expression, identification with a club or tribe and for religious purposes.

Tattoos are quite a tribal and pagan concept and for that reason Israel were prohibited from having them. The passage in Leviticus that deals with them reads:

> "You shall not round off the hair on your temples or mar the edges of your beard. You shall not make any cuts on your body for the dead or tattoo yourselves: I am the LORD. Do not profane your daughter by making her a prostitute, lest the land fall into prostitution and the land become full of depravity." (Leviticus 19:27-29)

God in this commandment is prohibiting the Israelites from following the cultural practices of the day. Is the same command still relevant today, and what are the principles imbedded in the command?

1. God created us in His image and likeness (Genesis 1:26,27).

2. Our bodies are the dwelling place for God; so they are not our own in that sense (1 Corinthians 6:19,20).

3. We are not to be conformed to the present world but to present our bodies as a living sacrifice (Romans 12:1,2).

There are actually five prohibitions made in the Leviticus passage and they relate not so much to any inherent immorality in the action (with the obvious exception of prostitution) but these things were all involved in idolatry, and in the times in which they were written, identified one with idolaters. Notice the phrase central to the regulations reminding Israel that their God was Yahweh, in contrast to the false gods about them. Actually, considering what idolatry has largely become (sporting and pop culture) this passage might be given a modern interpretation, 'do not imitate the styles of hair, body art and sexual freedoms of the idols around you'. There is then a context to the prohibitions – they are not (prostitution excepted) immoral things in themselves. If those laws were written today, they would almost certainly have contained different regulations while preserving the same intent. While we do not need to keep the laws of the Mosaic covenant, the principle behind them is as binding today as then; John simply wrote, "keep yourselves from idols" (1 John 5:21).

As previously noted, tattooing and marking the body was widespread in Egyptian and Canaanite culture particularly around religious and fertility cults; recall the prophets of Baal cutting themselves (see 1 Kings 18:28).

What is our motive?

- Rebellion against parents and society is clearly not acceptable (see Ephesians 6:1-3).

- Artistic expression may be okay – but does it glorify God or us (see 1 Corinthians 10:31)?

Seeking to direct people's attention to oneself goes against the principle of modesty (see 1 Peter 3:3,4). We are Christ's ambassadors – is the message conveyed by a tattoo in keeping with that profession? God spoke of engraving Israel on his hands so as not to forget them (see Isaiah 49:16) though in all probability this is a figure of speech from God and not literally the case. However, it has been suggested that some Jews from the time followed this custom on themselves so they would not forget Israel or the temple. Some may use this principle to justify having a tattoo, saying it helps remind them of their commitment and servitude to God or to bring to mind an inspiration verse of scripture or the date of their baptism. Some point to Revelation 19:16 and suggest that Jesus has a tattoo on his thigh, "King of kings and Lord of lords", but this is at best inconclusive.

In conclusion, scripture offers no clear guidance and the matter would seem to fall into the category of disputable matters of the conscience.

Questions to ask ourselves in this regard would be:

- Will my tattoo be a cause of contention for my ecclesia and loved ones?

- Will my tattoo cause someone to stumble in the faith?

- Do I have any doubts about whether my tattoo will please God?

We cannot demand that religious tattoos must be wrong but they are certainly unnecessary. Tattooing and scarification carry intrinsic health risks that make them unwise.

In summary, we see no reason to have religious tattoos and several sound reasons not to. We must be careful that we do not take the freedoms we have in Christ in directions Christ would not go. Any who choose tattoos must take care that they are not merging their identity with the world and thereby failing to follow Christ.

Lots of Christadelphians are just hypocrites aren't they?

Sadly, to some extent we all are! If we were able to be perfect and follow Christ with a pure heart it follows that we wouldn't need him. To be sure, we ought not to be hypocrites (professing one thing and deliberately practising another) but sadly all too often we are.

This does not mean (as the question infers) that our faith is wrong, merely that our discipleship needs improvement. It would be lovely to be as black and white as John when he writes of the principles of faith and say that 'no man who is a hypocrite is a true believer'. In practice however, things are quite grey. There would be no need for Peter to write that believers should, "put away all malice and all deceit and hypocrisy and envy and all slander" (1 Peter 2:1) if hypocrisy were not an evil that we may all fall into.

The accusation that Christadelphians are all hypocrites is usually levelled by way of self-justification. The argument runs like this, 'My stand in not being a believer is justified by my observation that you are all hypocrites'. The idea behind the word hypocrite is that of pretence. A genuine believer would not do or say this or that. Unhappily all believers have fickle constitutions rooted in human nature and in practice we often fail to measure up to the ideal. The Apostle Paul lamented:

> "I have the desire to do what is right, but not the ability to carry it out. For I do not do the good I want, but the evil I do not want is what I keep on doing."   (Romans 7:18,19)

Did that make him a hypocrite? We say no – it made him human. As humans, we are prone to failure; Jesus would have us rise above it (see Matthew 5:20).

We cannot excuse and tolerate hypocrisy on the grounds of human weakness; we must always strive to be genuine and sincere in our faith and practice. Brother Dennis Gillett succinctly wrote: "True discipleship does not encourage impersonation."[3] It does us well to remember these words of our Lord when warning of hypocrisy, "Nothing is covered up that will not be revealed, or hidden that will not be known" (Luke 12:2). It would be disastrous if our actions brought shame upon the name of God. Peter advises us to live such an honourable life that unbelievers, "may see your good deeds and glorify God" (1 Peter 2:12).

What can I do if my love for God grows cold?

If you are baptized remember back to that time when you were baptized into Jesus Christ – I'm sure like us you felt so much love, joy and peace. Sometimes we can feel like we are losing or have lost the feeling of love for God and the Lord Jesus and inevitably along with this our love for our brothers and sisters in Christ as well; we are not feeling any love or the joy of salvation. This is not an uncommon place to be; it can creep up on us and one day we can just think to ourselves, 'I don't love God any more – or the ecclesia – and in fact I don't think I believe any more'. In that frame of mind we can be tempted to turn our back on God and our brothers and sisters. It is a spiritual truth that our love to God needs to be protected and made to grow stronger as in any relationship. Jesus predicted that it would get difficult to keep loving and not abandon the faith because of the relentless winds of wickedness that blow against our love and faith in God.

---

3   *The Genius of Discipleship*, page 4.

Our Lord specifically warned that in the dark days of his absence, "because lawlessness will be increased, the love of many will grow cold" (Matthew 24:12). It is easy to be caught up in the spirit of disobedience and so our love grows cold. Implicit in the warning is part of the answer. If "lawlessness" is the problem, obedience is the solution. We will return to that thought, but first some Biblical context.

While love of God is commanded, it must be given voluntarily or it is not love. Seventeen times in scripture we are told to "love the Lord" (nine times in Deuteronomy, two in Joshua, three in the Psalms and three by Christ). Several of these provide motivation for us. Moses informs us that, "He [God] is your life and length of days, that you may dwell in the land that the LORD swore to your fathers" (Deuteronomy 30:20). David wrote, "I love the LORD, because he has heard my voice and my pleas for mercy" (Psalm 116:1). Simply put, considering what God has done for us is an inspiration to love. John picks up on this in his simple yet profound style and distils it into "We love because he first loved us" (1 John 4:19).

It is not however particularly helpful to be reminded that we should love. Presumably the believer who has lost love for God is aware of that and is concerned by it. How do we get love back when we are just not feeling it? Some might say, 'you need to pray more' or 'you need to read the Bible more'. Those things go without saying, but a believer who is struggling to love is probably struggling in these as well.

In six of the references to loving God we are specifically told to keep the commandments. It was the Lord who twice said, "For where your treasure is, there your heart will be also" (Matthew 6:21; Luke 12:34). He meant that our hearts will follow the things we accumulate. This principle may be amplified to – do the deeds of love and love will follow. The deeds of love are the commandments. If we set our mind to obey God (even in a mechanical fashion) love will be the inevitable consequence. Obedience is the path to love. Jesus recommended this to the entire ecclesia at Ephesus who had "abandoned the love you had at first" and he advised them to "do the works you did at first" (Revelation 2:4,5) Can we see the connection? To get back the love you had at the beginning do the things you did back then. This is very practical advice; there is something we can do – and it is the works of God.

Another practical thing we can do is be present at the gatherings of the ecclesia and especially the memorial meeting. In Psalm 73 Asaph was struggling. He describes his attitude toward God as "brutish and ignorant; I was like a beast toward you" (Psalm 73:22). What did Asaph do when he found his love for God flagging, when he looked around at the wicked who seemed to be prosperous? He "went into the sanctuary of God" and understood the end of the wicked (Psalm 73:17). When our hearts and minds are misaligned and we can't seem to process the issues of life correctly or feel the love of God we once did, the answers are to be found in the sanctuary of God. Precisely what Asaph saw or what happened in the sanctuary, we are not told, but we know the result – Asaph said, "it is good to be near God". When we are near God, it strengthens our love for Him, and when we love Him it strengthens our desire to be with Him. This is a positive feedback loop (the exact opposite of a vicious circle) and makes love easier. The message to the Hebrews was very much the same:

> "Let us consider how to stir up one another to love and good works, not neglecting to meet together, as is the habit of some, but encouraging one another, and all the more as you see the Day drawing near." (Hebrews 10:24,25)

Again in this passage the connection between love and attendance is emphasised.

In helping to encourage and increase our love for God and His people, it is helpful to think of our love for God as:

1. **A muscle to be exercised.** If love is like a muscle – the more we use it, the more we put it under load, the more we do 'love', the bigger and stronger it gets. Love can be a thought, a feeling but primarily in scripture love is defined as things we do. Some of the key spiritual exercises to maintain and grow our love are:

   - Reading the Bible – because we love God and want to hear Him speak to us His wisdom (2 Timothy 3:15-17).

   - Praying – because we love God and want to praise, thank and petition Him (Luke 18:13).

   - Watching – Because we want to be spiritually alive and aware (Matthew 26:41).

   - Fellowshipping – Remembering our Lord Jesus' love for us in the way he appointed. This Jesus taught is essential to maintain our love.

   - Serving – Just start being kind to everyone you meet – kindness is love in action.

2. **Love as a fire to be stoked.** A fire will go out if not refuelled constantly with more wood. A fire needs more than one piece of wood. The more pieces of wood, the more warmth is generated as the logs burn against each other. This is like fellowship – burning for and with each other. Therefore, love for God and love for the brethren go hand in hand. If there is no love in our fellowship it will burn out. The fire needs to be protected – shielded from the cold winds of lawlessness that would blow against it.

3. **Love as sailing together in a boat.** Think about Paul sailing on the way to Rome and the catastrophic events as recorded in Acts 27. If we sail a big boat with a precise destination in mind it takes constant watching, navigation and working together to steer the boat using the wind against the currents and storms that arise. Note in Acts 27 how Paul

demonstrated love in all his actions – because he had a clear vision of how his captain the Lord Jesus would want him to sail and a clear vision of his purpose. This purpose was to save all on board and get to the destination. Paul did not stand back but got in and helped. This is a wonderful example for us. If we stand back and are observers in the spiritual boat our love will not be exercised.

Putting the information together, there are (at least these) practical things to do:

- Make sure we attend ecclesial gatherings and fellowship others.
- Be diligent to obey the commands of God.
- Remember what God has done for us.
- Read the Bible.
- Pray.
- Watch to stay spiritually alive and alert.

They may seem mechanical and little more than going through the motions. Perhaps it is somewhat like cardiac compressions in resuscitation – external, and physical but often enough to get the heart going again. We might also point out that these things are all best done when our hearts are robust. When love comes easy, we need to make good habits that will sustain us when love is challenging. The above advice is both prevention and cure. Obedience, attendance and remembrance will help our hearts stay warm as well as rekindle them should they grow cold.

How do I hate the world and love my neighbour?

This is one of the scriptural paradoxes to which we referred earlier. The atheist looks at this and declares God to be irrational and therefore irrelevant. How can we both love and hate the same people? To be fair, scripture does not say, 'hate the world', it says:

> "Do not love the world or the things in the world. For all that is in the world – the desires of the flesh and the desires of the eyes and pride of life – is not from the Father but is from the world. And the world is passing away along with its desires, but whoever does the will of God abides forever." (1 John 2:15-17)

The word "world" is the Greek word *kosmos* from which our English word cosmopolitan (to be at home in all parts of the world) comes. "World" in its context means, the material things or influences that tend to affect us adversely in our effort to do the will of God – which is to love Him and love our neighbour as ourselves. John describes the world's influences as:

1. "The lust of the flesh" – or evil desires.

2. "The lust of the eyes" – or false values.

3. "The pride of life" – or self-will and egotism.

Any part of our will that rebels and defies God could be described as the worldly thinking. In Bible terminology we are to crucify or put to death this kind of thinking.

We are not to be happily integrated and peacefully content in the society of this world. Jesus told Pilate, "My kingdom is not of this world" (John 18:36) by which he meant that he and his followers were different in origin and purpose from the arrangements that exist in everyday society. Jesus knew that this kind of existence (living in the world but not belonging) is hard and so he prayed for us:

> "I have given them your word, and the world has hated them because they are not of the world, just as I am not of the world. I do not ask that you take them out of the world, but that you keep them from the evil one. They are not of the world, just as I am not of the world." (John 17:14-16)

"The world" is what collective human nature has established as its social, political and religious systems and values. The Apostle Paul speaks of the same influences as the "elemental spirits" or attitudes of the world and describes them as human philosophy and the traditions of men:

> "See to it that no one takes you captive by philosophy and empty deceit, according to human tradition, according to the elemental spirits of the world, and not according to Christ."
>
> (Colossians 2:8)

The world is ruled by lust and because of that will be destroyed by God. If we join with the world and allow the lust to have unbridled space in our lives then we will pass away with it. There are essentially only two choices – love God or love the world. They are mutually exclusive.

Both the Apostle John and the Apostle Paul are taking (by inspiration) their view of the world from the teaching of Jesus. Consider the following quotes and the combined message that they teach:

> "The world cannot hate you, but it hates me because I testify about it that its works are evil."   (John 7:7)

> "I am the light of the world. Whoever follows me will not walk in darkness but will have the light of life."   (John 8:12)

> "... even the Spirit of truth, whom the world cannot receive, because it neither sees him nor knows him. You know him, for he dwells with you and will be in you."   (John 14:17)

> "If the world hates you, know that it has hated me before it hated you. If you were of the world, the world would love you as its own; but because you are not of the world, but I chose you out of the world, therefore the world hates you."
>
> (John 15:18,19)

> "In the world you will have tribulation. But take heart; I have
> overcome the world."   (John 16:33)

Jesus is clearly teaching that he is different from the world and we must be also. The *people* who live about us are not the same as the *arrangement* of things in the world. John says of the one 'don't love it' and of the other 'love them'. The conundrum evaporates. One is talking of the present arrangement of things and the other of the people. We are to "love your neighbour as yourself" (Leviticus 19:18) amplified by Jesus to mean, "love your enemies and pray for those who persecute you" (Matthew 5:44).

Our attitude towards the system and arrangement of things must not be love, but detachment. However, Jesus did not intend isolation for then we will not be in a position to love the people of the world. We love the people of the world in the same way that Jesus did, by care, compassion and preaching. Our love for people, while modelled on the love God has for us is not the same as our love for God. We can (and we should) love God deeply and trust Him implicitly. Our Lord did this, but he was less committed in his love for those about him than for God. We read:

> "Now when he was in Jerusalem at the Passover Feast, many
> believed in his name when they saw the signs that he was
> doing. But Jesus on his part did not entrust himself to them,
> because he knew all people."   (John 2:23,24)

In this respect the love was one-sided. Jesus knew that before long they would turn on him and reject him. While Jesus had love for them and showed it in his actions, he did not unreservedly give himself to all others. Our love for the brothers and sisters of Christ can be deeper and more committed than our love for the 'man in the street'. This is no licence to treat one better and the other worse, but a reminder of the words of Jesus, "Behold, I am sending you out as sheep in the midst of wolves, so be wise as serpents and innocent as doves. Beware of men ..." Perhaps we might say we show love to them but are wise not to expect love from them. With fellow believers it should be mutual love.

Ultimately the greatest love we can show to those about us is to bring Christ to them, and hopefully in consequence, bring them to Christ. This does not preclude or absolve us from the more practical expressions of love, but it reminds us of the greatest need they have. James wrote:

> "If a brother or sister is poorly clothed and lacking in daily food, and one of you says to them, 'Go in peace, be warmed and filled,' without giving them the things needed for the body, what good is that?" (James 2:15,16)

It is hard for hungry and cold people to hear the Gospel.

Loving people who are lost is God's way of saving. We should love others with the goal that they too can renew their hearts and minds with God's truth.

A good example of how not to love the world but love our neighbour is Jesus' story of the 'Good Samaritan'. The story highlights the danger when we view the world incorrectly and narrowly as just people and particularly anyone who is not part of a 'Christadelphian club'. This was the problem of the Jewish spiritual elite at the time of Jesus. They viewed the injured and dying man as the world, from which it was best to keep away in order to avoid any contamination or condemnation. The Samaritan demonstrated the love of God in this situation by loving the man. There is danger of going to the other extreme. You have probably heard of the saying, 'hate the sin – but love the sinner'. This saying can be true, but it is not true for all time. If people wilfully continue sinning once they know better, at some point God will not love them evidenced by his judgement on them. At the judgement God will hold us all accountable for our actions according to our knowledge.

Perhaps the final word on this question should also be from James. He explained the twofold objective of love and care for people whilst remaining distant from the world. He wrote:

> "Religion that is pure and undefiled before God the Father is this: to visit orphans and widows in their affliction, and to keep oneself unstained from the world."   (James 1:27)

Do miracles happen today?

Sometimes we can feel very disconnected from the amazing miracles and wonders that are recorded in the Bible. We can wonder, 'Is God still working today? Does he have any power in my life? Where is the evidence of His existence?'

A miracle can be defined as an extraordinary event that is not explicable by natural or scientific laws and is therefore attributed to a divine agency. For example, the sun stops moving in the sky, a pair of shoes never wears out, someone coming alive from the dead, a person being able to walk on water, water in a jar made into excellent wine.

Biblical miracles have several purposes:

- To accomplish the purpose of God by supernatural means.

- To proclaim and prove that Yahweh is God and can control events according to His will. God's signs and wonders to Israel and Pharaoh would fall into this category. "But I will harden Pharaoh's heart, and though I multiply my signs and wonders in the land of Egypt ..." (Exodus 7:3).

- To demonstrate that someone like a prophet was speaking on behalf of God and that the message carried God's authority. Moses, Jesus and the apostles fall into this category.

> "Men of Israel, hear these words: Jesus of Nazareth, a man attested to you by God with mighty works and wonders and signs that God did through him in your midst, as you yourselves know ..." (Acts 2:22)

> "The signs of a true apostle were performed among you with utmost patience, with signs and wonders and mighty works." (2 Corinthians 12:12)

- To point to a new reality and creation and to increase people's faith.

> "And he went throughout all Galilee, teaching in their synagogues and proclaiming the gospel of the kingdom and healing every disease and every affliction among the people." (Matthew 4:23)

Perhaps the greatest miracle, and one upon which the entire Christian faith is based, is the resurrection of Jesus Christ. Much has been written to demonstrate the historical accuracy of the claims of the resurrection documented in the New Testament Gospels. Paul wrote:

> "I delivered to you as of first importance what I also received: that Christ died for our sins in accordance with the Scriptures, that he was buried, that he was raised on the third day in accordance with the Scriptures, and that he appeared to Cephas, then to the twelve. Then he appeared to more than five hundred brothers at one time, most of whom are still alive, though some have fallen asleep. Then he appeared to James, then to all the apostles. Last of all, as to one untimely born, he appeared also to me." (1 Corinthians 15:3-8)

Books such as *Who Moved the Stone?* by Frank Morison, or *Evidence that Demands a Verdict* by Josh McDowell demonstrate the truth of this quite forcibly. Written in a less accessible older style but with good material is *The Trial* by Robert Roberts.

Most people would say, if God or an agent of God could demonstrate to them a miracle they would believe in His powers. If God could and would do a miracle like that it would make God greater and give them real proof that God is the creator of the natural laws of the world that we see around us every day.

It is interesting to note that in the face of real divine miracles some people still refused to believe in the author of the miracle. In fact, they became more resistant to God, maybe because of their pride. Perhaps they just didn't like the God of the miracle – Pharaoh is a case in point. Some people who witnessed Jesus' miracles first hand did not believe in him and even attributed his miracles to an evil force. The same is true today: it is possible for some to see miracles and still not believe in the agency of God.

The power of God was present in the apostolic era to enable the spread of the Gospel through the pagan world:

"These signs will accompany those who believe: in my name they will cast out demons; they will speak in new tongues; they will pick up serpents with their hands; and if they drink any deadly poison, it will not hurt them; they will lay their hands on the sick, and they will recover."   (Mark 16:17,18)

The question remains – Does God do miracles today? We believe that God does not empower people today to do specific miracles through the power of the Holy Spirit, as was given to the first century believers described in the verses above. The main purpose of those powers in the first century was to help convince people of the resurrection and the Gospel message in a very hostile environment.

Having said this, God can do miracles now – however and whenever He so chooses. As Creator, God is free to work without, above or against the natural laws we see. From our reading of scripture and experience we would say that God does perform miracles today in the following ways.

- In a response to prayer or just because it is in accordance with His will God can heal or control circumstances which seem miraculous to those who experience it.

  "And the prayer of faith will save the one who is sick, and the Lord will raise him up. And if he has committed sins, he will be forgiven. Therefore, confess your sins to one another and pray for one another, that you may be healed. The prayer of a righteous person has great power as it is working. Elijah was a man with a nature like ours, and he prayed fervently that it might not rain, and for three years and six months it did not rain on the earth. Then he prayed again, and heaven gave rain, and the earth bore its fruit." (James 5:15-18)

- God is controlling and intervening in the nations to achieve His purpose. To the untrained, unspiritual eye the history and destiny of the nations is seemingly at the whim of a multitude of random factors – but to those who understand God's grand plan, it is a miracle the way God rules in the kingdom of men and most are totally unaware of it (see 2 Chronicles 10:15; Daniel 4:25).

- The process of spiritual birth is a miracle. Spiritual birth is the process whereby we come to believe in God and then live according to the influence of the spirit – rather than the influence of flesh, which is natural to us (see 1 Peter 1:23; John 1:12,13). This transformation of us by God's Spirit is indeed a miracle in the same way that a grub can turn into a butterfly (see Romans 12:2).

- The miracle of creation and life itself. We cannot really explain life – what causes it and what sustains it? What is the essence, spark, power that is life? If we open our eyes to it, we will see the miracle of life and creation every day. "O LORD, how manifold are your works! In wisdom have you made them all" (Psalm 104:24). "I praise you, for

I am fearfully and wonderfully made. Wonderful are your works; my soul knows it very well" (Psalm 139:14).

- The modern nation of Israel. All natural and historical evidence would lead to the conclusion that the Jewish people should not exist and would never return to their land once they had been removed violently from it in AD 70 during the time of the Roman Empire – especially once they had apparently assimilated into the nations of Europe and then from the ashes of the holocaust. Yet despite these events they were miraculously regathered, and the ancient land of Israel was agreed upon as their new homeland. All this was in direct fulfilment of the ancient prophecies concerning their destruction and regathering (see Isaiah 43:10-12; Ezekiel 37).

Should believers take a stand on social injustice?

There are many problems in this world and the inequities are considerable. As we write, the world is gripped in the "Black Lives Matter" protests. Before that there were significant global protests about climate change. The reality is there have always been issues that don't seem fair and against which people feel they should protest. The voice of the people crying for liberty, equality and fraternity is the voice of madness drawing the world towards Armageddon (see Revelation 16:13,14).

What should a believer do? Paul made it quite clear that participating in a protest is not a course a believer should choose. He wrote:

> "The Lord's servant must not be quarrelsome but kind to everyone, able to teach, patiently enduring evil, correcting his opponents with gentleness." (2 Timothy 2:24)

The issue is not so much whether the cause would be just in the eyes of Christ (and some of them seem as if they might be) but whether the Lord would condone our participation at all. Isaiah wrote of the coming Messiah, "he will bring forth justice to the nations. He will not cry aloud or lift up his voice, or make it heard in the street" (Isaiah 42:1,2). Clearly there are just causes that are of concern to Jesus that he will address, but protest and social disturbance are not his method. Jesus made it clear to Pilate that his "kingdom is not of this world. If my kingdom were of this world, my servants would have been fighting, that I might not be delivered over to the Jews" (John 18:36). There has probably never been so great a social injustice as the wrongful abuse and death of Jesus and yet his servants neither protested nor fought. We are to see ourselves as citizens of a heavenly kingdom rather than belonging to this world.

There are two frequent features of modern protests regardless of the justice (or otherwise) of the cause:

- Civil disturbance and violence.
- Political agendas.

Neither of these ought to be features of the life of a believer. If we join a protest we will almost always find that it takes on characteristics that we would not endorse, even if we agreed with the primary cause. Civil disobedience and vandalism are things we should stand apart from. Paul reminds us that, "whoever resists the authorities resists what God has appointed, and those who resist will incur judgement" (Romans 13:2).

Do we feel that unless we protest nothing will change? Do we distrust the ways and schedule of God? Scripture has made it clear that, "the way of man is not in himself, that it is not in man who walks to direct his steps" (Jeremiah 10:23). We await a time when Jesus will return to correct the social injustices, as David predicted:

"May he defend the cause of the poor of the people, give deliverance to the children of the needy, and crush the oppressor!" (Psalm 72:4)

What should we do until then? We ought to be a personal example for good to all we meet both within and outside of our brotherhood. We should pray and long for the return of Jesus when the problems will all be fixed and we ought to live our lives as though we are part of Christ's kingdom now.

Chapter 9

Questions about life

"*Happiness is the meaning and the purpose of life, the whole aim and end of human existence.*" (Aristotle, Greek philosopher)

"*The chief purpose of life, for any of us, is to increase according to our capacity our knowledge of God by all means we have, and to be moved by it to praise and thanks.*" (J. R. R. Tolkien, author)

What is the purpose of my life?

"Without a purpose, life is motion without meaning, activity without direction and events without reason. Without a purpose life is trivial, petty and pointless", so wrote Rick Warren in his popular book, *The purpose-driven life*. Sometimes we can ask ourselves what is the point of my life, does God really need me, does God really care about me, and does God have a purpose for me?

A broader question sits behind it – what is the purpose of life? This is a question that has exercised the minds of people for thousands of years. Unhappily without God there are no definitive answers and so for thousands of years the purpose of human existence has been debated endlessly. There are two basic schools of thought that emerge strongly answering to the basic philosophies of the Epicureans and the Stoics that were encountered by Paul in Acts 17. The one says the purpose of life is self-fulfilment and the other self-betterment. We see these philosophies play out in the lives of men and women who seek pleasure or enjoyment in their various endeavours. The question is asked by the wise man in Ecclesiastes, "What benefit do people get from all the effort which they expend on earth? A generation comes and a generation goes" (Ecclesiastes 1:3,4, NET). At both the individual level and the collective level there seems to be no progress or profit. Death is the victor and it ultimately brings all human schemes to dust. It matters not what our philosophy, character or achievement, death wins in the end. It is as the wise man said:

> "I reflected on everything that is accomplished by man on earth, and I concluded: Everything he has accomplished is futile – like chasing the wind!"   (Ecclesiastes 1:14, NET)

If there is no God, and no ultimate purpose beyond what we can do and what we can achieve in our brief time on this earth then it does all seem pointless. Happily we can confidently assert that there is a God and life has purpose and meaning. There are three Biblical metaphors of life that help explain the meaning of our existence:

1. Life is a test.
2. Life is a trust.
3. Life is a preparation.

The first of these suggests that God is placing challenging circumstances in our path to see how we respond; the second proposes that life is a sacred trust from God and He wants to see how we use it; and the third that this life is a temporary assignment preparing us for a greater future. Should we fail the test, abuse the trust or not prepare adequately then we may find that God excludes us from His eternal family. This is by no means to suggest that we will earn God's favour in the next life by behaving appropriately now; it will be by grace that we are saved. However, we cannot expect Him to value our self-importance and self-interest. This life is all about the next. If we make no choices that render us suitable for God's eternal family, even in the smallest of ways, we cannot anticipate He will find room for us.

God specially created us, and He has a purpose with us. There are a number of basic inter-related ideas that it is clear God had in creation.

- We were made to give God glory (Revelation 4:11).

- We were created to become like Christ (Ephesians 2:10a).

- We were shaped for service (Ephesians 2:10b).

- We were designed for godliness (Titus 1:3).

- We were made to be part of God's family (Ephesians 3:15).

With these thoughts in mind the believer needs to address five critical questions about their own existence:

1. *What will be the centre of my life?* This is the question of worship. Who are we going to live for? What / who are we going to build our life around? Who will be at the centre of our choices? Moses encourages us to love "the LORD your God, obeying his voice and holding fast to him, for he is your life" (Deuteronomy 30:20).

2. *What will be the character of my life?* This is the question of discipleship. What kind of person will we be? Who will be our role model? "Let this mind be in you which was also in Christ Jesus" (Philippians 2:5). And, "let your manner of life be worthy of the gospel of Christ" (Philippians 1:27).

3. *What will be the contribution of my life?* This is the question of service: knowing your gifts and how you can serve in the family of God.

> "For the ministry of this service is not only supplying the needs of the saints but is also overflowing in many thanksgivings to God." (2 Corinthians 9:12)

4. *What will be the communication of my life?* This is the question of our mission to preach the Gospel. The Lord said:

> "Let your light shine before others, so that they may see your good works and give glory to your Father who is in heaven." (Matthew 5:16)

5. *Who will be the community of my life?* This is the question of fellowship. How will we demonstrate our commitment to other believers and our connection to the family of God? Where will we practise the "one another" commands?

> "That which we have seen and heard we proclaim also to you, so that you too may have fellowship with us; and indeed our fellowship is with the Father and with his Son Jesus Christ." (1 John 1:3)

We do not wish the reader to imagine that believers always have the objectives in focus and their life well adjusted. Sometimes we lose the meaning for our life and we feel hopeless and lost – struggling with our purpose even though we know God is not uncommon. It can arise from the seeming monotony of day-to-day existence or from traumatic experiences in our lives. Consider how even great Bible characters at times struggled to make sense of life.

- *Isaiah.* "I have laboured in vain; I have spent my strength for nothing and vanity" (Isaiah 49:4).

- **Job.** "My days are swifter than a weaver's shuttle and come to their end without hope ... I loathe my life; I would not live forever. Leave me alone" (Job 7:6,16).

- **Asaph.** "The sinners; they do well at all times, and their wealth is increased. As for me, I have made my heart clean to no purpose, washing my hands in righteousness; for I have been troubled all the day; every morning have I undergone punishment ... When my thoughts were turned to see the reason of this, it was a weariness in my eyes; till I went into God's holy place, and saw the end of the evil-doers" (Psalm 73:12-17, BBE).

The last of these quotes provides the answer that rebalanced Asaph and will ultimately restore all who trust in God. The destiny of those who trust in God is assured but those who do not will perish. We only find purpose and meaning by listening to God. If we find that purpose seems to have disappeared from our life, we will only find it again with God.

Are people basically good or evil?

Most people would think that all humans have the capacity for both good and evil. People are then divided between those who think humans are primarily good and those who think we are basically evil and driven by powerful self-centred forces that in the end will be self-destructive. What does the Bible say about our nature?

The Bible states that God created Adam and Eve to be in His image and likeness and having made us, "God saw all that he had made – and it was very good!" (Genesis 1:31). "Very good" means that there was no evil present, nothing that would spoil God's creation. They were very good – because they were made in the image (physical shape) and likeness (moral / intellectual capacity) of the angels. The comment in Hebrews makes the connection with humans and angels and implies they are similar.

> "For it was not to angels that God subjected the world to come, of which we are speaking. It has been testified somewhere, 'What is man that you are mindful of him, or the son of man, that you care for him? You made him for a little while lower than the angels; you have crowned him with glory and honour.'" (Hebrews 2:5-7)

In creating Adam and Eve, God gave them the capacity of free will. God gave man purpose and a law:

> "The LORD God took the man and put him in the garden of Eden to work it and keep it. And the LORD God commanded the man, saying, "You may surely eat of every tree of the garden, but of the tree of the knowledge of good and evil you shall not eat, for in the day that you eat of it you shall surely die." (Genesis 2:15-17)

They could choose to obey or disobey God's law – sadly they chose to disobey. Human free will used to disobey God's laws since creation has led to much evil and suffering. It seems God has allowed it so we can understand more fully the vast difference between good and evil; but the Bible puts the responsibility for the evil that humans do squarely on us. The wise man Solomon noted, "See, this alone I found, that God made man upright, but they have sought out many schemes" (Ecclesiastes 7:29). God Himself stated, "The heart is deceitful above all things, and desperately sick; who can understand it?" (Jeremiah 17:9). Jesus said, "Out of the heart come evil thoughts, murder, adultery, sexual immorality, theft, false witness, slander" (Matthew 15:19). The combined message of these verses is that we are not now the same as the "very good" state in which man was created.

The resultant enmity produces a battle within us between good and evil. Paul gives insight into this battle:

"For I do not do the good I want, but the evil I do not want is what I keep on doing. Now if I do what I do not want, it is no longer I who do it, but sin that dwells within me. So I find it to be a law that when I want to do right, evil lies close at hand. For I delight in the law of God, in my inner being, but I see in my members another law waging war against the law of my mind and making me captive to the law of sin that dwells in my members. Wretched man that I am! Who will deliver me from this body of death?" (Romans 7:19-24)

Paul taught that there are two forces (principles or laws) that can govern our thoughts and actions.

1. The law of sin (Flesh) – also described as "my flesh", "sin that lives in me" and "evil".

2. The law of God (Spirit) – also described as "inner being", "conscience", and "good".

Paul expands on this teaching in Galatians.

"Now the works of the flesh are evident: sexual immorality, impurity, sensuality, idolatry, sorcery, enmity, strife, jealousy, fits of anger, rivalries, dissensions, divisions, envy, drunkenness, orgies, and things like these. I warn you, as I warned you before, that those who do such things will not inherit the kingdom of God. But the fruit of the Spirit is love, joy, peace, patience, kindness, goodness, faithfulness, gentleness, self-control; against such things there is no law. And those who belong to Christ Jesus have crucified the flesh with its passions and desires." (Galatians 5:19-24)

So, in summary the Bible teaches that God made us very good, but we chose to disobey. Consequently, humans now have a bias towards evil that is part of our nature. The good news is we still have free will by which we can choose to follow the Spirit (God's law). The word of God is where we learn about the law of God and living by the spirit. If we choose to follow God's law the fruits of our obedience will be evidenced in the wonderful characteristics of "love, joy, peace, patience, kindness, goodness, faithfulness, gentleness, self-control". Our destiny will be largely governed by what we allow to direct our lives. If we allow the evil within to reign unchallenged, our destiny will be very different than if the spirit directs us.

Why do believers get depressed?

Behind the question is possibly the thought that as believers in the good news about the kingdom of God and the saving name of Jesus Christ, coupled with the promised wisdom, joy and strength from God and His word, we should be far less susceptible to depression, perhaps even immune? Let's be clear – sadness and grief are normal human emotions that God expects us to experience as part of a normal life. We all have these feelings from time to time, but they usually go away within a few days or weeks. Believers are human and as such subject to a fallen and broken world. All people at some time will be sad, down or depressed. Because we are human, we are not immune from these feelings and neither was our Lord Jesus.

The Psalmist writes, "Why are you cast down, O my soul?" (Psalm 42:5) He was sad, troubled, perplexed, disquieted, unhappy and spiritually depressed. Obviously he felt overwhelmed within himself. Possibly he had no idea how common these feelings are and how much a part of normal life they can be. Considering the list of those in scripture that had symptoms identifying them as suffering from depression, we can readily dismiss the notion that depression is caused by a lack of faith. Much harm has been done through the suggestion that those with depression are faithless.

Major depression can bring about long-lasting symptoms such as overwhelming sadness, emptiness, blackness, hopelessness, worthlessness, desolation, low energy, loss of appetite, and a lack of interest in things that used to bring pleasure. Left unrecognised and untreated, depression can lead to serious health issues, including putting your life at risk. Fortunately, there are effective treatments for depression through options like talking to a professional, medication, diet, and exercise. It is likely that anybody suffering depression will require assistance from professionals competent to help.

Since depression is not caused by a lack of faith or a lack of spirituality, it follows that merely endeavouring to increase these components of Christian life will not provide solutions. Despite this fact, it is known that believers are less likely to get depression, likely to have milder symptoms than those who are unbelievers and likely to have a better recovery than unbelievers.[1] That is to say, faith in God and Christ is both protective and curative for depression. We do not for a moment intend to say that faith will either prevent or cure depression, but that it can be helpful. Spiritual help can be found by focussing on the comfort and encouragement in scripture. We find the words, "be strong and of good courage" and other similar expressions many times in scripture. There are many encouraging passages in scripture that take us in positive directions – read them, think about them and live by them.

The article referenced above also details how in some cases a spiritual component can make depression worse because of feelings of guilt and fear. Could it be that believers may have to struggle against depressive thoughts and environments more than unbelievers because of their faith? Jesus did say, "Blessed are those who mourn, for they shall be comforted." (Matthew 5:4). We will return to this thought a little later and will explore some spiritual causes for depression and offer some suggestions that may be of benefit.

---

1   See "Religious and Spiritual Factors in Depression: Review and Integration of the Research"; Raphael Bonelli, *Journal of Mental Health and Economics*, August 2012.

- **Fear of the past.** No matter how dark the stains may be, they have all been blotted out! It is finished! Never look back on your sins again – they will only depress you! If you focus on 'your sinfulness' you will only conclude that 'you are not good enough'. Whether you believe it or not, nobody is good enough! The issue is not our goodness ... the issue is God's goodness. Paul wrote:

> "One thing I do: forgetting what lies behind and straining forward to what lies ahead, I press on toward the goal for the prize of the upward call of God in Christ Jesus. Let those of us who are mature think this way ..."
> (Philippians 3:13-15)

The American Christian writer John Piper wrote, "Mental health is, in great measure, the gift of self-forgetfulness. The reason is that introspection destroys what matters most to us – the authentic experience of great things outside ourselves."

- **Fear of the future.** The concluding thoughts of the Lord's Prayer remind us of the timelessness and the greatness of God. For us the future is an unknown and perhaps a frightening thing. We can be comforted in the thought that wherever the future takes us God (the same God as always) will be there. Moses comforted Israel with these thoughts, "The eternal God is your dwelling place, and underneath are the everlasting arms" (Deuteronomy 33:27). When Moses said, "underneath" we might well ask, "underneath what?" The answer is us. However low we may have sunk, however further we may yet fall, the arms of the everlasting God will be beneath us to catch us and support us. We will explore the issues of confidence at the judgement later, but suffice to say for now that we need have no fear of the future if our faith abides in God. The Apostle John expressed it this way:

> "Little children, abide in him; that, when he shall appear, we may have confidence, and not be ashamed before him at his coming." (1 John 2:28)

- *Works-based salvation.* Aside from being incorrect, the entire notion of legalism is unhelpful to our spiritual psyche. If we believe that salvation is the result of works, we are setting ourselves up for failure. When (not if!) we fail to measure up to the example of Christ, it can be so demoralising that we slump into depression. Faith is (and is intended to be) a liberating concept. Paul wrote:

> "There is therefore now no condemnation for those who are in Christ Jesus. For the law of the Spirit of life has set you free in Christ Jesus ..." (Romans 8:1,2)

Sin need no longer be viewed as a destructive and crippling limitation – Christ has dealt with it. We may still be subject to it, but we have the promise that one day the present curse will be removed (see Romans 8:21). A works-based approach removes that confidence and places salvation subject to performance (rather than faith) and therefore we doubt our salvation.

- *Too much focus on ourselves.* The unfortunate reality is that humanity is fundamentally weak. We are not able adequately to plan our direction (see Jeremiah 10:23), nor have we the ability always to perform what we want, either spiritually or physically (see Romans 7:18). This means that we will inevitably fail at some point. When failure comes despite our best endeavours, it can be so depressing that it precipitates mental illness. The antidote is to focus on God and not ourselves. God will not fail us or disappoint us. In contrast we limp from one disappointing failure to another. Having unreal expectations of what is possible is not likely to assist our mental outlook. "I can do all things through him who strengthens me" was the confidence of the Apostle Paul (Philippians 4:13). Paul's confidence was not in himself but in God and Christ. This allowed Paul to report to the Corinthians, "For when I am weak, then I am strong" (2 Corinthians 12:10). It seems the inverse is also true, 'When I am strong then I am weak' – that is to say, focus on personal strength leads to weakness.

- *The Elijah syndrome.* After the conquest on Mount Carmel, Elijah was depressed. He thought he was a failure and the only believer left. It seemed to Elijah that he was a righteous minority and everything else was falling apart. His words were:

> "I have been very jealous for the LORD, the God of hosts. For the people of Israel have forsaken your covenant, thrown down your altars, and killed your prophets with the sword, and I, even I only, am left, and they seek my life, to take it away." (1 Kings 19:10)

Clearly, the perspective that the spiritual state of the nation was terrible and he had failed his mission in part caused Elijah's depression. While there might be some added onus on leaders, for the most part we need only concern ourselves with our spiritual health. That does not mean we are to be insular and selfish, but that we recognise that we answer to the Master for ourselves, and only ourselves. Elijah's perspective was out by a factor of 7,000 (see 1 Kings 19:18) and this clearly took him into a very dark place. If we mourn that things are not good and we really would prefer them to be better, we have the assurance from the Lord that He (not us) will deal with that and we thereby will be comforted.

Can I be good enough for God?

Some people have lost faith or slumped into depression by thinking and worrying that they are not good enough for God.

We can begin doubting the ability of God to love us or save us. We may feel inadequate when we compare ourselves with others or are constantly struggling with the same sin. We can think to ourselves, 'I'm no good for God; He would be better off without me'. Many people, of *all* ages, struggle with this feeling. It is hard to see any good in ourselves, especially because we know who we really are deep down. Paul affirms that, "all have sinned and fall short of the glory of God" (Romans 3:23). God is all knowing and quite familiar with who we really are deep down, as the words of Jeremiah testify, "I the LORD search the heart and test the mind" (Jeremiah 17:10).

We have all done things for which we are ashamed, and many have done things that we might feel are unforgivable sins. We know and experience that we are stained with sin (Ephesians 2:3; 1 John 1:8; Romans 5:12). Jeremiah said, "The heart is deceitful above all things, and desperately sick; who can understand it?" (Jeremiah 17:9).

There is only one way to be right with God and feel right with God and that is through Jesus Christ who is our righteousness. John 3:16 sometimes goes over our heads because we hear it so many times, but read it again with new eyes: "For God so loved the world, that he gave his only Son, that *whoever* believes in him should not perish but have eternal life."

The phrase 'good enough' or the opposite, 'not good enough' imply that there is some kind of gradation, a benchmark that we are required to achieve. It is our faith in Jesus Christ that makes us acceptable to God – not anything we *do* (see Ephesians 2:8,9). Faith, not only makes us accepted, but counted righteous – that is, without condemnation. This is how the Apostle Paul saw it:

> "God chose what is low and despised in the world, even things that are not, to bring to nothing things that are, so that no human being might boast in the presence of God.

And because of him you are in Christ Jesus, who became to us wisdom from God, righteousness and sanctification and redemption, so that, as it is written, 'Let the one who boasts, boast in the Lord.'" (1 Corinthians 1:28-31)

None of us can do any works 'good enough' to erase all the sins we have ever committed in our lifetimes.

God did not send Christ because humanity was capable of being good enough. Isaiah wrote, "We are all like one who is unclean, all our so-called righteous acts are like a menstrual rag in your sight" (Isaiah 64:6, NET).

This does not mean that we accept mediocrity or stop trying to be like Christ – but it does lift from our shoulders the burden of failure. There is no sense in which we should feel detached and aloof from our sins – as if sin didn't matter and God will deal with it. This takes us perilously close to saying, "Are we to continue in sin that grace may abound?" (Romans 6:1). David felt very deeply the thankfulness that came when the weight of his darkest sin was lifted; he wrote, "Blessed is the one whose transgression is forgiven, whose sin is covered" (Psalm 32:1).

We should rather focus more positively on the question, 'is God good enough for us'? David challenged his readers to "taste and see that the LORD is good!" (Psalm 34:8). While we will never be good enough for God, we will always find that God is more than good enough for us. This will find ultimate expression in the future when God rewards our faithfulness in just a few things with an exalted position over many things (see Matthew 25:21,23).

Do not be weighed down by self-judgement and concern regarding your ability to make God accept you. Our loving heavenly Father loves us enough to sacrifice *His own Son* in order to give us the hope of life. As Jesus tells us, "Let not your hearts be troubled. Believe in God; believe also in me" (John 14:1).

Should you feel confident about salvation?

People respond differently to this question. Some would say, 'Absolutely'! Others might say, 'I'm hopeful but I would not want to presume on God's grace'. Some might say, 'If my good deeds outweigh my bad deeds, then I would feel more confident'. Some would say, 'I'm not really sure'.

We believe we should be able to feel confident about salvation. God and the Lord Jesus Christ have done everything necessary to save you – and they really want to save you. This is what faith is – being sure and confident in receiving what we hope for.

Under Moses, the people of Israel were saved out of Egypt, but despite God showing them continually that He was with them they would not, could not, believe that God would fulfil His promise to them and bring them into the Promised Land. They were not confident about their salvation and this was demonstrated in their actions. This is contrasted with the faithful who were totally and fully persuaded that God could do far more than all they thought possible.

Feeling confident in God about our salvation is a sign of faith. Paul wrote:

> "*He has* delivered us from the domain of darkness and transferred us to the kingdom of his beloved Son, in whom we have redemption, the forgiveness of sins."
>
> (Colossians 1:13,14)

To the Hebrews was written:

> "Do not throw away your confidence, which has a great reward. For you have need of endurance, so that when you have done the will of God you may receive what is promised. For, 'Yet a little while, and the coming one will come and will not delay; but my righteous one shall live by faith, and if he shrinks back, my soul has no pleasure in him.' But we are not

of those who shrink back and are destroyed, but of those who have faith and preserve their souls." (Hebrews 10:35-39)

Such confidence is not in our ability but in God. It is not presumption, but faith that provides such a firm foundation. Balaam correctly observed:

"God is not man, that he should lie, or a son of man, that he should change his mind. Has he said, and will he not do it? Or has he spoken, and will he not fulfil it?" (Numbers 23:19)

The last word surely belongs to Christ who said, "Fear not, little flock, for it is your Father's good pleasure to give you the kingdom" (Luke 12:32).

Why do bad things happen to good people and good things happen to bad people?

At the root of this question is our idea of justice and fairness. Sometimes, when life seems to be unfair for good people, we question God. We may be able to accept that for bad and good people outside of God's specific calling and care, time and chance happens to them all and that the laws of a fallen world where people are subject to misfortune, disease, mortality and death is somehow reasonable. But what about when bad things happen to those who God has called and chosen and loved and when they have genuinely loved and sought to please Him? What are we to make of this? When godly people die suddenly in their prime, or are diagnosed with a terminal illness, or lose children or suffer painful injuries. How do we reconcile God allowing such things happening to good people?

Asaph was a man who struggled with this and was tempted to question God when he saw the prosperity of the wicked and he himself bowed down with problems:

"As for me, my feet had almost stumbled, my steps had nearly slipped. For I was envious of the arrogant when I saw the prosperity of the wicked. For they have no pangs until death; their bodies are fat and sleek. They are not in trouble as others are; they are not stricken like the rest of mankind."

(Psalm 73:1-5)

Asaph looked around him and lost perspective of God's long-term plan. He was viewing life as if he was to have only one life. He was missing God's long-term purpose for him.

Asaph goes on to say:

"When I thought how to understand this, it seemed to me a wearisome task, until I went into the sanctuary of God; then I discerned their end."
(Psalm 73:16,17)

When Asaph went to the sanctuary of God – that is he sought to see life from God's perspective – then he understood the real end of the wicked. The wicked only live for this one life – that is all they will get. But by the grace of God the godly will live forever – with a noble character forged by the experiences of life and the sufferings that God has called upon them to endure in this life. So Paul could say:

"We do not lose heart. Though our outer self is wasting away, our inner self is being renewed day by day. For this light momentary affliction is preparing for us an eternal weight of glory beyond all comparison."
(2 Corinthians 4:16,17)

And Asaph could end his Psalm with some encouraging thoughts:

"I am continually with you; you hold my right hand. You guide me with your counsel, and afterward you will receive me to glory. Whom have I in heaven but you? And there is nothing on earth that I desire besides you. My flesh and my heart may fail, but God is the strength of my heart and my portion forever. For behold, those who are far from you shall perish;

you put an end to everyone who is unfaithful to you. But for me it is good to be near God; I have made the Lord GOD my refuge, that I may tell of all your works." (Psalm 73:23-28)

Essentially it is about viewing life from the correct perspective – the eternal. Psalms 42, 49 and 77 are some other wonderful Psalms to ponder on this subject.

We may be tempted to think that because we are suffering, God doesn't love us; nothing could be further from the truth. It is often that we are suffering *because* God loves us (see Hebrews 12:6-13). In suffering we are drawn to understand and know God more. Suffering and trial *is* the path to deeper spiritual insight. Solomon wrote:

"My son, do not despise the LORD's discipline or be weary of his reproof, for the LORD reproves him whom he loves, as a father the son in whom he delights. Blessed is the one who finds wisdom, and the one who gets understanding, for the gain from her is better than gain from silver and her profit better than gold. She is more precious than jewels, and nothing you desire can compare with her. Long life is in her right hand; in her left hand are riches and honour." (Proverbs 3:11-15)

How does God view believers who subsequently suffer a brain injury or dementia?

We believe God would view these believers with compassion and a longing to heal them to a right mind in the kingdom. Consider the thoughts from Isaiah that support this view:

"Say to those who have an anxious heart, 'Be strong; fear not! Behold, your God will come with vengeance, with the recompense of God. He will come and save you.' Then the eyes of the blind shall be opened, and the ears of the deaf unstopped; then shall the lame man leap like a deer, and the tongue of the mute sing for joy. For waters break forth in the wilderness, and streams in the desert." (Isaiah 35:4-6)

The overarching principle must be that God will do what is right. Abraham was confident, "Shall not the Judge of all the earth do what is just?" (Genesis 18:25).

Jesus had so much compassion for the mentally sick and unstable. "When he went ashore he saw a great crowd, and he had compassion on them and healed their sick" (Matthew 14:14). It is difficult to believe that God feels differently.

It was the confident expectation of Paul that:

"He who began a good work in you will bring it to completion at the day of Jesus Christ. It is right for me to feel this way about you all, because I hold you in my heart, for you are all partakers with me of grace." (Philippians 1:6,7)

We cannot think that brain injury though disease or illness will be allowed to thwart Paul's confidence.

Some are born with intellectual disabilities ranging from minor to profound. What of them? Let God be the judge (see 1 Corinthians 4:5). What is more important is how we love and care for them after the example of our Lord Jesus with compassion, patience, gentleness, kindness and understanding.

We all need to be aware that at any time we could be overcome by an accident, illness or disease that takes from us our right mind. Before this happens we can pray for others and ourselves Nehemiah's prayer: "Remember me, O my God, for good" (Nehemiah 13:31). We are encouraged to consider that when we have a sound mind it is the time to serve the Lord while we can; for if the Lord tarries and we grow old, senility is a strong possibility. The preacher details an inevitable slide into physical and mental deterioration as we age and therefore recommends that we remember our Creator "in the days of your youth, before the evil days come" (Ecclesiastes 12:1).

Chapter 10

Questions about death

"The boundaries which divide life from death are at best shadowy and vague. Who shall say where the one ends, and where the other begins?" (Edgar Allan Poe, author)

"I look upon death to be as necessary to our constitution as sleep. We shall rise refreshed in the morning." (Benjamin Franklin, American President)

What happens at death?

From a biological perspective, when we stop breathing and our heart stops beating, unless there is immediate and successful resuscitation, in a few minutes we will die, a process of decay will be irreversibly instituted and we will return to the natural elements that constitute us. Scripture succinctly puts it, "when you take away their breath, they die and return to their dust" (Psalm 104:29).

Almost nobody has any argument with the above explanation. That this is what occurs to the human body at death is almost never in dispute. There are a few hopeful (and wealthy) people who with considerable faith in science, trust that by cryopreservation they might be preserved in death and somehow be reanimated. This idea flies in the face of both science and scripture. At best it can prevent the ugliest ravages of decay, but will ultimately only ensure the preservation of a corpse. A vast number of people place their hope in the idea of an immortal soul that consciously lives on in death in an afterlife – generally a pleasant one.

The Bible presents death as an enemy, "The last enemy to be destroyed is death" (1 Corinthians 15:26). Death cannot of itself be the gateway to something greater; it is an enemy and until it is vanquished remains an enemy. In Psalm 49 the word "perish" is used repeatedly. This gives us clearly to understand that there is finality and hopelessness in death. Whatever constituted the person has reduced to nothingness and eventually the body will follow.

The real question is, what happens to the essence of a person? Are we just the sum of biochemical processes or is there a higher and enduring consciousness that exists extra-corporeally? Some people have what are known as 'near-death experiences'. Without arguing about the nature of these and what they may or may not represent, we may simply say they are not 'death experiences'. There have been no resurrections since apostolic times so we cannot ask anybody who died and was brought back to life what it was like. By definition a near-death experience is not death. Near death events are clearly reversible while death is not. We cannot therefore extrapolate with any confidence from near-death experiences to determine what happens at death and what it feels like.

The Bible is very clear that there is no lingering personality in death:

"The living know that they will die, but the dead know nothing ... Their love and their hate and their envy have already perished."   (Ecclesiastes 9:5,6)

When a person dies, their thoughts cease and there is no consciousness. Death is mental extinction. Psalm 146:4 records, "in that very day his thoughts perish". The only hope of reanimation known to the scriptures is resurrection. The Bible knows nothing of the pagan notion of disembodied souls surviving death.

That being said, a divine record is being kept of the lives and characters of those God wishes to raise and accept, and they are described as being written "in the book of life" (Philippians 4:3; see also Daniel 12:1). The Greek word used often in the New Testament scriptures for tomb is the word *mnēmeion*, from which we get the concept of mnemonics (systems of memory) – this makes it clear that the graves of believers are somehow etched in divine memory.

How God achieves resurrection and creates again the exact person who had died, with their precise personality and memories, is beyond human ability either to know or describe. However, Job was confident in the certainty and reality of this hope and he said, "after my skin has been thus destroyed, yet in my flesh I shall see God" (Job 19:26).

What is the purpose of a funeral service?

For people of some religious faiths a funeral has specific religious significance and is believed to benefit the soul of the dead. For example, the Roman Catholic Church offers a Mass for the soul so that the temporal effects of sin in purgatory may be extinguished. Islamic funerals are said to offer good hope for the afterlife. Hindu adherents have a service to liberate the soul for an ascent into heaven. Clearly, funerals of Christadelphians (who do not believe in immortal souls) will not be conducted for such purposes. Since the deceased has no consciousness and no eternal soul, a funeral cannot advantage them at all; it is only of value for those who remain.

So why have a funeral service and what does it accomplish? There are several benefits to having a funeral service:

- By showing care and respect for the person who has died, the family may be encouraged.

- It can help provide closure and assist the grieving process for relatives and friends.

- It is an opportunity to give thanks to God for the life of the deceased.

- It is an opportunity to reaffirm our belief in the resurrection.

- It can be a witness to unbelievers.

- It is a sobering reminder to us all that life is the time to serve the Lord.

A public service or indeed any service for that matter is by no means mandatory, though some of the points listed above may not be so readily achieved in its absence. There is no particular form that a service should take; however, the tendency of modern funerals to be merely a celebration of life, reflects to a considerable extent a life lived without God and has little to commend it to the believer. On the other hand, a funeral service that is respectful to God, and full of the hope of the resurrection, may be quite a moving tribute to a faithful friend.

The question of children's attendance at funerals is a very personal subject and is best left for individual choice. We have seen the levity and guilelessness of children both enhance and detract from the proceedings. Particularly with young children (who in all probability don't fully appreciate what is occurring) we might carefully weigh up whether attendance is in the best interests of all concerned.

Is cremation acceptable for believers?

The reverence with which ancient (and more modern) tombs are treated requires no further comment. It was considered a mark of disgrace not to be interred in the family sepulchre. For example we read of Jehoram, "he departed with no one's regret. They buried him in the city of David, but not in the tombs of the kings" (2 Chronicles 21:20).

Burial is almost the universal method for disposing of a dead body recorded in scripture. Today most Jews believe that the words of Genesis 3:19, "By the sweat of your face you shall eat bread, till you return to the ground, for out of it you were taken; for you are dust, and to dust you shall return" demand the body should be returned to the ground. Some demand that our body in life belongs to God (see 1 Corinthians 6:13-20) so the body should belong to God in death and man has no right to interfere with it. This seems an extreme position, which, if true should demand that surgery such as amputation must almost certainly be wrong. Some modern Christians would say that since baptism is symbolic of burial, cremation inappropriately destroys the type. Cremation historically is most commonly (though not always) a pagan practice.

The references to death by burning and / or cremation in scripture are rare and we have space to consider them all. First we read of Achan and his family, "all Israel stoned him with stones. They burned them with fire and stoned them with stones" (Joshua 7:25). This would seem to be describing the execution of Achan and his family as the punishment for sin. There was at the very least enough of Achan remaining for Israel to raise "over him a great heap of stones". In Leviticus we read,

"If a man takes a woman and her mother also, it is depravity; he and they shall be burned with fire" (Leviticus 20:14). Presumably they were to be burnt as a means of execution rather than executed and cremated. It appears that Gentile nations made a habit of executing by fire and then cremating in the same fire; the Jews did not. They maintained that as Nadab and Abihu were not consumed by divine fire, and their bodies were taken out of the camp – presumably for burial (see Leviticus 10:2-5) – so judicial execution by fire should not destroy the body.

Of the work of Josiah we read:

"Moreover, the altar at Bethel, the high place erected by Jeroboam the son of Nebat, who made Israel to sin, that altar with the high place he pulled down and burned, reducing it to dust. He also burned the Asherah. And as Josiah turned, he saw the tombs there on the mount. And he sent and took the bones out of the tombs and burned them on the altar and defiled it, according to the word of the LORD that the man of God proclaimed, who had predicted these things. Then he said, 'What is that monument that I see?' And the men of the city told him, 'It is the tomb of the man of God who came from Judah and predicted these things that you have done against the altar at Bethel.' And he said, 'Let him be; let no man move his bones.' So they let his bones alone, with the bones of the prophet who came out of Samaria. And Josiah removed all the shrines also of the high places that were in the cities of Samaria, which kings of Israel had made, provoking the LORD to anger. He did to them according to all that he had done at Bethel. And he sacrificed all the priests of the high places who were there, on the altars, and burned human bones on them. Then he returned to Jerusalem."   (2 Kings 23:15-20)

Clearly this cremation was intended to desecrate the memory of those in tombs associated with idolatry as well as the altar erected to the idol. In contrast, the tomb of the faithful prophet was undisturbed.

In Amos 2:1 one of the reasons for judgement against Moab was that, "he burned to lime the bones of the king of Edom". It seems that the king of Edom may have been buried and the Moabites disinterred his remains and desecrated them. This appears to be a condemnation against violating a tomb rather than a denouncing of cremation *per se*.

One thing is certain, God can re-create from either dust or ashes. God requires neither a body nor a grave for resurrection to take place. We do not imagine that those who were torn apart by wild animals and consumed, or torched by the Roman and Holy Roman Empires, will in any sense be disadvantaged in the resurrection. It follows then that the physical act of cremation is no barrier to being raised.

There is only one positive reference to cremation and it was the occasion of the death of Saul and Jonathan:

> "When the inhabitants of Jabesh-gilead heard what the Philistines had done to Saul, all the valiant men arose and went all night and took the body of Saul and the bodies of his sons from the wall of Beth-shan, and they came to Jabesh and burned them there. And they took their bones and buried them under the tamarisk tree in Jabesh and fasted seven days."   (1 Samuel 31:11-13)

Here we have a combination of cremation and burial. Clearly it was done as a mark of respect and not as abuse or displeasure.

Paul wrote to those in Corinth, "If I give away all I have, and if I deliver up my body to be burned, but have not love, I gain nothing" (1 Corinthians 13:3). There seems to be an element of choice in the apostle's suggestion that would favour the idea that he is referring to the Roman practice of making living torches of

Christians who refused to recant, by way of execution, rather than cremation.

Some might argue that cremation merely hastens the process of returning the body to the earthy elements of which it is made; others that it belongs to God and should be left to naturally decay.

Summarising the Biblical evidence, burial seems to be the overwhelming choice. However, with at least one honourable mention, outright condemnation of cremation is unwarranted. Burial or cremation would seem to be a matter best left to the personal choice and conscience of those involved.

How should we understand suicide?

Suicide is the act of intentionally causing one's own death.

"Every year close to 800,000 people around the globe take their own life and there are many more people who attempt suicide. Every suicide is a tragedy that affects families, communities and entire countries and has long-lasting effects on the people left behind. Suicide occurs throughout the lifespan and was the second leading cause of death among 15-29-year-olds globally in 2016."[1]

"In Australia in 2018, suicide accounted for over one-third of deaths (38.4%) among people 15-24 years of age and 29.4% of deaths among people 25-34 years of age. In 2018, there were 105,730 years of life lost to suicide. On average, a person who died by suicide in 2018 lost 36.7 years of life."[2]

These are sobering statics. Every suicide is a tragedy, and for those left behind very difficult to understand. Suicide

---

1   WHO website.

2   Australian Bureau of Statistics.

often stems from a deep feeling of hopelessness. The inability to see solutions to problems or to cope with challenging life circumstances can lead people to consider taking their own lives. These feelings and circumstance for most are a temporary situation – most survivors of suicide attempts go on to live full, rewarding lives. Depression is a key risk factor for suicide; others include mental disorders, substance use, chronic pain, a family history of suicide, and a prior suicide attempt. Impulsiveness often plays a role among adolescents who take their life.

Traditionally many churches have had a harsh view on the matter. The Catholic Church has taught that suicide is a sin against God that has dire penalties. Those who had committed suicide were unable to be buried on sacred ground or to receive a funeral Mass.

What can we understand from the Bible regarding God's view of this tragic matter?

We find that examples of suicide appear in the both the Old and New Testaments: Samson (Judges 16:23); Saul (1 Samuel 31:4,5); Ahithophel (2 Samuel 17:23); Zimri (1 Kings 16:18); and Judas Iscariot (Matthew 27:3-5). What we find is people who were overcome by circumstances and their emotions; we do not find a message or judgement about suicide from God's perspective.

God has given commands against taking any human life unauthorised by Him; this must surely include taking our own life:

- "Whoever sheds the blood of man, by man shall his blood be shed, for God made man in his own image" (Genesis 9:6).

- "Thou shalt not kill" (Exodus 20:13).

There are Bible texts that reveal our life is a gift from God and that He has lordship over our life. For example:

- "Only take care, and keep your soul [life] diligently, lest you forget the things that your eyes have seen, and lest they depart from your heart all the days of your life ..." (Deuteronomy 4:9).

- "I call heaven and earth to witness against you today, that I have set before you life and death, blessing and curse. Therefore, choose life, that you and your offspring may live, loving the LORD your God, obeying his voice and holding fast to him, for he is your life and length of days ..." (Deuteronomy 30:19,20).

- "Do you not know that you are God's temple and that God's Spirit dwells in you? If anyone destroys God's temple, God will destroy him. For God's temple is holy, and you are that temple" (1 Corinthians 3:16,17).

- "Do you not know that your body is a temple of the Holy Spirit within you, whom you have from God? You are not your own, for you were bought with a price. So, glorify God in your body" (1 Corinthians 6:19,20).

Throughout history suicide has been viewed seriously, though on occasion it might have been seen to be right for a person to lay down their life because of their faith. The mass suicide at Masada for example has been justified by some as an honourable example of the taking of one's own life.

Samson's death is a challenging example. It certainly seems that Samson's final act was allowed and empowered by God for His glory and purpose. Samson's life is briefly, but honourably mentioned in Hebrews 11, suggesting that what he did was sacrificial rather than selfish. Behind the example of Samson and of those who would lay down their life because of their faith is the idea that there are principles or goals that can be more important than life itself. And so, self-sacrifice is not suicide: letting go of life because of faith is different from letting go of life because of lack of hope.

Suicide has a very negative impact on the family and wider community. The commands, "Love thy neighbour as thyself" and Paul's words, "husbands should love their wives as their own bodies. He who loves his wife loves himself. For no one ever hated his own flesh" (Ephesians 5:28,29) enshrine this principle and teach that suicide is the denial that self-preservation is the first law of life.

Doing harm to ourselves invariably causes harm to our neighbour. Think about those who are left to deal with the pain and grief. Not accounting for these consequences is falling short of loving and supporting our families and neighbour.

As mentioned before, people take their own lives for many reasons. Among them are:

- Shame and guilt.

- Those who cannot face life due to bereavement.

- Those who feel that death is better than life due to the circumstances they are in.

- A complete loss of hope in this life.

- Mental illness.

No one who commits suicide would in that moment be of normal sound mind. Mental illness or circumstances have defeated their will to live. Suicide is an act of insanity. It could be said that none of us are completely sane all our lives and we all most likely will have moments of insanity – as Job did when he uttered, "Why was I not as a hidden stillborn child?" (Job 3:16). We may well have moments or days or months when we lose the will to live and question our worth. Many of us have had these suicidal thoughts at some point in our lives. Feeling suicidal is not a character defect, and it doesn't mean that we are crazy, or weak, or flawed. It only means that we have more pain than we can cope with. Those who commit suicide are deep in this emotional place.

Nevertheless, in committing suicide we put our will before God's will, before our family's will, before our community's will. Our loving heavenly Father and our loved ones want us to live. The following quotes teach powerfully that our Heavenly Father wants us to live:

- "Fear not, for I am with you; be not dismayed, for I am your God; I will strengthen you, I will help you, I will uphold you with my righteous right hand" (Isaiah 41:10).

- For I know the plans I have for you, declares the LORD, plans for welfare and not for evil, to give you a future and a hope. Then you will call upon me and come and pray to me, and I will hear you. You will seek me and find me, when you seek me with all your heart" (Jeremiah 29:11-13).

In suicide we take our life into our own hands, instead of trusting our life into God's loving hands. We must say again that no one who commits suicide is in that moment of normal, rational and sound mind. To commit suicide is to run away from life and it involves taking that which belongs to God alone – the gift of our life. In suicide we take the times and seasons of life into our own hands.

What should be our response to those who commit suicide and their loved ones?

Words from William Barclay put this well:

"If there is one place where condemnation should be silent, and where sympathy should be paramount, and where self-condemnation should be in the heart, it is here. The person who commits suicide does so because they find life intolerable ... and when people are defeated by life then we may leave them with trust to the mercy of God. For the Christian the taking of one's life is forbidden, but we must regard with nothing but loving sympathy the person who in their loneliness and lostness seeks their final way to escape."[3]

The forgoing thoughts may have raised some strong feelings as many have been affected by suicide or you may have these feelings right now.

How can we help those contemplating suicide?

If you feel suicidal, no matter how much pain you're experiencing right now, you are not alone. Remember again that many of us have had suicidal thoughts at some point in our lives. Remember, feeling suicidal is not a character defect, and it doesn't mean that you are crazy, or weak, or flawed. It only means that you have more pain than you can cope with right now. With time and support, you can overcome your problems and the pain and suicidal feelings will pass. God is looking at you with compassion and wants you to reach out to Him and others. Remember:

- Your emotions are not fixed, they are constantly changing. How you feel today may not be the same as how you felt yesterday or how you will feel tomorrow or next week.

- Your absence would create grief and anguish in the lives of friends and loved ones.

- There are so many things God has in store for your life. There are sights, sounds, and experiences in life that can delight and lift you.

- Your ability to experience pleasurable emotions is equal to your ability to experience distressing emotions.

- God loves you dearly and will never leave or forsake you. Talk to Him.

3   *The Plain Man's Guide to Ethics*, page 78.

The Psalmist wrote:

"The LORD is near to the brokenhearted and saves the crushed in spirit. Many are the afflictions of the righteous, but the LORD delivers him out of them all." (Psalm 34:18,19)

This is a wonderful quotation as it shows us that the emotions surrounding a broken heart and crushed spirit do not exclude us from being righteous in God's eyes.

Why suicide can seem like the only option

If you are unable to think of solutions other than suicide, it is not that other solutions don't exist, but rather that you are currently unable to see them. The intense emotional pain that you are experiencing can distort your thinking so it becomes harder to see possible solutions to problems, or to connect with those who can offer support. Doctors, counsellors, friends or loved ones can help you to see solutions that otherwise may not be apparent to you. Give them an opportunity to help.

A suicidal crisis is almost always temporary

Although it might seem as if your pain and unhappiness will never end, it is important to realise that crises are usually temporary. Solutions are often found, feelings change, unexpected positive events occur. Remember, suicide is a drastic solution to a temporary problem. Give yourself the time necessary for things to change and the pain to subside.

Even problems that seem hopeless can have solutions

Mental health conditions such as depression, schizophrenia, and bipolar disorder are all treatable with changes in lifestyle, therapy, and medication. Most people who seek help can improve their situation and recover. Even if you have received treatment for a disorder before, or if you have already made attempts to solve your problems, know that it is often necessary to try different approaches before finding the right solution or combination of solutions. When medication is prescribed, for example, finding the right dosage often requires an ongoing process of adjustment. Don't give up before you have found the solution that works for you. Many problems can be treated or resolved.

Even if it doesn't feel like it right now, *there are many people who want to support you during this difficult time*. Reach out to someone. Do it now. Tell someone what is going on with you. Talk to someone who won't try to argue about how you feel, judge you, or tell you just to 'snap out of it'. Find someone who will simply listen and be there for you. It doesn't matter who it is, as long as it is someone you trust and who is likely to listen with compassion and acceptance.

How to talk to someone about your suicidal thoughts

Even when you have decided who you can trust to talk to, admitting your suicidal thoughts to another person can be difficult.

- Tell the person exactly what you are telling yourself. If you have a suicide plan, explain it to them.

- Phrases such as, 'I can't take it any more' or 'I'm done' are vague and do not illustrate how serious things really are. Tell the person you trust that you are thinking about suicide.

- If it is too difficult for you to talk about, try writing it down and handing a note to the person you trust. Or send them an e-mail or text and sit with them while they read it.

If you think someone is suicidal you can just say, 'Are you feeling okay?' and then listen, encouraging them to talk. Do not judge them.

Is euthanasia acceptable to God?

Euthanasia and voluntary assisted dying (VAD) are topical issues around the world. A physician intentionally ending the life of a patient was considered unthinkable for centuries, but Western sentiment seems to be changing. In fact, both euthanasia and voluntary assisted dying are sometimes referred to as "death with dignity". Pressure for the liberalisation of the laws on euthanasia and voluntary assisted dying will probably continue to grow as it is viewed primarily as a human rights issue.

We might note before continuing that in scripture the life of animals is considered differently from humans. It is permissible to kill animals for food but killing a person for any reason is forbidden (see Genesis 9:3-5). We need therefore to exclude from consideration the compassionate euthanasia of animals from our debate. Since animals may be killed, their euthanasia provides no precedent for humans. For our purposes, we will confine the term euthanasia to humans.

Euthanasia is a deliberate, intentional act of someone to end the life of another person in order to relieve that person's suffering. For example, a doctor injects a patient with a lethal substance to relieve that person from unbearable physical pain. The term euthanasia is often used in different ways. Three of the most common are:

- *Voluntary euthanasia.* Euthanasia is performed at the request of the person whose life is ended, and that person is competent. For example, a doctor injects a lethal substance into a competent patient, at their request, to relieve that person from unbearable physical pain.

- *Non-voluntary euthanasia.* Euthanasia is performed, and the person is not competent. For example, a doctor injects a patient in an unresponsive state (sometimes referred to as a persistent vegetative state) with a lethal substance.

- **Involuntary euthanasia.** Euthanasia is performed, and the person is competent but has not expressed the wish to die or has expressed a wish that he or she does not die. For example, a doctor injects a competent patient who is in the terminal stage of a terminal illness such as cancer with a lethal substance without that person's request.

VAD (sometimes called assisted suicide) is a process where an eligible person under the law who is at the end of their life, and suffering, may choose the timing and manner of their death. The patient themself administers the lethal dose provided by a medical practitioner.

In June 2019 the Voluntary Assisted Dying Act came into effect in Victoria, Australia and most other states will most likely follow their lead. Victorians who are at the end of life and who meet eligibility criteria can now request access to VAD. The following is from the website of Victoria Health and is helpful to understand the issues involved.

"Voluntary assisted dying is only for people who are suffering from an incurable, advanced and progressive disease, illness or medical condition, who are experiencing intolerable suffering. The condition must be assessed by two medical practitioners to be expected to cause death within six months. There is an exception for a person suffering from a neurodegenerative condition, where instead the condition must be expected to cause death within twelve months. Voluntary assisted dying will only be available to Victorians who are over the age of 18 who have lived in Victoria for at least twelve months, and who have decision-making capacity. To be eligible for voluntary assisted dying they must be experiencing suffering that cannot be relieved in a manner the person considers tolerable. Mental illness or disability alone are not grounds for access to voluntary assisted dying, but people who meet all other criteria, and who have a disability or mental illness, will not be denied access to voluntary assisted dying."

There are three primary arguments used by those in favour of euthanasia and voluntary assisted dying:

1. The autonomy and rights of the patient over their life.

2. Minimising pain and suffering.

3. There is no morally relevant difference between taking steps to hasten death and allowing the dying process to occur.

For the believer in Christ only the second of these reasons carries any weight. Palliative and end of life care has improved such that most pain can now be managed and controlled. Those who champion euthanasia or VAD make it plain that a key objective is not concerned so much with the pain and suffering but rather with a very individualistic, philosophical commitment to human autonomy. The belief is, if I am sick and want to end my life, I should have the freedom to do so via euthanasia or VAD.

Euthanasia and VAD reject the inherent dignity that God has given human beings. Participants seek to eliminate suffering, but they instead eliminate the objective value of life. Although the Bible does not speak of either euthanasia or VAD directly, the same principles that were laid down regarding suicide in the previous answer are largely relevant.

The Catholic catechism has this matter right: "We are stewards, not owners, of the life God has entrusted to us and, thus, our lives are not ours to dispose of."

God has also given commands against taking any human life unauthorised by Him: "Whoever sheds the blood of man, by man shall his blood be shed, for God made man in his own image" (Genesis 9:6).

There are Bible texts that reveal our life is a gift from God and that He has lordship over our life. The passages in Deuteronomy 4:9, 1 Corinthians 3:16,17 and 1 Corinthians 6:19,20 that were considered in the previous answer are worth revisiting here. The value of human life in all its forms and at all stages is the central theme of the Gospel, for it is the very purpose of Christ's birth, death, and resurrection.

Having said this, the process of dying does not seem straightforward in our modern world. With the advancement of modern medicine, where should we draw the line with such things as medical intervention to keep people alive longer than they would naturally live? Passive euthanasia is when death is brought about by an omission, i.e., when someone lets the person die. This can be by withdrawing or withholding treatment. Even though the two things might sound quite similar and the results (death) are the same, the two things are quite different in intent. Withholding measures to prolong life is very different from providing the means to end it.

End of life care involves bringing together health professionals to help manage impending death. Increasing pain relief with the drugs currently available may contribute to an earlier death. It needs also to be recognised that modern medical care such as is available in many countries has often extended the life and thereby prolonged the suffering and pain well beyond what would be natural. Medical care might thus be a two-edged sword. Terminal disease with prolonged suffering is relatively common, but for much of the world's history death was often quite rapid. We have not conquered death, and the extension of life does not always come with quality. All of this makes end of life care a considerably greyer zone than we may have at first thought.

Two abiding principles seem to guide us.

1. The Lord gives life and the Lord takes away life. Our life is not our own and we do not have the right to choose when we die.

2. Pain and suffering are real, and we should do all that we can to alleviate this for our fellow humans.

It is worth considering whether God would expect us to preserve our life at all costs. The decision to turn off a life-support machine, or to refuse treatment, to increase pain medication knowing it may hasten death, or to refuse medical intervention entirely may in each case represent a person's faithful freedom and responsibility before God. In these grey areas and in the grim reality of end of life and suffering, it will be a matter of conscience.

Chapter 11

Questions about morals and ethics

"We keep on being told that religion, whatever its imperfections, at least instils morality. On every side, there is conclusive evidence that the contrary is the case and that faith causes people to be more mean, more selfish, and perhaps above all, more stupid." (Christopher Hitchens, atheist)

"Let us with caution indulge the supposition that morality can be maintained without religion. Reason and experience both forbid us to expect that national morality can prevail in exclusion of religious principle." (George Washington, American President)

Why does the Bible condone slavery?

It does not! The question is an attack on the righteousness of God. The reasoning flows like this: if the Bible condones slavery then God condones slavery and God is therefore unrighteous. Let us be clear from the outset, the Bible does not condone the abduction of people for slavery. God absolutely prohibited this, "Whoever steals a man and sells him, and anyone found in possession of him, shall be put to death" (Exodus 21:16).

Slave traders who abduct people and oppress them are utterly condemned in scripture.

We need to remember that slavery was commonplace in ancient society. Often people from nations conquered in war were taken captive and used as slaves. One might ask, if God could make laws prohibiting abduction why not prohibit slavery in all forms? Why wasn't slavery absolutely condemned? One might also ask, 'Is God powerless to prevent slavery? Surely if He were omnipotent He could?' Of course, but it would involve the revoking of human free will and that is probably not on any human agenda, nor the divine at this present time.

We need to be careful that we don't see laws aimed at regulation of slavery as approval of the concept of slavery. They are two quite different things. God for His part created us all equal and never intended slavery. Slavery is a human invention that God regulated without ever approving. Historically, God tolerated slavery. The very notion of 'tolerance' implies disapproval; else tolerance would be approval. The regulations concerning divorce were necessitated because of human "hardness of heart" (Matthew 19:8); it is easy to suggest that laws regulating slavery were made for similar reasons.

However, there are other forms of servitude and God placed regulations around these. The kind of service envisaged in the beginning of Exodus 21 and for which regulations were made was more like a personal mortgage. In times of significant personal hardship one elected to be sold (or to sell a child) as a slave for a certain time (maximum six years) in exchange for an amount of money.

There are in scripture several types of service that were permitted and regulated. These are:

- Service to pay off a debt or relieve hardship (see Leviticus 25:47-55; Deuteronomy 15:7-15).

- Voluntary servitude (see Exodus 21:6) in exchange for food and shelter.

- Hired service as a daily labourer (see Deuteronomy 24:14).

When we come to the Greco-Roman concept of slavery, the New Testament did not approve it, but rather in acknowledgment that it existed, regulated the practice so far as believers were concerned. The regulations suggest the master (if he were a believer) should treat his slaves as employees might be treated today: "Masters, treat your bondservants justly and fairly, knowing that you also have a Master in heaven" (Colossians 4:1). This is not licence to have slaves, nor the approval of the concept, but the regulation of the arrangements. Paul went as far as recommending to Philemon that his runaway slave (Onesimus) not be punished but received as a brother (see Philemon verses 16-18). Rather than approve the concept of slavery God tolerated and regulated it in the same way He did divorce. As Christians the obligation to treat everybody fairly completely transcended the customs and laws of the Roman world.

In the first century ecclesia there was no difference in value of people before God:

> "For as many of you as were baptized into Christ have put on Christ. There is neither Jew nor Greek, there is neither slave nor free, there is no male and female, for you are all one in Christ Jesus. And if you are Christ's, then you are Abraham's offspring, heirs according to promise." (Galatians 3:27-29)

Why does the Bible approve polygamy?

The answer to this question is essentially the same as the previous one. The Bible never approved polygamy, it regulated it. In ancient times polygamy was common. The divine model is one man with one woman for life as Jesus made clear:

> "Have you not read that he who created them from the beginning made them male and female, and said, 'Therefore a man shall leave his father and his mother and hold fast to his wife, and the two shall become one flesh'? So they are no longer two but one flesh." (Matthew 19:4-6)

There were Old Testament commands against kings having many wives, "he shall not acquire many wives for himself" (Deuteronomy 17:17) and New Testament injunctions for elders and deacons to be "the husband of one wife" (1 Timothy 3:12; Titus 1:6). This suggested that while God might tolerate (without approving) polygamy for an ordinary person, those who were an example to others were held to a better standard. We do not find a record in scripture of anybody with multiple wives escaping the problems one might expect to find in those circumstances. Rather the rivalry, jealousy and anxiety produced through polygamy demonstrate why monogamy, as God intended, is in every way superior.

Why does the Bible accept concubines?

Concubinage was an ancient Eastern custom that persisted in some areas down to the twentieth century. A concubine was a slave who had a personal, lifelong and exclusive relationship with her master as a wife. A popular misconception is that a concubine was simply a sex slave. It is true that a concubine remained a slave, but they were also regarded as a wife. This is illustrated by the status of Hagar of whom we read, "Sarai, Abram's wife, took Hagar the Egyptian, her servant, and gave her to Abram her husband as a *wife*" (Genesis 16:3); and later, "Cast out this *slave woman* with her son, for the son of this *slave woman* shall not be heir with my son Isaac" (Genesis 21:10).

The words "cast out" are one Hebrew word used elsewhere for divorce (e.g., Leviticus 21:7,14). Clearly Hagar was considered both a slave and a wife. The following extract from Judges 19 further illustrates this. It concerns a Levite –

> "who took to himself a concubine from Bethlehem in Judah. And his concubine was *unfaithful* to him, and she went away from him to her father's house at Bethlehem in Judah, and was there some four months. Then her *husband* arose and went after her, to speak kindly to her and bring her back. He had with him his servant and a couple of donkeys. And she brought him into her father's house. And when the girl's father saw him, he came with joy to meet him. And his *father-in-law*, the girl's father, made him stay, and he remained with him three days." (Judges 19:1-4)

The language used makes it clear that the man was considered a husband, the woman's father as the father-in-law, and there was an expectation of faithfulness as one might expect in a marriage.

That faithfulness as a wife was expected of a concubine is emphasised by the rebuke from Jacob to Reuben (the latter having slept with Jacob's concubine) because "you went up to your father's bed; then you defiled it" (Genesis 49:4). Jacob had the expectation that his concubine was his alone and was not pleased his son had behaved inappropriately.

Some concubines were slaves first and wives second, usually to provide an heir when the wife was barren as in the case of Abraham and Hagar and others were purchased to be wives (e.g., the Levite in Judges 19). While the sons of concubines were sometimes accepted as *bona fide* heirs (as in the case of Jacob's children), in many respects a concubine still had much in common with a servant.

A father was permitted (presumably during hardship) to sell a daughter as a concubine. Possibly the father then received a greater bride price than he might otherwise have done. There was an expectation that she would remain a concubine forever. Male servants were released after six years but a girl who became a concubine was "not to go free as male servants do" (Exodus 21:7, NIV). This reflects that while still a servant, she was also a wife. The record in Exodus 21 goes on to demand that if she was designated a concubine for a master's son, she was to be dealt with "as with a daughter". A concubine was clearly part of the family.

What was the difference between a concubine and a second wife? It seems merely the status within the family. Of one there was the expectation of household service while the other was free to do as she pleased. Of both was the expectation of faithfulness and to both were due obligations of decent treatment (see Exodus 21:10).

In common with the two previous answers, scripture neither condones nor approves of the practice of taking a concubine; it simply regulated what was already occurring. It certainly seems an odd (if not improper) practice to us today and is clearly not what God originally intended. We cannot be sure why God allowed the practice – was it preferable for destitute families rather than resorting to prostitution or starvation?

The practice of Solomon taking hundreds of concubines (along with hundreds of wives) suggests that in his case it was more to do with satisfying lust than heirs. Scripture is not silent as to the folly of this behaviour.

Considering the last three questions, we are led to the conclusion that God is remarkably tolerant and flexible concerning human foibles. We, and our circumstances are often far from ideal, yet God still works with us and accepts our weakness with a generosity of spirit that is utterly unsurpassed among the human population of this earth.

How was it right for Cain and Seth to marry their sisters?

The Bible records that God created Adam and Eve and they had other sons and daughters in addition to Cain and Seth (see Genesis 5:4). The Jewish historian Josephus records, "the number of Adam's children, as says the old tradition, was thirty-three sons and twenty-three daughters".

Genesis 4 gives several indications that a significant amount of time likely passed between the birth of Cain and Abel and the murder of Abel. If humanity was being fruitful and multiplying as God commanded (Genesis 1:28), it is reasonable to assume that Adam and Eve were not waiting many years before conceiving their next child. If they had a single child every two years (i.e., no twins), and their children began marrying at the age of twenty and immediately began having children as well, there would have been roughly 300 people on the Earth by the time Cain was 100 – a plausible age for when Cain may have killed his brother.

Although not stated, the conclusion is that Cain and Seth married their sisters or nieces and had children together. As the entire human race came from an original pair this was unavoidable. If they did marry their sisters was this considered to be incest and how can this be reconciled with God's later laws prohibiting sexual relations within the family unit?

Is God inconsistent with His own moral laws and does this weaken our faith in a God who can change His mind. This seems to be an obvious contradiction and how can it be defended?

Some suggest that Cain and Seth's wives came from a race of people that lived before and contemporary with Adam and Eve. This idea creates more problems than it solves regarding Bible teaching about creation and sin and death entering the world through the one man – Adam. The scriptures are clear that Adam was the first man created (see Genesis 2:7,18,19; 1 Corinthians

15:45) and that Adam and Eve were to be responsible to populate the earth. Adam, when naming the creatures, couldn't find a mate – there was none of his kind. This indicates that there was no creature in existence even close to resembling him. Eve was given her name because she was the mother of all living. Paul said, "he has made from one blood all nations on the earth" (Acts 17:26). We can rule out the idea of some pre-Adamic race from which Cain and Seth chose their wives.

Another possibility suggested is that God could have formed wives for Cain and Seth in the same way that He had done for Adam. There is no support for this in scripture.

Consider the following points:

- Cain and Seth were not breaking any law. God had not yet given specific laws regarding sexual relations between families at the time. The definition of marriage in Genesis 2:24 only prohibits parents and children marrying each other.

- Cain and Seth were not subject to the law later given in Leviticus 18:6-17.

We may reasonably assume that God forbade intermarriage between family members at the time of Moses to protect the increasing chance of deformed offspring. God created our genetic material and therefore knew of the growing dangers of inbreeding long before humans had any idea. The law prohibiting incest was given at the right time to protect against genomic deformities.

Why was it right for God to order killing in the Old Testament?

We read, "in the cities of these peoples that the LORD your God is giving you for an inheritance, you shall save alive nothing that breathes, but you shall devote them to complete destruction, the Hittites and the Amorites, the Canaanites and the Perizzites, the Hivites and the Jebusites, as the LORD your God has commanded." (Deuteronomy 20:16,17)

Add to this the demand made of Saul:

"Thus, says the LORD of hosts, I have noted what Amalek did to Israel in opposing them on the way when they came up out of Egypt. Now go and strike Amalek and devote to destruction all that they have. Do not spare them, but kill both man and woman, child and infant, ox and sheep, camel and donkey." (1 Samuel 15:2,3)

Clearly God commanded destruction. We cannot wish it away, suggest it was a Jewish invention or exaggeration or suggest that God is now different. This is an issue that we must come to terms with. We must seek to understand God.

Men such as Richard Dawkins make no effort to understand God or His perspective and simply denounce it.[1]

How do we respond? The atheist attacks on divine credibility are increasingly giving some believers cause for concern and are creating doubt regarding the character of God. Let us summarise the case for God:

1. God created life, and He (only) has the right to take it.

2. God has the right to bring judgement against sin / evil and wickedness as and when He sees fit.

3. Judgement against the Canaanites was for outright wickedness and terrible immorality.

4. God was very patient with the Canaanites and gave them opportunity to repent and change.

---

1 See Richard Dawkins, *The God Delusion*.

5. Salvation was offered to those who converted or vacated the land ahead of Israel entering it.

We will now explore the summary points in some greater detail. Scripture says, "Has the potter no right over the clay?" (Romans 9:21). In Ecclesiastes we read:

> "Walk in the ways of your heart and the sight of your eyes. But know that for all these things God will bring you into judgement." (Ecclesiastes 11:9)

These together speak of the sovereignty and majesty of God. The atheist may rant that God has no right to do this or that, and they are completely wrong. God has the sovereign right to do as He pleases.

The question then comes from the atheist, 'Is what God chooses the morally right choice?' Most of them would not contemplate for even a moment before rejecting God's perspective. This will not be our method. We will explore the issue and then arrive at a reasoned position.

First concerning the moral state of the Canaanites, Moses said to Israel:

> "Do not say in your heart, after the LORD your God has thrust them out before you, 'It is because of my righteousness that the LORD has brought me in to possess this land,' whereas it is because of the wickedness of these nations that the LORD is driving them out before you. Not because of your righteousness or the uprightness of your heart are you going in to possess their land, but because of the wickedness of these nations the LORD your God is driving them out from before you, and that he may confirm the word that the LORD swore to your fathers, to Abraham, to Isaac, and to Jacob." (Deuteronomy 9:4-6)

Moses later listed the evils and warned Israel not to follow them:

"You shall not learn to follow the abominable practices of those nations. There shall not be found among you anyone who burns his son or his daughter as an offering, anyone who practices divination or tells fortunes or interprets omens, or a sorcerer or a charmer or a medium or a necromancer or one who inquires of the dead, for whoever does these things is an abomination to the LORD. And because of these abominations the LORD your God is driving them out before you." (Deuteronomy 18:12)

The Canaanite immorality was dictated by their religion that was based around fertility. It tied fruitfulness of the land, harvests and people to a bewildering array of deviant sexual practices. Practices such as divination, witchcraft, temple sex priests and priestesses, adultery, homosexuality, paedophilia, sex with all sorts of animals (does this explain why even animals were to be destroyed?) were all part of an ingrained culture of gross immorality. After the Canaanite cities of Sodom and Gomorrah were destroyed, Lot's daughters seduced their drunken father, most likely imitating the sexual practices of the cities they had just left behind (see Genesis 19:30-36). Worse yet, Canaanites practised child sacrifice. Rotherham simply asks, "Who shall say that the Most High has not the right to extinguish such polluters of the earth and contaminators of mankind as these?"[2]

There was a reason God had said, "Do not give any of your children to be sacrificed to Molech" (Leviticus 18:21). The attraction of Canaanite religion was obvious – sex and pleasure – a self-serving religion that gratified the basic desires of people at the expense of children. We know the result of failing to eradicate the Canaanites fully:

"The people of Israel lived among the Canaanites, the Hittites, the Amorites, the Perizzites, the Hivites, and the Jebusites.

---

2   Special Note on the destruction of the Canaanite nations, *Emphasised Bible*, page 259.

And their daughters they took to themselves for wives, and their own daughters they gave to their sons, and they served their gods. And the people of Israel did what was evil in the sight of the LORD. They forgot the LORD their God and served the Baals and the Asheroth." (Judges 3:5-7)

The atheist may argue, 'But they never had a chance!' Not so. God waited from Abraham's time down to Joshua and gave them opportunity to change. We read:

"As for you [Abraham], you shall go to your fathers in peace; you shall be buried in a good old age. And they [Israel] shall come back here in the fourth generation, for the iniquity of the Amorites is not yet complete." (Genesis 15:13-16)

Abraham lived among the Canaanites and was very well known, as was the God who he worshipped. Melchizedek was a king – priest of the "most high God" in Jerusalem at this time (see Genesis 14:18). There were people who had heard and responded, like Rahab, and they were saved. The Gibeonites (Joshua 9-11) who although deceptive were faithful enough to understand the foolishness of trying to resist God's will and sought peace with Israel. Moses had specifically instructed Israel, "When you draw near to a city to fight against it, offer terms of peace to it" (Deuteronomy 20:10). Sadly the book of Joshua records:

"There was not a city that made peace with the people of Israel except the Hivites, the inhabitants of Gibeon. They took them all in battle." (Joshua 11:19)

In that sense the Canaanites' stubborn refusal to submit to God and renounce their wickedness saw them destroyed. The Canaanites had an opportunity and they almost entirely failed to grasp it.

Having put forward God's Biblical perspective we can still feel uneasy or troubled about this. The thought of God asking His people to execute others is difficult to comprehend. But comprehend we must, and we must come to terms with our own feelings of injustice. The ultimate challenge behind Old Testament divinely sanctioned killing, be it the flood, Sodom or Gomorrah, the Canaanites, the death of the children of Israel by divinely directed serpents, or any other calamity, is a challenge of the sovereignty of God. The prime reason for these things is for the judgement of God on sin and the destruction of sin. God has, does, and will bring judgement on those who wilfully rebel and sin against Him. According to the scripture all sin is judged by death – and we consequently all deserve death because we are all sinners. If we refuse to accept this truth, we are rejecting the truth of God and in danger of judgement ourselves.

God punishes evil, but for many in this world the Canaanite offences are simply not offensive. They think that sexual deviation, adultery, bestiality, witchcraft, etc. are not to be punished but expressed freely. God hates sin because He understands and feels the consequence of sin so much more than we. God hates sin and so often we do not – so we can lose perspective on the reality of sin.

God is no different with us today: there is a time of judgement coming on this world, and God has given plenty of warning. We do not need to perish at God's hand but we can turn to Him in humility and faith. If we repent, God will not give us what we deserve, but what we need – forgiveness and life. If we reject God we can expect judgement as was made clear to the Hebrews: "how shall we escape if we neglect such a great salvation?" (Hebrews 2:3).

How did a God of love order parents to kill disobedient children?

In Deuteronomy 21 we read:

> "If a man has a stubborn and rebellious son who will not obey the voice of his father or the voice of his mother, and, though

they discipline him, will not listen to them, then his father and his mother shall take hold of him and bring him out to the elders of his city at the gate of the place where he lives, and they shall say to the elders of his city, 'This our son is stubborn and rebellious; he will not obey our voice; he is a glutton and a drunkard.' Then all the men of the city shall stone him to death with stones. So you shall purge the evil from your midst, and all Israel shall hear, and fear. And if a man has committed a crime punishable by death and he is put to death, and you hang him on a tree, his body shall not remain all night on the tree, but you shall bury him the same day, for a hanged man is cursed by God."

(Deuteronomy 21:18-23)

An atheist might superficially read a passage like this looking for evidence that God is malevolent and assume that they have found it. Our task is to read the passage carefully and consider the entire picture to make sure we understand before leaping to conclusions.

We note first that the parents were clearly upset with the behaviour and had unsuccessfully tried to curtail it with both reason and discipline. The relationship had clearly deteriorated to a point where the parents were ashamed of his behaviour. Careful reading reveals that God was not commanding the parents to kill their son at all, let alone against their will, but demanding recourse to appropriate communal judgement. The facts as outlined are as follows:

- The son is stubborn and rebellious.

- He is an overindulgent drunkard.

- He refuses to listen to correction.

- He refuses to change despite discipline.

- He was to be taken before the elders (to be judged).

This law was not going to be enacted against a son who refused to pick up his clothes or make his bed and merely sat about eating pizza and chocolates; the matters were considerably more serious than that. The list of sins given demonstrates that the son has scorned the laws of God, refused parental example and correction and is now set in a course against God.

The parents are legally restrained from impulsive violence and must (if they desire) take the matter to the courts. Note that both parents were united in the attempts to turn him about. The elders at the gate represented the judicial system in Jewish society. There is not an absence of due process in the text, but rather, considering the overwhelming evidence of guilt and intransigence in the example presented, a presumption that the decision will be unfavourable. We also note that the parents were not required to be personally involved in the execution. Capital crimes required two or three witnesses and women were not permitted under Jewish law to give witness; this means that for a guilty verdict other witnesses must also have testified to the truth of the allegations. The trial was to be in the city of the accused. This meant that the character of the son as well as the trustworthiness (or otherwise) of the parents and other witnesses would be well known. The way Jewish justice was enacted came down heavily in favour of the accused. Thus, this law was not about flippant, hasty and ill-conceived judgement.

Parents tend to make excuses for their children and to side with them even well into adulthood. The old saying that "blood is thicker than water" has a good basis. When evil is concealed rather than exposed, it grows and festers. In ancient Israel there was a direct link between prosperity and a lack of godliness. There is a worked example of this in Joshua 7 regarding the sin of Achan.

There is another passage with similar intent regarding exposing evil; it reads:

"If you hear in one of your cities, which the LORD your God is giving you to dwell there, that certain worthless fellows have gone out among you and have drawn away the inhabitants of their city, saying, 'Let us go and serve other gods,' which you have not known, then you shall inquire and make search and ask diligently. And behold, if it be true and certain that such an abomination has been done among you, you shall surely put the inhabitants of that city to the sword, devoting it to destruction, all who are in it and its cattle, with the edge of the sword."   (Deuteronomy 13:12-15)

It is clear that the actions of the son in chapter 21 and the men in chapter 13 were essentially the same. It was in everyone's interest to have gross evil exposed. If the entire city was complicit in the evil (by refusing to expose it) then they were considered culpable. Likewise in the original command in Deuteronomy 21, had the parents failed to expose the evil they would have been judged.

The principle that underlies this provision, is respect of persons. Of Jehoshaphat it is recorded:

"He appointed judges in the land in all the fortified cities of Judah, city by city, and said to the judges, 'Consider what you do, for you judge not for man but for the LORD. He is with you in giving judgement. Now then, let the fear of the LORD be upon you. Be careful what you do, for there is no injustice [KJV, respect of persons] with the LORD our God, or partiality or taking bribes.'"   (2 Chronicles 19:5-7)

Judgement was to be just and not perverted by filial connections on the part of family or friendship on the part of the rulers. Decisions had to be fair and not influenced adversely by friendship or family. These same questions challenge us in our dealings with each other to this day. If our children are astray from God in a grossly immoral fashion we must likewise side with God and denounce the evil.

There are at least three sound reasons behind the provision of this law:

1. To limit the influence of ungodliness and expose it.
2. To give godly parents an option when all else had failed.
3. To reinforce the principle that there is no respect of persons with God.

The law was not designed to harm families emotionally and there is no evidence that it ever did. Despite all of this, the law seems very harsh to our modern ears – but we need to remember that the parents were very much in control of the enactment of the law.

Why did David's sin result in the death of his child?

Sin always has consequences. Often these are borne by others – there is an inescapable yet inherent unfairness in that fact. Sin is not fair and neither is it kind. The nature we bear as mortals is an eloquent testimony to it. We are all born into a troubled world with an inferior constitution. This is a consequence of the first sin. From the moment we are born we bear the effects of this hideous truth. This is one of the reasons why sin is so noxious – it hurts others who are innocent. The effect of Cain's murder of Abel rippled through the entire family. Sin is short-sighted and does not see consequences. A child born to an alcoholic mother will almost certainly have significant physical and mental problems – a direct physical consequence of the sin of the mother. In such a case there is a physical link between the behaviour of the mother and the disease of the child. We may be distressed at the fate of the innocent child suffering because of the sins of the mother, but realise that it is an inescapable physical consequence.

In the case of David's unnamed son there is no suggestion of a physical link (to the contrary it appears to have been born healthy) but rather evidence of divinely directed consequences. Nathan pronounced, "because by this deed you have utterly scorned the LORD, the child who is born to you shall die". It is precisely the involvement of God that causes our concern. Can that be right? It seems to fly in the face of the statement of God through Ezekiel where we read, "The soul who sins shall die. The son shall not suffer for the iniquity of the father" (Ezekiel 18:20). In the case in question David had sinned and it appears that the child suffered.

The record shows that the baby born became sick and despite the fervent prayers of David, it died seven days after birth, unnamed and uncircumcised. More than that the record specifically details that, "the LORD afflicted the child" (2 Samuel 12:15). Had Bathsheba drunk heavily during the entire pregnancy, we might have thought, you can't escape cause and effect. Had the child, like so many others died in infancy without the direct involvement of God we would almost certainly not have the same concern. We might say somewhat philosophically, "time and chance happen to all". However, we are particularly informed that this death was at the hand of God. There is no escaping the conclusion that divine intervention was the cause of the sickness and death of the child.

It might seem to us that the child suffered for the sins of the father and this doesn't feel right. However, careful reading of scripture tells us who suffered – it was David. In anguish of soul David languished for seven days just lying on the floor refusing comfort and food. When the child died the servants were afraid to tell David and said to each other:

> "While the child was yet alive, we spoke to him, and he did not listen to us. How then can we say to him the child is dead? He may do himself some harm." (2 Samuel 12:18)

The servants had seen the torment of David and reasoned, wrongly as it turned out, that in such anguish of soul, suicide was a real possibility. We might like to imagine that the child was punished, but scripture does not record it like that. God was not punishing the child – He was punishing David. The record clearly shows that it was David who was in anguish under the punishment of God and there is no injustice in that.

It might seem to us that this punishment of David was intolerably harsh, but there is no complaint from David. He was later to write:

> "The LORD is merciful and gracious, slow to anger and abounding in steadfast love. He will not always chide, nor will he keep his anger forever. He does not deal with us according to our sins, nor repay us according to our iniquities."
>
> (Psalm 103:8-10)

Limited by human ignorance and restricted with myopic vision, we can wrongly assume that for David's child, premature death was the most terrible outcome. Imagine what his future may have been like had he lived. The very public humiliation of illegitimacy in the royal family, the anguish caused through the circumstances of Tamar, Amnon, Absalom and Adonijah may have all been too much? What if God foresaw that if the child lived, he would grow up to reject Him? Any trials he endured would not be outweighed by immortality. Perhaps God could foresee no good in his life and spared him the anguish? These are at the very least, real possibilities. As it was, the child died unaccountable to God, and unjudged.

Is death always the worst option? The Apostle Paul suggests not. For him, given the reality of reunion with Christ at his next waking moment and the certainty of immortality, he could write, "to die is gain" (Philippians 1:21). Clearly this introduces us to the concept that in some circumstances death may be preferable to life. Isaiah on reflecting on the same matter records, "the righteous man is taken away from calamity; he enters into peace" (Isaiah 57:1,2). When somebody is in the last throes of a terrible terminal illness we might describe death as a blessing – we don't mean that death is good, but that the alternative for them would have been worse. Even we who do not (and cannot) know the future are sometimes able to see that death can be a kindness rather than an evil. Job, in the dark times of tribulation reflecting on his suffering, lamented his existence and believed things to be so bad that he would have been better off dying soon after birth. Job said:

> "Why did I not die at birth, come out from the womb and expire? ... For then I would have lain down and been quiet; I would have slept; then I would have been at rest."
>
> (Job 3:11-13)

Had it not been for "the purpose of the Lord" (James 5:11) perhaps Job might have been right. In his misery Job had forgotten the "eternal weight of glory beyond all comparison" (2 Corinthians 4:17). The observation of the Preacher was:

> "If a man fathers a hundred children and lives many years, so that the days of his years are many, but his soul is not satisfied with life's good things, and he also has no burial, I say that a stillborn child is better off than he." (Ecclesiastes 6:3)

With the hope of eternal life, present trial and even death has no sting; without the hope of eternity, life has no meaning – we might well be better off dying as a baby.

If the end result was to be death, God may have graciously prevented an unnecessary life of misery. We may not say it with supreme confidence, but it is at least possible that premature death was a preferable alternative. The bigger picture seen from the divine perspective may make all the difference. We don't know, we can't know, and more than that – we don't need to know what might have been, we just need to trust that God with foreknowledge, wisdom and righteousness made the best choice.

How was it right to slay the unnamed prophet, and forgive the worst king the nation of Israel had?

The record of these events is found in 1 Kings 13. It may seem an odd story to consider; perhaps few people might recall it and fewer still be perplexed by it. There are, however, significant issues that arise from it that teach us about God and His dealings with us. There are two interrelated narrative threads in the record – the circumstances of the divine condemnation and healing of Jeroboam and the demise of an unnamed prophet who had denounced Jeroboam and cursed the altar that he had made.

An unnamed prophet from Judah was sent to Bethel at the command of God to pronounce judgement upon Jeroboam. Because of his rebellion and evil designs against the prophet of God, Jeroboam was struck with a withering paralysis as recorded:

"Jeroboam, standing at the altar, extended his hand and ordered, 'Seize him!' The hand he had extended shrivelled up and he could not pull it back." (1 Kings 13:4)

Jeroboam then begged the prophet to request God on his behalf to heal him, and he was healed. The prophet was then invited home to dine with the King and offered a reward – but he refused citing an instruction from God:

"So was it commanded me by the word of the LORD, saying, 'You shall neither eat bread nor drink water nor return by the way that you came.'" (1 Kings 13:9)

So far the story seems quite in order – the prophet had done the work of God faithfully, had been protected from the evil intent of the King who then had been smitten, repented and was healed. The prophet went home a different way as he had been instructed.

However, another older prophet of God upon hearing of the story went and found the younger prophet and invited him home to refresh himself. The younger prophet refused citing again the instruction from God. The older prophet responded:

> "I also am a prophet as you are, and an angel spoke to me by the word of the LORD, saying, 'Bring him back with you into your house that he may eat bread and drink water.' But he lied to him." (1 Kings 13:18)

As they sat at dinner the older prophet pronounced a sentence of doom against the younger prophet who was subsequently killed by a lion on his way home. The older prophet then went and collected the body and buried it. The narrative concludes with the words, "After this thing Jeroboam did not turn from his evil way" (1 Kings 13:33).

The conundrum is this: how was it right for God to heal the worst king Israel ever had and who went on his merry way continuing in evil, while at the same time destroying a prophet who was deceived into disobedience? This may be further divided into two questions that we will consider separately:

1. Was it fair to test the unnamed prophet in that way?

2. Was God unjust in His treatment of the two men?

It is perfectly reasonable for God to test the obedience of His servants even with deception. You will note that this was the circumstances of the first sin which follows a similar pattern – a straightforward command by God, an affirmative restatement of the command by Eve, a beguilingly attractive lie from the serpent, followed by failure to keep God's instruction with the resultant punishment.

The invitation of Jeroboam (when he was presumably not in great need of refreshment and didn't care for the man much) was easily refused. The invitation of the older prophet was far more testing and he succumbed to temptation. The original command had been received directly from God and he should not have allowed the word of a man (prophet or not) to change it. In truth the command of God was onerous: he had to take a circuitous route home and was not permitted refreshment on the way. We get a sense in the record of the arduous nature of the journey because the older prophet found him "sitting under an oak", presumably recuperating from the rigours of travel. The proposition put by the older man was considerably inviting and taken up without complaint.

The principle is this: nothing should be allowed to countermand a direct command from God, but God Himself (see Genesis 22:2,12). The unnamed man, being a prophet should have realised this but he seemed all too ready to accept the hospitality of the older prophet. We must not give the word of man greater value than the word of God. The Apostle Paul warned the Galatians:

> "I am astonished that you are so quickly deserting him who called you in the grace of Christ and are turning to a different gospel – not that there is another one, but there are some who trouble you and want to distort the gospel of Christ. But even if we or an angel from heaven should preach to you a gospel contrary to the one we preached to you, let him be accursed. As we have said before, so now I say again: If anyone is preaching to you a gospel contrary to the one you received, let him be accursed." (Galatians 1:6-9)

The divine punishment for disobedience of the prophet (under testing) was reasonable. There is a principle:

> "Everyone to whom much was given, of him much will be required, and from him to whom they entrusted much, they will demand the more." (Luke 12:48)

The prophet was in a position of considerable privilege and responsibility and was held to a high standard. The consequences of sin are extreme!

Did the older prophet take it upon himself to test the younger man, or was there some divine prompting? Did God suggest to the older man that he should test the faithfulness of the younger? We cannot say, but there is no problem in God supplying the test of obedience if He did. We know that God brought difficult circumstances upon Israel, "testing you to know what was in your heart, whether you would keep his commandments or not" (Deuteronomy 8:2).

We turn now to the question of the apparent injustice in the story. One man, a horrid idolater of whom it was frequently said "made Israel to sin", was shown mercy; the other, a prophet who was deceived into what seems to us a relatively minor disobedience was killed. How is that fair?

What is not immediately evident in the narrative is the final end of the two men. We may surmise that the older prophet in requesting his sons, "When I die, bury me in the grave in which the man of God is buried; lay my bones beside his bones" (1 Kings 13:31) had in mind the resurrection when they would both together rise to immortality. However the fate of Jeroboam and his house was, "to cut it off and to destroy it from the face of the earth" (1 Kings 13:34). It is of no significance what happens in this short life, eternal destiny is the concern of God. Despite the immediate circumstances, it would appear that the destiny of one man was eternal life and the other eternal death. "What shall we say then? Is there injustice on God's part? By no means!" (Romans 9:14).

Why is there evil and suffering?

"Is God willing to prevent evil, but not able? Then he is not omnipotent. Is he able, but not willing? Then he is malevolent. Is he both able and willing? Then whence cometh evil? Is he neither able nor willing? Then why call him God?"[3]

---

3   Attributed to Epicurus, Greek Philosopher.

The quote above summarises the way the human mind agonises over the question. Epicurus, the father of the Epicureans (see Acts 17:18) did not believe in life after death and thus could see no purpose in suffering. Nor could he comprehend divine timeframes to appreciate the duration of suffering.

To a human observer, the matter may seem unreasonable; from a divine perspective not so. Let us ask a hypothetical question to commence our exploration: who would not be prepared to undergo intense trial for less than a second in order to secure a happy, fulfilled and long life in this world? If we were able to undergo one moment of agony that secured wealth, health, happiness in order to die peacefully in our sleep at ninety-six, who would not sign up? We reason that a moment of pain that guarantees stability and happiness would be well worth it. Admittedly the pain might be great, but fleeting – so fleeting that it hardly rates a mention. The equation is absolutely favourable.

What fraction of eternity is the present? The answer is zero! That means that the suffering of the present in eternal terms is for so short a time that it hardly counts at all. This was the inspired assessment of the Apostle Paul when he wrote, "For this light momentary affliction is preparing for us an eternal weight of glory beyond all comparison" (2 Corinthians 4:17). Notice that Paul deems the equation favourable not merely for chronological reasons (momentary versus eternal) but he reasons that the suffering is light compared to the glory which is weighty. Seen from a divine perspective our present suffering is light and momentary and the glory is weighty and eternal.

We note also from scripture that when it comes to believers, suffering is not arbitrary but preparative. To the Romans Paul wrote, "for those who love God all things work together for good, for those who are called according to his purpose" (Romans 8:28). This means that for believers there is divine oversight of our lives so that every experience (good and evil as we see it) is used by God to further His purpose with us. This is further explained in Hebrews to be part of a divinely regulated discipline:

> "We have had earthly fathers who disciplined us and we respected them. Shall we not much more be subject to the Father of spirits and live? For they disciplined us for a short time as it seemed best to them, but he disciplines us for our good, that we may share his holiness. For the moment all discipline seems painful rather than pleasant, but later it yields the peaceful fruit of righteousness to those who have been trained by it."   (Hebrews 12:9-11)

What about those who are not believers? Aren't they still sons and daughters of God in a creative sense? God allows evil that we might be disillusioned with the present age and seek for something greater. This was the essence of Paul's message to the Epicureans – that divine control of this world should cause people to, "seek God, and perhaps feel their way toward him and find him" (Acts 17:27). The reason why God has allowed the futility and chance of this world, is to inspire hope for something better as Paul wrote to the Romans:

> "For I consider that the sufferings of this present time are not worth comparing with the glory that is to be revealed to us. For the creation waits with eager longing for the revealing of the sons of God. For the creation was subjected to futility, not willingly, but because of him who subjected it, in hope."
> (Romans 8:18-20)

Here Paul takes our earlier theme and amplifies it with the added dimension of hope. If the present were all we might wish it to be, we may well lose sight of the future; but if the present seems pointless and miserable then our longing for something better is fanned into flame.

Suffering can be evidence in favour of God. A loving God uses it to try to save us eternally. This makes sense of the passage that reads:

> "I am the LORD, and there is no other. I form light and create darkness; I make well-being and create calamity; I am the LORD, who does all these things." (Isaiah 45:6,7)

Suffering has been divinely created and is regulated by God to achieve His purpose. We might ask, what possible purpose could there be in the death of thousands of children from famine and starvation? Not having the wisdom or knowledge of God we may never see any reason – that doesn't mean there isn't one. We must be careful not to assume that something we can't understand is meaningless. It may not be intelligible to us and yet at the same time be perfectly reasonable to God, and it might be reasonable to us also if only we had divine power.

A world without pain and suffering would not allow us to grow, develop and improve in the way we do. It was necessary even for Jesus to learn through suffering as scripture records, "although he was a son, he learned obedience through what he suffered" (Hebrews 5:8). If God treats us as His children, we can expect the same also. This is explicitly stated later in Hebrews:

> "The Lord disciplines the one he loves, and chastises every son whom he receives. It is for discipline that you have to endure. God is treating you as sons." (Hebrews 12:6,7)

Through suffering and trial we grow. Paul went as far as saying that we can thereby rejoice in sufferings and there are records (see Acts 16:25) to detail that he did. To the Romans he wrote:

> "We rejoice in our sufferings, knowing that suffering produces endurance, and endurance produces character, and character produces hope." (Romans 5:3,4)

We have seen that there is perspective and purpose to suffering which human eyes cannot easily discern. It is up to us to trust that God is in control and will ultimately bring good from evil. When God's purpose is realised we have the assurance that:

> "He will wipe away every tear from their eyes, and death shall be no more, neither shall there be mourning, nor crying, nor pain any more, for the former things have passed away."
>
> (Revelation 21:4)

Why doesn't God stop mass murder and genocide?

We might accept the previous answer on an individual basis, yet feel that when things reach a massive scale it becomes unreasonable and God should intervene. Perhaps it is the scale that horrifies us.

The question arises, at what point does murder become acceptable? 6,000,000 Jews murdered in World War Two was horrific, but what about 5,999,999 or 5,999,998 or 5,999,997? Where do we draw the line? We are drawn to the obvious conclusion that we would not condone any number of deaths. The acceptable level of murder is zero. All of those involved in mass murder are individuals and each death is no more tragic than another. If God is the creator and hence father to all people then surely the pointless deaths of thousands in a short space ought to move Him?

Death is an evil whenever and however it occurs. We must remember that the natural effects of sin have down though the ages been responsible for vastly more deaths than the unnatural causes even on a massive scale. God has already worked to eliminate death and in His good time it will be achieved. When scripture revealed the heart of God to "have no pleasure in the death of anyone" (Ezekiel 18:32), this can only mean that there must be significant divine purpose to God allowing death as He does. All deaths are tragic: natural deaths, unnatural deaths, individual deaths and mass death – they are all tragedies. God does not wish any of us to die and remain dead. Ezekiel adds that it is God's wish that we turn to Him and live.

Only God has the right to take life. The scriptures recall that He has done so in the past and will do so again. When divine judgements are unleashed, they are always justified by gross wickedness and always preceded by warnings to repent. Two examples will serve to illustrate the point. One of the greatest acts of mass killing was inflicted by God Himself on a violent and corrupt world out of control. Having warned the world (for years!) and pleaded with them through faithful men like Noah, the situation got so bad that God washed the earth with a cleansing flood and began again with Noah and his family. It would have been unjust for God to allow the situation to continue. Secondly we take the example of the Assyrian capital of Nineveh. The Assyrians were cruel, heartless and violent. God gave them forty days' warning at the hand of Jonah that He would destroy them all unless they repented. They responded to Jonah's preaching and from the king down there was national repentance. Consequently there was no divine destruction. It would have been unjust for God to destroy the people when they had repented.

We might thus accept the actions of God, but the thrust of the question is not so much the divine judgements but what seems to be divine inaction when men unjustly murder each other. Why doesn't He intervene? If the angels are manipulating world events to achieve His purpose, why doesn't He arrange them differently?

The first point to note is this: we are too small to see how the threads of global incidents combine to achieve God's purpose. We already discussed how that the Holocaust may have been a trigger that set in motion a series of events leading ultimately to the kingdom of God. If we are unable to see purpose, or appreciate that there is a just divine reason, let us not draw the conclusion that there cannot be purpose or it cannot be just.

Part of our troubled human existence is the evil that people inflict on each other. It is a consequence of sin. This evil cannot be removed while human free will remains. It is in God's ultimate purpose to remove our capacity to make poor choices and He will do so in one of two ways:

1. Removing the capacity for sin in the bodies of those who hate sin and freely choose to serve God (by granting immortality).

2. Removing the entire person of those who delight in sin and refuse to serve God (death).

When human ability to sin has been removed, there will only be loving, obedient and immortal people remaining. The horrid actions (including mass murder) of evil people will have been removed.

The question then is a matter of timing. When do we want God to eliminate mass murder and genocide? The person who has not yet found God might respond, "right now", without realising that this solution would at the same time eliminate them. For example, if the purpose of God was brought to a conclusion prior to World War Two in order to ensure that the horrors of the Holocaust never happened, then both the authors and most of the readers of this book will have missed out on God's purpose because they would never have been born, and others would miss out because they had not yet found God. The tragedy of murder is as ancient as Cain and Abel. Had God intervened with His ultimate plan then, not one of us would have the opportunity to be included in God's kingdom. It is true that much evil has occurred in human history that would thereby have been avoided, but it is also true that countless thousands would never have received an opportunity to join God's family. Who are we to say that the one does not outweigh the other? Logic demands that the balance favours the eternal.

We must also remember that when humans kill each other, this does not preclude God from resurrecting them to eternal life. When (as happened in World War Two) the saints of God are caught in man's violence and killed, God can and will raise them. Given the length of the divine timeline they will have missed out on a fraction of a moment. The apparent injustice evaporates.

God on His part has told us that He is waiting patiently for as many as possible to be included. The Apostle Peter expressed it this way:

> "The Lord is not slow to fulfil his promise as some count slowness, but is patient toward you, not wishing that any should perish, but that all should reach repentance."
>
> (2 Peter 3:9)

We may summarise the matter this way:

- God is in control.

- God is saddened by any death.

- Most of the horrid events in this world exist because of the exercise of human free will.

- God can use calamity to further His purpose.

- God has a plan to eliminate violence which involves removing evil people and saving faithful ones.

- God is working to His own timeline which is right, and He has the right to choose when to act.

If God put sexual desire in place, why is it wrong to indulge it?

Desire is a powerful emotion or feeling. Desire can be defined as a strong physical longing for something. The desire or craving to have sex can be very powerful. When God created sexual desire,

He did so to bind marriage partners together, the man and the woman becoming a stronger unit. God has given us a legitimate outlet for sexual desire and at the same time forbidden its exercise in other directions.

It seems to be part of human nature that we desire what is unlawful or prohibited. Paul makes this point:

"If it had not been for the law, I would not have known sin. For I would not have known what it is to covet if the law had not said, 'You shall not covet'. But sin, seizing an opportunity through the commandment, produced in me all kinds of covetousness. For apart from the law, sin lies dead."

(Romans 7:7,8)

God has made us with the ability to desire and the free will to make choices about what we will do with our desire. We have been designed so that these instinctive desires are the most powerful part of our nature. The desire to eat food is essential to our life. These basic desires are the real passions that drive us. The virtue or vice of any of these powerful forces in us – such as the sex drive – depends entirely on the use of it. If we are master of the desire and use it legitimately as God has allowed, then it is a virtue; but if the desire masters us in such a way that it causes us to disobey God and harm ourselves and others, then it becomes a vice.

God created sexual intimacy to be enjoyed between a man and woman within the marriage bond. It is a wonderful desire within this relationship (see Genesis 2:21-23). Sexual intimacy outside of this relationship is forbidden in the Bible. God put unlawful sexual desire at the head of the list of covetousness (see Deuteronomy 5:21). Jesus forbids the look of lustful desire (see Matthew 5:27). We can ask ourselves, Why? Surely, it would be so much more fun to indulge our desires to the full. However, God knows, and we can witness for ourselves the power of pain, consequences, tragedy and emptiness that are unleashed by acting upon ungodly sexual desire. Consider the tragedy of David's illicit love for Bathsheba and its horrendous consequences. The Proverbs are full of warning against unlawful sexual desire (see Proverbs 5 for example).

To desire a person sexually that we have no right to desire is the pathway to disaster for more than just the two people involved. God always has good reason for His moral and ethical laws – which are underpinned by the principles of wisdom in obeying Him as our Creator and the wisdom of conforming to the society and family structures that God knows give us the most joy and satisfaction. The wisdom of God is seen when we seek to understand what is behind God's laws. Some of the reasons are here listed:

- To prevent unwanted, unplanned children outside a family unit.
- To preserve the family unit and protect children.
- To prevent the emotional dead-end of casual relationships.
- To prevent sexually transmitted diseases.

Paul made it clear that sexual immorality can disqualify us for the kingdom of God. He wrote:

"Do you not know that the unrighteous will not inherit the kingdom of God? Do not be deceived: neither the sexually immoral, nor idolaters, nor adulterers, nor men who practise homosexuality, nor thieves, nor the greedy, nor drunkards, nor revellers, nor swindlers will inherit the kingdom of God."
(1 Corinthians 6:9,10)

However, this is not an irreversible circumstance. When we repent there is forgiveness as the next verse goes on to show:

"Such were some of you. But you were washed, you were sanctified, you were justified in the name of the Lord Jesus Christ and by the Spirit of our God."   (verse 11)

Is abortion acceptable to God?

Abortion can be defined as the intentional ending of a pregnancy by removal or expulsion of an embryo or fetus before it is able to survive outside the uterus. Abortion is a very ancient practice, dating back thousands of years. Throughout history women have resorted to a range of methods to effect an abortion from taking potions to using sharp objects. Vast numbers of women died as a result of blood loss and infection. Today there are methods that are safe for the mother though just as lethal for the unborn child. According to Wikipedia, around fifty-six million abortions are performed each year in the world, with about forty-five per cent done unsafely.

There is much debate over the religious, moral, ethical, and legal issues surrounding abortion. Those who oppose abortion argue that an embryo or fetus is a human or at the very least a potential human with a right to life, and they may compare abortion to murder. Those who support abortion hold that it is part of a woman's right to make choices about her body and that the woman's rights are greater than those of the unborn fetus.

What are the reasons that a woman would choose to end a pregnancy? Consider the lengthy list below:

- The timing for a child is not right for the woman or couple.
- Social or economic reasons.
- A child would interfere with a career or education.
- The fetus is not the desired gender.
- The 'parents to be' are not married.
- The woman is (or is considered to be) too young to be a mother.
- One or both parents is disabled.
- The pregnancy jeopardises the health of the mother.

- The fetus has a significant disease.
- The child is the product of incest.
- The woman has been raped.

The list has been compiled from medical data of the causes for elective termination of pregnancy from Australia and the USA. Having read the list, are there any that your conscience would allow as a legitimate reason for terminating a pregnancy? Some reject abortion for any cause, others might accept a compelling medical or psychological cause such as the final four reasons. You will notice that as the list progressed, the reasons became more compelling, yet sadly the first three reasons account for approximately ninety-five per cent of all abortions and all the remaining reasons between them only five per cent. Perhaps the one most people would have the most sympathy with would be a child conceived from rape, yet this accounts for about 0.1% of the reasons. Pressure for population control – i.e., the one child policy of China can sometimes result in compulsory abortion or selective sex abortion.

It is worth noting that throughout history countless millions of children have been born but then taken from their mothers for all sorts of reasons and disposed of in a culturally acceptable way for those times. In Greek / Roman times the child would not be named and left in a remote area where wild animals would dispose of it. Roman law, religion and the entire ethos of the ancient world saw nothing morally wrong with infanticide or with abandoning their newborns on the dung heaps or garbage dumps of cities!

If we conduct our lives and relationships God's way, children will not be born out of wedlock or from casual relationships. This would significantly reduce the number of women that even considered the idea of abortion. Perhaps we could all agree that abortions conducted for convenience (ninety-five per cent of all terminations) should not take place.

This leaves us with a fraction of cases to consider. Abortion is a subject that arouses deep emotions, with people having arguments for and against. What would God think about terminating a pregnancy? What are the Biblical arguments? The Bible does not say anything obvious about abortion. However, we can look at some principles and draw some conclusions.

God commanded in the sixth commandment that we should not kill – or more strictly – murder. That is, you must not take the power of life and death into your own hands and kill anyone for your own selfish reasons. Debate among Christians centres around when God views a person as being a person with some saying it is only when a baby is born and others saying at conception and every stage of development in between.

How does God regard a fetus? There is a law in Exodus 21 that states that if a man injures a pregnant woman so that she has a miscarriage, the man must pay her husband compensation. He is not considered in this instance a murderer or charged with manslaughter.

"If men fight and hit a pregnant woman and her child is born prematurely, but there is no serious injury, he will surely be punished in accordance with what the woman's husband demands of him, and he will pay what the court decides. But if there is serious injury, then you will give a life for a life."
(Exodus 21:22,23, NET)

The sense of the passage suggests that the "serious injury" relates to the woman. This reading suggests that the penalty for causing a miscarriage is different from that of causing serious injury or death. Some demand that the "serious injury" refers to both the woman or the fetus. This would give the passage a narrow interpretation as follows: if a pregnant woman is struck and her child is born prematurely, but both it and she live and suffer no serious harm then the man who struck her shall be punished according to the verdict of the court. One wonders why there would be a punishment in such a case? Clearly the parents to be in the scenario, have suffered loss as a result of the action. But, however this is interpreted the fact remains that an accidentally caused and undesired miscarriage is very different from premeditated termination of a pregnancy.

Evidence that God considers breathing to be the start of life is taken from the following texts:

> "The LORD God formed the man of dust from the ground and breathed into his nostrils the breath of life, and the man became a living creature." (Genesis 2:7)

You could say that God breathing into Adam's nostrils made him a living creature. Without that breath in the nostrils he was not a living creature. It can be argued that the Bible seems to define living persons as those who have the breath of life in their nose. "All in whose nostrils *was* the breath of life ... died" (Genesis 7:22). Living creatures appear to be defined in terms of having the breath of life in their nostrils. Job 27:3 says, "All the while my breath is in me, and the spirit of God is in my nostrils". Job's description of being alive and not dead, is "having breath in me" and "the spirit of God in my nostrils". Some use the fact that God only numbered people from the age of one month old whenever He numbered His people. For example:

> "Those that were numbered of them, according to the number of all the males, from a month old and upward, even those that were numbered of them were seven thousand and five hundred." (Numbers 3:22)

Why did God only count those older than one month old?

It would appear that unborn babies are not considered living in the same way as the rest of us. Before we leap to the conclusion that they are not living we need to look at some more passages.

"Did not he who made me in the womb make him [a servant]? And did not one fashion us in the womb?" (Job 31:15)

"For you formed my inward parts; you knitted me together in my mother's womb. I praise you, for I am fearfully and wonderfully made. Wonderful are your works; my soul knows it very well. My frame was not hidden from you, when I was being made in secret, intricately woven in the depths of the earth. Your eyes saw my unformed substance; in your book were written, every one of them, the days that were formed for me, when as yet there was none of them." (Psalm 139:13-16)

"Thus says the LORD who made you, who formed you from the womb and will help you ... Thus says the LORD, your Redeemer, who formed you from the womb." (Isaiah 44:2,24)

"Before I formed you in the womb I knew you, and before you were born I consecrated you; I appointed you a prophet to the nations." (Jeremiah 1:5)

The above passages all make it clear that God can be intimately involved with an unborn child and is aware of the developing child. Further to this, the scriptures declare that God can be involved in the birth:

"Yet you are he who took me from the womb; you made me trust you at my mother's breasts. On you was I cast from my birth, and from my mother's womb you have been my God." (Psalm 22:9)

"Upon you I have leaned from before my birth; you are he who took me from my mother's womb." (Psalm 71:6)

"The LORD called me from the womb, from the body of my mother he named my name ... he who formed me from the womb to be his servant, to bring Jacob back to him." (Isaiah 49:1,5)

"... he who had set me apart before I was born, and who called me by his grace." (Galatians 1:15)

There are a number of scriptures that make it clear that a fetus can be aware of its surrounding environment:

"The children struggled together within her, and she said, 'If it is thus, why is this happening to me?' So she went to inquire of the LORD. And the LORD said to her, 'Two nations are in your womb, and two peoples from within you shall be divided; the one shall be stronger than the other, the older shall serve the younger.'" (Genesis 25:22,23)

"... when the sound of your greeting came to my ears, the baby in my womb leaped for joy." (Luke 1:44)

So while it is clear that unborn babies are not independently living, they are clearly not dead and unfeeling. Scripture uses terms for the unborn like man and son, suggesting that they are potential miniature people.

"Let the day perish on which I was born, and the night that said, 'A man is conceived.'" (Job 3:3)

"And behold, your relative Elizabeth in her old age has also conceived a son, and this is the sixth month with her who was called barren." (Luke 1:36)

So, while it is clear that the life of an unborn child is treated differently in scripture from those who are independently alive, there are quite a number of features making it clear that they are not merely growing collections of cells. Where does all of this leave us with respect to answering the question? The Judeo-Christian idea that each individual person has worth because they were created by God and in His image was foreign to pagan society where the State, the tribe, the collective was the only value they knew. The teaching of Judaism and then Christianity was profound in changing attitudes to women and children.

God's love and concern for the fatherless, widows and children should point us in the right direction.

"He executes justice for the fatherless and the widow, and loves the sojourner, giving him food and clothing. Love the sojourner, therefore, for you were sojourners in the land of Egypt." (Deuteronomy 10:18,19)

The following Bible principles will be helpful in forming our understanding and our conscience.

- God created man to be the highest form of life on earth and we are made in His image and likeness (Genesis 1:26-28).

- God commanded marriage and reproduction within marriage (Genesis 1:28).

- Children belong to God and are a blessing from God (Psalm 127:3).

- Human life is very precious to God. In fact, it is so precious that God Himself instituted the death penalty for anyone who takes the life of another (Exodus 21:12).

In Matthew 7:12, the Lord Jesus Christ said, "So whatever you wish that others would do to you, do also to them, for this is the Law and the Prophets". This is a very challenging passage for all of us, but particularly for those who advocate abortion. Paul tells us in 2 Timothy 3:3 that the last days will be characterised by people who lack "natural affection" (KJV). Clearly, in the context a lack of natural affection is a bad thing. It is natural to conceive a child, grow to love that child, take care of the child during pregnancy, give birth to the child, and then raise the child with the best care possible – that is the natural process that God has ordained.

Based on all of these Biblical principles we conclude that God would not condone abortion. However, we understand that in our community, abortion (like birth control) has been a matter of conscience and that in some cases for health reasons or as a result of traumatic circumstances such as rape a woman may decide to terminate a pregnancy. This decision will be between God and them and we should be loving and withhold condemnation in such circumstances.

Are alternative sexual orientations wrong?

This answer and the two that follow are closely related. While the answers are specific, there is considerable overlap and there are concepts relevant to more than one question that are only presented once. It may be worthwhile to read all three responses to obtain a fuller perspective.

Around the year 2000 LGBT (**L**esbian, **G**ay, **B**isexual and **T**ransgender) were letters used to describe those who identified with alternative sexual orientations from heterosexuals. Since then there has been a rapid increase in sexual orientation and gender identity labelling. Then it became common for LGBTQ to be used; the addition of "Q" some say stands for **Q**uestioning, representing people who are uncertain of their sexual orientations or gender identities. Others say it stands for **Q**ueer, a catch-all term for anyone who is not heterosexual. Now there is also "I", for **I**ntersex; "A", for **A**lly or **A**sexual and often a plus sign meant to cover anyone else who is not included: in point of fact, intersex doesn't really belong in this space as it refers to a group of medical conditions that affect biological sex (discussed in the next answer) and isn't necessarily about sexual orientation. For the others in that list there are usually no biological abnormalities that are able to be identified. So LGBTQIA+ is a designation for any who may have a sexual orientation that is not heterosexual.

Words and phrases have been developed to describe sexual deviation and freedom. Sexual orientation is about who someone is attracted to and who they feel drawn to romantically, emotionally, and sexually. In the next answer we will address gender identity, which is about what a person feels themselves to be.

What does God think of all this – and what does His word teach?

The Bible overwhelmingly teaches that sexual intimacy is given by God as an expression of love to be shared and enjoyed exclusively between a husband and wife. God's teaching in the Bible leaves no room whatsoever for confusion or ambiguity when it comes to sexual orientation. The Bible never tries to justify deviant feelings or behaviours that are contrary to God's moral code. We could discuss and debate at length why some people have a predisposition or choose to have homosexual relationships. For example, is it due to their nature (i.e., their genetic make-up) or is it nurture (the way they have been raised and conditioned by society)? No doubt both play a part in shaping and informing our sexuality.

In our opinion, the clarity of God's truth on this matter remains unchanged despite humanistic arguments and imaginative Biblical interpretation designed to justify homosexual behaviour and sexual freedoms generally. The Bible prohibits *all* kinds of sexual promiscuity – heterosexual as well as homosexual. Logical consistency demands that individuals and groups who want to reinterpret scripture to sanction free sexual expression among homosexuals should extend the same concession to heterosexual singles; and, in fact, some have already taken this next step. But none of this can alter the facts: there is simply no scriptural support for endorsing sexual immorality (i.e., sexual activity outside the bond of heterosexual marriage) for anyone, no matter what his or her personal sexual feelings may be.

As for same-sex "marriage", we see no place for it within the context of consistent Bible teaching on the subject of marriage. According to the Bible, marriage is *heterosexual by definition*. Jesus, when expressing his understanding of the scriptural foundation for the divine purpose and design in marriage, referred to its origins in the creation of man and woman.

Sodom has become so associated with homosexual conduct that its name was for many years a byword for it. The Genesis account describes the men of the city attempting forcibly to have sex with two angelic visitors, who have appeared in the form of men. Later parts of the Old Testament accuse Sodom of a range of sins: oppression, adultery, lying, abetting criminals, arrogance, complacency and indifference to the poor. None of these mentions homosexual conduct. This has led some people to wonder if we have read homosexuality into the Genesis narrative, when in fact the real issue was social oppression and injustice. But a straightforward reading of the text makes it clear that homosexuality was in fact involved.

Although the Hebrew word for "know" (*yada*) can just mean to 'get to know' someone (rather than to "know" them sexually), it is clear from the crowd's aggression, and Lot's dreadful attempt at offering them his daughters as an alternative, that they were looking for much more than social acquaintance. Hence what happens next – the angels warned Lot that judgement was imminent (Genesis 19:13).

In the New Testament, Jude adds an important insight:

"Just as Sodom and Gomorrah and the surrounding cities, which likewise indulged in sexual immorality and pursued unnatural desire, serve as an example by undergoing a punishment of eternal fire."   (Jude, verse 7)

What happened at Sodom is clearly meant to be a warning. Jude makes it clear that their ungodliness involved sexual immorality.

They were punished for sexual sin along with the other sins of which they were guilty.

Jude also highlights the nature of their sexual desires: they pursued "unnatural desire" (literally, unnatural "flesh"). Some have suggested that this relates to the fact that the visitors to the city were angelic. But these angels appeared as men, and the crowd outside Lot's house showed no evidence of knowing they were angelic. Their desire was to have sex with the "men" (Genesis 19:5) staying with Lot. It was the homosexual nature of their desires, and not just the violent expression of them, that is highlighted in the New Testament.

Leviticus contains two well known statements about homosexual activity:

- "You shall not lie with a male as with a woman; it is an abomination" (Leviticus 18:22).

- "If a man lies with a male as with a woman, both of them have committed an abomination; they shall surely be put to death; their blood is upon them" (Leviticus 20:13).

Sometimes people claim that these verses appear in a book of laws in the Old Testament that Christians are not obliged to follow today. Hence, they say, the prohibitions on same-sex intercourse do not now apply. We note that both passages contain the word "abomination". In Hebrew, this is a word applied to any act that is excluded by its very nature or is dangerous or sinister. It is the word used elsewhere for various idolatrous practices (Deuteronomy 7:5; 13:14) which has led some to suggest these verses do not condemn all homosexual behaviour, but only cultic prostitution connected to pagan temples. However, the language used is not that specific – it refers in general terms to lying with a man "as with a woman". In addition, the surrounding verses describe other forms of sexual sin (such as incest, adultery and bestiality). Christians would recognise that these are still forbidden today. Furthermore,

Leviticus 20:13 highlights both male parties equally. This also suggests that general, consensual homosexual activity is in view (as opposed to rape or a forced relationship).

Turning to the New Testament, Romans 1 has much to say about the nature and character of homosexual behaviour. In Romans 1:18–3:20, Paul shows that the whole world is unrighteous in God's sight, and therefore in need of salvation. In Romans 1:18-32 Paul describes how the Gentile world has turned away from God and embraced idolatry. The details in the passage may indicate that Paul is using the Greco-Roman culture surrounding his readers, as a case in point. Pagan and humanistic society faces God's wrath because it has suppressed the truth that God has revealed about Himself in creation (verses 18-20). Paul then illustrates how this has happened. He gives three examples of how what has been known about God has been exchanged for something else. They exchanged the glory of God for images of creatures (verse 23). They exchanged the truth of God for a lie, worshipping created things, i.e., the human form and mind (verse 25). And they rejected the knowledge of God (verse 28), exchanging "natural" relations for "unnatural" ones:

> "For this reason, God gave them up to dishonourable passions. For their women exchanged natural relations for those that are contrary to nature; and the men likewise gave up natural relations with women and were consumed with passion for one another, men committing shameless acts with men and receiving in themselves the due penalty for their error." (Romans 1:26,27)

Two important truths are apparent from these verses:

1. Homosexual desire is not what God originally intended.

This does not mean that homosexual desire is the only thing that God did not originally intend. All of our desires have the capacity to be distorted by sin. Paul describes both lesbian and male homosexual behaviour as "unnatural".

Some have argued that this refers to what is "natural" to the people themselves – heterosexual people engaging in homosexual activity and thereby going against their "natural" orientation. According to this view, Paul is not condemning all homosexual behaviour, but only that which goes against the person's own sexual inclinations. But this view cannot be supported by the passage itself. The words for "natural" and "against nature" refer not to our subjective experience of what feels natural to us, but to the fixed way of things in creation. The "nature" that Paul says homosexual behaviour contradicts, refers to God's purpose for us, revealed in creation and reiterated throughout scripture. Paul's reference to male and female homosexual conduct supports the idea that he is condemning all homosexual activity, and not just the Pederastic (man-boy) relationships that occurred in Roman culture.

The strength of Paul's language should not make us think that homosexual conduct is the worst, or only form of sinful behaviour. Paul may be highlighting it because it is a particularly vivid example, or because it was especially relevant for his readers in Rome given their cultural context. Either way it illustrates something that is the case for all of us: as we reject God, we find ourselves craving what we are not naturally designed to do. Even those desiring heterosexual sex find themselves doing so in a way that does not fully accord with the Creator's design for sex. There are no grounds in this passage for singling out homosexual people for any kind of special condemnation. The same passage indicts all of us.

2. Distorted desires are a sign that we have turned away from God.

Paul writes that alongside the Gospel, "The wrath of God is being revealed from heaven against all ungodliness and unrighteousness of men" (Romans 1:18). Though there will one day be a "day of wrath when God's righteous judgement will be revealed" (Romans 2:5), there is already a present-day expression of God's anger against sin. We see God's wrath in this: He gives us what we want. In response to the exchanges Paul has described, we see three instances of God giving societies over to live in the wreckage of our sinful desires. This is His present-day judgement against sin. We ask for a reality without Him and He gives us a taste of it.

In each case the "giving over" results in an intensification of the sin and the further breakdown of human behaviour. God gives humanity over to impure lusts and dishonourable bodily conduct (Romans 1:24), and to "dishonourable passions" (verse 26). The exchanging of natural relations for unnatural leads to being given over to a "debased mind" and the flourishing of "all manner of unrighteousness" which Paul unpacks in a long list of antisocial behaviours (verse 28-31). Sin leads to judgement, but judgement also leads to further sin.

The presence of all these sinful acts is a reminder that we live in a world that has deliberately turned away from God in all sorts of ways and is therefore experiencing a foretaste of God's anger and courting its final outpouring on the day of judgement.

It is important to recognise that Paul is talking here in social rather than individual terms. He is describing what happens to society as a whole – rather than of particular individuals. The presence of same-sex desire is not an indication that we have turned from God more than others; it is a sign that humanity as a whole has done so. It is not the only sign, but it is a sign that human nature has been changed from what God originally intended.

"Or do you not know that the unrighteous will not inherit the kingdom of God? Do not be deceived: neither the sexually immoral, nor idolaters, nor adulterers, nor men who practise homosexuality, nor thieves, nor the greedy, nor drunkards,

nor revilers, nor swindlers will inherit the kingdom of God."
(1 Corinthians 6:9,10)

In these verses Paul describes different kinds of people who (unless they repent) will be excluded from the kingdom of God. Four kinds relate to sexual sin, and two of those specifically to homosexual behaviour. The ESV takes the latter and puts them together as "men who practise homosexuality", while the NIV translates them as "male prostitutes and homosexual offenders".

The first of the words relating to homosexuality is *malakos*, which translated literally means "soft ones". In classical literature it could be used as a pejorative term for men who were effeminate, for the younger, passive partner in a pederastic relationship, or to refer to male prostitutes (hence the NIV's translation). In 1 Corinthians 6, *malakos* comes in a list describing general forms of sexual sin, and the context suggests Paul is probably using it in a broad way to refer to the passive partners in homosexual intercourse. The second word Paul uses is *arsenokoites*. This word is made by adding *arsen* (male) to *koite* literally "bed" and hence intercourse. These two words are used in the Septuagint translation of Leviticus 18:22 and 20:13, which suggests that Paul is linking back to those two passages. (Paul has already just made a connection with Leviticus in 1 Corinthians 5, where he condemns their acceptance of a man living with his father's wife using language that echoes Leviticus 18:7,8. For Paul, the sexual sins that Leviticus prohibits remain forbidden for New Testament Christians.) *Arsenokoites*, then, is a general term for male-male intercourse. Its pairing with *malakos* indicates that Paul is addressing both the active and passive partners in homosexual intercourse.

The unmistakeable conclusion is that homosexual sin is serious. Active unrepentant sinners (including those actively involved in same-sex relationships) will not enter God's kingdom. Paul urges us not to be deceived on this point. He assumes there will be those who deny this teaching and argue that some forms of homosexual conduct are acceptable to God. But Paul is clear – homosexual conduct leads people to destruction in God's eyes. This is a serious issue.

In 1 Timothy Paul writes:

> "The law is not laid down for the just but for the lawless and disobedient, for the ungodly and sinners, for the unholy and profane, for those who strike their fathers and mothers, for murderers, for the sexually immoral, men who practise homosexuality, enslavers, liars, perjurers, and whatever else is contrary to sound doctrine." (1 Timothy 1:9,10)

He again uses the term *arsenokoites* (translated by the ESV as "men who practise homosexuality" as a catch-all term for all forms of homosexual conduct). Also, in common with the list in 1 Corinthians, same-sex intercourse is mentioned among other wide-ranging sins, non-sexual as well as sexual.

These forms of behaviour characterise those who are not "just" and for whom the law was given, in order to bring conviction of sin and the need for mercy. All these practices contradict "sound doctrine" and the Gospel. They do not conform to the life Christians are now to lead. They go against the grain of the new identity we have in Christ.

Attempts to read these texts as anything other than prohibitions of homosexual behaviour do not ultimately work. The plain reading of each passage is the right one. It is homosexual practice in general, rather than only certain expressions of it, which are forbidden in scripture. To attempt to demonstrate otherwise is to violate the passages themselves. These very same texts list homosexuality alongside many other forms of behaviour that are also against God's will. The very passages that show us that homosexual activity is a sin, make it very clear that it is not a unique sin. It is one example of what is wrong with all of us.

What if I feel uncertain or confused whether I am a male or female?

This question has largely to do with what is now termed "gender identity". Before attempting an answer, it will be helpful to define some current biological and psychological terms:

- *Primary sex characteristics* – The internal and external reproductive organs.

- *Secondary sex characteristics* – Non-reproductive physical differences between sexes that appear during puberty, such as body shape, voice pitch and hair distribution.

- *Biological sex* – The structural and functional characteristics of a person that underlie assignment as either male or female. It is determined by a person's chromosomes, hormones, primary and (to a much lesser extent) secondary sex characteristics.

- *Assigned sex* – The sex assigned to us at birth usually based on primary sex characteristics.

- *Intersex* – A general term that covers a range of rare and complex disorders resulting in ambiguity with respect to biological sex. These people either have genetic abnormalities, sexual characteristics that do not fit with medical norms for male and female bodies and / or sexual characteristics that do not match their genetic makeup.

- *Gender* – In the past the terms "biological sex" and "gender" have often been used interchangeably. Even today drawing a distinction between them is not universal. Where a distinction is made, however, gender is often intended to emphasise the social and cultural, as opposed to the biological, distinctions between the sexes. As such, the term usually encompasses the psychological, social and cultural aspects of being male or female.

- **Gender identity** – The way individuals perceive themselves and wish to name and identify themselves.

- **Gender expression** – The psychological and social aspects of how masculinity and femininity are presented in things like dress, demeanour, social roles and conventions and other cultural gender norms.

- **Gender incongruence** – The mismatch an individual feels as a result of a discrepancy between their gender identity and their assigned sex.

- **Gender dysphoria** – Dysphoria is the opposite of euphoria. Gender dysphoria refers to the distress experienced by people with gender incongruence. Some people with gender dysphoria have a strong desire to live according to their gender identity, rather than their assigned sex.

- **Gender bending** – The intentional crossing, bending or blending of accepted gender roles or behaviours, by adopting the dress, mannerisms or behaviours of the alternative gender (often referred to as transvestitism), or through the attempt to obscure one's gender or to appear as neither gender or both at the same time.

- **Transgender** – people whose gender identity differs from their biological sex (to varying degrees), and who seek to express the difference through gender bending, and / or cross-hormone therapy, and / or 'sex reassignment surgery'. The term transsexual is sometimes used interchangeably with transgender, though sometimes only of those who seek medical assistance to transition.

As is evident from the number of definitions there has been a rise in awareness and discussion on the issue of gender identity. It is a fact that for various reasons, some people experience a mismatch between their biological sex and their psychological sense of gender identity.

The development of modern "Gender Theory" argues that gender is not binary (limited to male and female) but that gender occurs on a broad spectrum; that gender is not fixed, but fluid. This is being promoted as both the justification for choosing one's own gender identity and the explanation of and the appropriate response to gender uncertainty and confusion.

We should be guided by God's word and its teaching on creation, including the ideas of corruption and disorder as a result of the human fall into sin, our redemption through Christ and the hope of salvation contained in the Gospel.

What does scripture say?

- "Then God said, 'Let us make man in our image, after our likeness' ... So God created man in his own image, in the image of God he created him; male and female he created them" (Genesis 1:26,27).

- "When God created man, he made him in the likeness of God. Male and female he created them, and he blessed them and named them Man when they were created" (Genesis 5:1,2).

- "Have you not read that he who created them from the beginning made them male and female" (Matthew 19:4).

The implication of these verses is clear: God intended and created only two sexes. The Biblical account of creation teaches that God has created each human being as either male or female. There is no room to consider male and female as two extremes at either end of a broad continuum, or to consider those with an intersex condition as additional sexes.

This male-ness and female-ness as revealed in Genesis 1,2 is not just a physical characteristic of the bodies of the man and the woman, but a part of their nature as beings made in the image and likeness of God. Man is intimately connected to the woman who is flesh of his flesh (Genesis 2:23), and to whom he holds fast (Genesis 2:24) and with whom he shares the responsibility of ruling the world under God (Genesis 1:28). Likewise, the woman's identity and purpose as God's image-bearer is intimately connected to the man, out of whom she is taken (Genesis 2:23), and whom she helps in their mutual task of care and procreation (Genesis 1:28; 2:20,21). The male-ness of Adam makes no sense without the female-ness of Eve as his counterpart, and vice versa. Each is defined in distinction from, but in relation to the other. The male and female reality of human sexuality revealed in Genesis 1 is both emphasised and developed in Genesis 2. Here we move from humanity being described in terms of the adjectival nouns "male" and "female" which are not unique to humans but also apply to animals (e.g., Genesis 6:19) to the nouns "man / husband" and "woman / wife".

"Therefore a man [ish] shall leave his father and his mother and hold fast to his wife [isha], and they shall become one flesh. And the man [adam] and his wife [isha] were both naked and were not ashamed." (Genesis 2:24,25)

The implication of this, contrary to current "Gender Theory", is that biological sex is inseparable from both gender identity and gender roles. Human males grow into men (and potentially husbands and fathers) and human females grow into women (and potentially wives and mothers). This is, once again, confirmed by Jesus, as he brings Genesis 1 and 2 into the closest possible connection.

"But from the beginning of creation, God made them male and female. Therefore a man will leave his father and mother and hold fast to his wife, and the two shall become one flesh." (Mark 10:6-8)

The implication is once again clear: men and women are not two poles at either end of a gender spectrum. Gender, like sex, and because it is an extension of sex is therefore only male or female.

However, in the reality of a post-Fall world, it is clear that human sexuality and gender identity are not straightforward. Clearly this is the case for some, and to some degree, for everyone. The Bible has much to say about the effects of the fall on every aspect of our humanity, including our sexual expression and gender identity. Sin and death have impacted every part of human existence and the whole created order has been subjected to frustration (Romans 8:20). Consequently, various forms of disease, disorder and disability are part of human experience. Things go wrong with us not only physiologically (with respect to our bodies) but psychologically (with respect to our minds) relationally and behaviourally.

One of the ways that the Bible acknowledges the reality of physiological sexual disability is by introducing us to the category of the eunuch – a term which generally referred to a castrated or otherwise impotent male. It is interesting to note that the eunuchs of scripture are all presented as male (as is indicated by the use of masculine words to describe them) but are unable to function sexually or reproductively (see Esther 2:3,14,15; Isaiah 56:3), either because of a birth defect or due to human interference. Following his discussion of the nature of marriage and the legitimate grounds for divorce, Jesus distinguishes between three types of eunuchs: two literal and one spiritual.

"For there are eunuchs, who have been so from birth, and there are eunuchs who have been made eunuchs by men, and there are eunuchs who have made themselves eunuchs for the sake of the kingdom of heaven. Let the one who is able to receive this receive it." (Matthew 19:12)

Jesus' first two categories were no doubt physical eunuchs whether made so by accident or design. Most likely, the first of these categories would have included conditions that today would be regarded as intersex. The Bible resists expanding sex

/ gender beyond male and female, even though some do not fit neatly into it. Scripture nowhere presents eunuchs as an additional sex. The words of Jesus, "let the one who is able to receive this receive it" suggest we should be careful not to judge these people too harshly.

But what about those whose bodily sex is obvious, and yet who claim to have been born in the wrong body; such as a male who is convinced he is a woman or a female who is convinced she is a man? How should we think about such a condition? Notwithstanding the fact that all kinds of things can and do go wrong with us psychologically, the Bible does not allow for the idea that one can actually be a man trapped in a woman's body or a woman trapped in a man's body. That may well be a person's subjective feeling, but it is not an objective fact. The Bible is also clear in its condemnation of a number of behaviours that would fall into the definition of "gender bending".

The first of these behaviours is that of cross-dressing, which is directly prohibited in Deuteronomy 22:

> "A woman shall not wear a man's garment, nor shall a man put on a woman's cloak, for whoever does these things is an abomination to the LORD your God." (verse 5)

There can be little doubt that this text condemns cross-dressing in the strongest terms. This is clear from the use of the word "abomination" that we explored when considering homosexuality. But why should cross-dressing be seen in such a light and condemned in such terms? It may have been to prevent licentiousness, or to oppose idolatrous practices but fundamentally it was to maintain the sanctity of that distinction of the sexes which was established by the creation of man and woman, and in relation to which Israel was not to sin. Therefore, while care is needed in applying old covenant commands to our situation under the new covenant, the abiding ethical principle behind Deuteronomy 22:5 is straightforward. This injunction seeks to preserve the order built into creation, specifically the fundamental distinction between male and female.

The second of the behaviours that scripture condemns is sexual effeminacy; that is, a man playing the part of a woman (by being the 'receiver') in homosexual intercourse. Paul's reference in 1 Corinthians 6:9 to the *malakos* therefore, is aimed at those who actively feminise themselves by (and for the purposes of) playing a passive homosexual role. See the previous answer for a more detailed consideration.

The third of the behaviours that the Bible opposes is gender ambiguity. That is, the attempt to blur the lines between man and woman by one's gender expression. This is Paul's concern in 1 Corinthians 11 and he challenges his readers accordingly:

> "Every man who prays or prophesies with his head covered dishonours his head. But every woman who prays or prophesies with her head uncovered dishonours her head – it is the same as having her head shaved ... Judge for yourselves: Is it proper for a woman to pray to God with her head uncovered? Does not the very nature of things teach you that if a man has long hair it is a disgrace to him, but that if a woman has long hair, it is her glory? For long hair is given to her as a covering."   (1 Corinthians 11:4,5,13-15, NIV)

While there are a number of complexities in the passage in which these verses appear (and we will not explore them here), what is clear is that Paul desires men and women both to maintain and celebrate the gender distinctions that reflect our God-given sex, and not take steps to either deny or diminish them.

The Bible's creation teaching and its post-Fall prohibitions against the abuse and misuse of sex and gender lead to the same conclusion: human beings have been created as either male or female, and it is God's will for us to embrace this even though it can be complex in a sin-cursed world.

We can further conclude that however we categorise the painful experience of gender dysphoria and incongruence – from a Biblical point of view it almost always involves a significant misperception of created reality. However, it is important to emphasise that this does not mean that sufferers of gender incongruence are necessarily responsible for their condition. The critical factor from God's perspective is how one responds to such a condition. Unlike wilful gender bending or deliberate gender erasing which, as we have seen, are clearly prohibited in scripture, the experience of gender dysphoria would seem to be an unsought affliction and, to that extent, a condition for which sufferers are not culpable. Consequently, our first response to those who struggle with their gender identity ought to be compassion and care, not condemnation or censure. The more difficult question is what should a person suffering from gender dysphoria do to resolve it? The Biblical teachings we have reviewed suggest that attempts to obliterate, disguise or live at odds with one's sex / gender are contrary to God's will and against human good. Consequently, any attempt to do so, no matter how well intentioned, is unlikely to bring the lasting relief that sufferers are seeking and may bring them even greater distress.

Does the Bible offer guidance concerning sexual orientation and identity challenges?

Absolutely! The Bible has been written with principles that are applicable to almost every circumstance and these two growing modern issues are comprehensively covered.

All who confess Jesus as Lord and believe in their hearts that God raised him from the dead and are baptized are not only justified from sin but brought to new birth and given a new identity as sons and daughters of the living God. "Therefore", writes Paul, "if anyone is in Christ, he [or she] is a new creation. The old has passed away; behold, the new has come" (2 Corinthians 5:17). This vital, spiritual union is necessarily determinative of a whole new self-understanding. As Paul writes elsewhere: "It is no longer I who live, but Christ who lives in me" (Galatians 2:20). In short, no Christian is what they once were (1 Corinthians 6:11). This new life entails a new lifestyle. Those in Christ are called to "no longer live for themselves but for him who for their sake died and was raised" (2 Corinthians 5:15). This does not mean the removal of all temptations, trials and afflictions in this age, but it does mean there is a new power at work in us to help us:

> "You have put off the old self with its practices and have put on the new self, which is being renewed in knowledge after the image of its creator." (Colossians 3:9,10)

This call to wrestle with our temptations and put them to death has deep implications for what we do with and to our bodies, for the Christian's body is now a temple of God's: "You are not your own," says Paul, "for you were bought with a price. So glorify God in your body" (1 Corinthians 6:19,20).

Such struggle with temptations should never be fought alone. This is one of the reasons why the risen Christ has given his followers the gift of brothers and sisters – not only that we might keep each other accountable, but that we might bear one another's burdens. Paul wrote to the Galatians:

> "Brothers, if anyone is caught in any transgression, you who are spiritual should restore him in a spirit of gentleness. Keep watch on yourself, lest you too be tempted. Bear one another's burdens, and so fulfill the law of Christ." (Galatians 6:1,2)

This text raises the important question: What counts as a "transgression" and what is simply a "burden"? In our view, the experience of gender dysphoria (for example) is a "burden" as might be the urges of homosexuality. Consequently, there is a need for ecclesias to be able to cope with the disclosure of these issues by those who have the courage to share what they are going through. Nevertheless, from a Biblical standpoint, attempts to alleviate the suffering by giving in to sin fall firmly into the category of "transgression".

When sin in these matters takes place, restoration must be in the "spirit of gentleness". A range of factors will need to be taken into account: e.g., whether the person is a believer or a seeker, how old they are, whether they are spiritually mature or immature, what steps they've taken, and whether they have other physical and / or mental health issues. Consequently, the nature and timing of restoration, and the kind of care and counsel required, will vary from person to person. Nevertheless, in light of the teaching of scripture, it is clear that all forms of cross-gender identification and homosexual acts are contrary to God's will and the good of sufferers. Therefore, the goal of restoration will be to work toward an acceptance of God's will for us.

Alongside our concern for the welfare of the person suffering with these problems, there is another important factor to be considered in our response. That is, the impact of the decisions we take or the strategies we adopt upon the ecclesial community. What message is being sent by an ecclesia that effectively condones that which scripture condemns? What effect will this have on other members of the body – particularly those who are vulnerable and impressionable or struggling in other areas of life? Paul's concern, "a little leaven leavens the whole lump of dough" (1 Corinthians 5:6) is relevant here. That said, needlessly imposing rigid gender stereotypes may not be helpful either. Provided believers are operating within accepted Biblical norms and cultural expectations for gender roles and gender expression, not all men and women need to look, dress or act in precisely the same way.

We should have compassion as Christ did to a needy and broken world, and take seriously the deeply personal and confusing thoughts of those who are genuinely struggling with the question, 'Who really am I'?

Having looked at some common threads we will now consider some advice particularly directed towards each of the challenges. Let us first consider homosexuality.

We note that homosexual sin is not uniquely horrid. Paul's list includes other forms of sexual sin (sexual immorality and adultery), and it includes non-sexual forms of sin (drunkenness and theft, for example). Homosexual sin is incredibly serious, but so is greed. We must not imply that homosexual sex is *the* sin of our age. If we are to be faithful to scripture, we must acknowledge theft, greed, drunkenness, reviling, and defrauding others, also characterise the unrighteous.

Homosexual sin is not inescapable. Paul wrote to the Corinthians:

"Such were some of you. But you were washed, you were sanctified, you were justified in the name of the Lord Jesus Christ and by the Spirit of God." (1 Corinthians 6:11)

These forms of behaviour are not appropriate for the ecclesia of Jesus Christ, precisely because it is not who we are any more. Clearly, some of the Corinthians had been active homosexuals. They did once live in these ways – but no more. They have been washed, sanctified and justified; forgiven, cleansed from their sins, and set apart for God. They have a new standing and identity before Him.

However ingrained it may be in someone's behaviour, homosexual conduct is not inevitable. It is possible for someone living a practising gay lifestyle to be made new by God. Temptations and feelings may well linger. That Paul is warning his readers not to revert to their former way of life suggests there is still some desire to do so. But in Christ we are no longer who we were. Those who have come out of an active gay lifestyle need to understand how to see themselves. What defined us then no longer defines us now.

The passages we considered concerning homosexuality should be read in the context of the wider teaching on sexuality in the Bible. We can only fully understand the goodness of the Biblical teaching on homosexuality when we appreciate God's design for sex within marriage, the design for community, the provision of non-sexual intimacy and ultimately transforming us into spirit beings.

To this we would add the crucial observation that, here as elsewhere in the Christian life, the example and commandment of Christ places us under obligation to proclaim both God's truth *and* His redemptive grace. We must "speak the truth in love" (Ephesians 4:15). There is no place for hatred, hurtful comments, or other forms of rejection toward those who experience same-sex attraction. Rather there should be understanding and patient grace that they will see the way to make right choices for Christ's sake despite their strong feelings – as we pray God does for us all.

How should we consider gender identity struggles? We have seen that the basic claims of "Gender Theory" are false and the goal of sex change is unrealisable. In light of the Bible's teaching, gender dysphoria (and the incongruence lying behind it) is best regarded as a psychiatric disorder. In other words, despite what is sometimes claimed, there is no reason to believe that a person can have either the brain of one sex, and the body of the other. Rather, it is a psychological pathology and, as such, one of the tragic effects of the Fall. Such clarity may do little, in and of itself, to alleviate the distress of those who suffer from gender incongruence. This is why responding compassionately and constructively to such felt experiences remains a paramount concern of the Christian community. The conclusions we have reached lay some important foundations upon which to build a Biblically informed and medically responsible pastoral and therapeutic approach.

Among the vices of the "old self" that all believers are called to discard are covetousness (Colossians 3:5) and falsehood (Ephesians 4:25). These sins are particularly pertinent to the subject at hand. Many who struggle with gender identity issues are sorely tempted to desire a body other than the one they have been given. That is covetousness. Likewise, the aim of those who seek to transition gender, is to pass themselves off as being different from what they actually are. This is falsehood. We appreciate that the person who is convinced they are 'in the wrong body' may wish to argue that their longing for a different body, or their attempts to disguise or change their body, are driven by a desire to present their "true selves". Our argument is that the physical body reveals the 'true self'. Such vices must be "put off". They are the opposites of contentment and truthfulness, and they undermine godly relationships. Consequently, faithfulness to Christ cannot be separated from how a person with gender incongruence manages their condition.

As there are vices to be "put off", so there are virtues that believers are called to "put on". Four are of special relevance to our subject: endurance, patience, joy and thanksgiving. The development of such Christlike characteristics is repeatedly encouraged in scripture. But these four are brought together in Colossians 1, where the Apostle Paul speaks of believers:

"Being strengthened with all power, according to his glorious might, for all endurance and patience with joy; giving thanks to the Father, who has qualified you to share in the inheritance of the saints in light." (verses 11,12)

Endurance and patience are vital for sufferers of gender incongruence, particularly for those whose cross-gender identification is strong and persistent. The distress caused by such a condition can be very painful, and the force of the temptation to alleviate it in destructive ways, very real. The battle to be faithful can therefore be exhausting. However, resistance and obedience are possible, and much prayer is needed that strength be given to this end. But, more than that, joy and thanksgiving are also possible – perhaps not for the affliction itself, but for the sufficiency of God's grace (2 Corinthians 12:9) and the fruit that suffering inevitably bears under the wise and sovereign hand of God (see Romans 5:3-5; James 1:2-4).

The final piece of scriptural teaching relevant to our question has to do with what is revealed about the nature of our resurrected bodies. Admittedly, there is much we cannot know on this score (1 Corinthians 15:35,36). Nevertheless, in broad terms, the Bible affirms a principle of both continuity and transformation (1 Corinthians 15:42-44). That is, following the pattern of Jesus' own resurrection, it is *this* earthly body that will be raised, but with different qualities and capacities. Christ, "will transform our lowly body to be like his glorious body" (Philippians 3:21). Curiously, the prospect of transformation has led some to speculate about the possibility of our being raised as either androgynous, monosexual or asexual beings. Given that our bodies in this world are sexed, and that the risen Jesus remains a man (see Acts 17:31), it would require a very clear statement of scripture to create the expectation that we will be raised as something other than sexed (and therefore gendered) beings. Certainly, when read in context, Galatians 3:28 teaches no such thing, nor does 1 Corinthians 6:13-15,30. Far from suggesting that sexual distinctions disappear in Christ, the first of these passages simply makes the point that one's sex is irrelevant to one's standing in Christ (Galatians 3:26,27). The second affirms, not the destruction of gender, but that our bodies will be raised just as the Lord's body was raised (1 Corinthians 6:14). In being raised, we will, of course, be changed (1 Corinthians 15:51,52), but nowhere does scripture suggest we will be changed from men or women into something else. Rather we will be changed from *mortal* men and women to *immortal* men and women (1 Corinthians 15:53,54). The one passage that some have thought teaches that we will be raised as asexual is where Jesus says, "For in the resurrection neither do they marry nor are they given in marriage but are like the angels in heaven" (Matthew 22:30). This passage clearly affirms that marriage, having served its purpose, belongs only to this age, but it says nothing about the elimination of human sexual distinctions.

The glorious prospect of bodily resurrection has two important implications. First, whatever disappointments and disabilities we may have to deal with in this life, it matters what we do with and to the bodies God has given us. In fact, even though Christians should be willing to spend and be spent in the cause of our Master, we are nonetheless to love our bodies. As Paul said, "no one ever hated his own flesh, but nourishes and cherishes it, just as Christ does the church" (Ephesians 5:29). What we do with our bodies is significant. The tragedy of self-rejection and self-mutilation needs to be seen in this light. This may well be an act of desperation, but it is also an assault upon the body and so ultimately sinful. The intensity of the struggle and the temptation to think about ourselves in ways other than those God encourages and directs in His word does not convey legitimacy upon such responses. Instead, we are called upon to take comfort in the Saviour who knows our weaknesses and is able not only to sympathise with them but to provide "grace to help in time of need" (Hebrews 4:16).

Secondly, in the resurrection at the last day, every form of disease, disorder, sickness and sadness will be healed and banished once and for all (Revelation 21:4). In fact, so wonderful will be the glory revealed both to us and in us that the sufferings of this present time will not be worth comparing with it (Romans

8:18). This is good news for all of God's people, but particularly for those whose gender incongruence proves irresolvable in this life. We have a real hope that will not disappoint us. This is why we are called to wait for it with patience (Romans 8:25), fixing our eyes not on what is seen and transient but on what is unseen and eternal (2 Corinthians 4:18).

The greatest need of those who experience gender dysphoria or who identify as transgender or have undergone sex reassignment procedures is not for their identity issues to be resolved (as wonderful as that would be), or their attempts at transitioning to be reversed (which may not be possible), but to be reconciled to God and adopted as His beloved children. In other words, like the rest of us, they too need the Gospel of Jesus Christ. Every human being has been created for Jesus Christ (Colossians 1:16) and will therefore be restless in heart unless and until they find their rest in him. Rest is precisely what Jesus promises to all who come to him in faith (Matthew 11:28) – irrespective of their past sins or present afflictions. This is the hope of the Gospel: that true life, lasting peace and eternal comfort can be found in Jesus Christ.

Why did God need a human sacrifice?

To modern minds the idea of human sacrifice is distasteful and reminiscent of pagan idolatry. What reason could God have in requiring the death of Jesus as a sacrifice?

We have already mentioned how much God hates sin because of its destructive consequences on people and His creation. When Adam sinned and as a result of sin entering the world God laid down a principle that sin could only be covered, atoned for and forgiven His way. And that way was through the shedding or spilling of blood. In the Bible, blood represents life – because if it is taken from an animal or human, life ends.

"For the life of the flesh is in the blood, and I have given it for you on the altar to make atonement for your souls, for it is the blood that makes atonement by the life."

(Leviticus 17:11)

God provided a covering for Adam and Eve's nakedness. In the Bible nakedness represents the guilt and shame that comes from sin. In the process of giving its skin for a covering the animal gave up its own life. "And the LORD God made for Adam and for his wife garments of skins and clothed them" (Genesis 3:21). This demonstrated to Adam and Eve the serious consequence of their sin – death; and that forgiveness and life could only come through the shedding of blood. Under the old covenant as described in the Law of Moses the repeated sacrifice of thousands of animals was a constant reminder of sin. We know from the teaching of Jesus and the apostles that these animals only taught principles of salvation; they were only a shadow of the reality that was Jesus Christ.

"For since the law has but a shadow of the good things to come instead of the true form of these realities, it can never, by the same sacrifices that are continually offered every year, make perfect those who draw near." (Hebrews 10:1)

Jesus Christ was a perfect man morally who totally obeyed God and never sinned. His sinless life can be credited to those who believe in his saving work. The ultimate obedience and sacrifice that Jesus had to make was to die as a sacrifice for the sin of the world.

"The next day he [John the Baptist] saw Jesus coming toward him, and said, 'Behold, the Lamb of God, who takes away the sin of the world!'" (John 1:29)

We can share in Jesus' perfect life, death and resurrection when we understand, believe and are baptized into his saving name.

Paul said:

"God has done what the law, weakened by the flesh, could not do. By sending his own Son in the likeness of sinful flesh and for sin, he condemned sin in the flesh." (Romans 8:3)

This means that no weak human was able to keep God's law. Everybody sinned and came up short – well short of perfect obedience to God. God looked at every human in all His creation and saw and knew that there was no one who could fulfil His righteous requirements for the way of salvation to be opened to us. So God sent His own Son conceived by the Holy Spirit in Mary, sharing in the effects of sin, and ultimately defeating it by his perfect obedience to his Father's will and in doing so is able to save us from our sins (Matthew 1:21).

The Apostle Paul gave a number of detailed explanations for the death of Christ. Consider the following from the letter to the Romans:

"For all have sinned and fall short of the glory of God, and are justified by his grace as a gift, through the redemption that is in Christ Jesus, whom God put forward as a propitiation [meeting place] by his blood, to be received by faith. This was to show God's righteousness, because in his divine forbearance he had passed over former sins. It was to show his righteousness at the present time, so that he might be just and the justifier of the one who has faith in Jesus." (Romans 3:23-26)

This particularly reinforces that it was right for Jesus to die in that way.

In the letter to the Hebrews this process is explained in considerable detail:

"But we see him who for a little while was made lower than the angels, namely Jesus, crowned with glory and honour because of the suffering of death, so that by the grace of God he might taste death for everyone. For it was fitting that he, for whom and by whom all things exist, in bringing many sons to glory, should make the founder of their salvation perfect through suffering. For he who sanctifies and those who are sanctified all have one source. That is why he is not ashamed to call them brothers, saying, 'I will tell of your name to my brothers; in the midst of the congregation I will sing your praise.' And again, 'I will put my trust in him.' And again, 'Behold, I and the children God has given me.' Since therefore the children share in flesh and blood, he himself likewise partook of the same things, that through death he might destroy the one who has the power of death, that is, the devil, and deliver all those who through fear of death were subject to lifelong slavery. For surely it is not angels that he helps, but he helps the offspring of Abraham. Therefore he had to be made like his brothers in every respect, so that he might become a merciful and faithful high priest in the service of God, to make propitiation for the sins of the people. For because he himself has suffered when tempted, he is able to help those who are being tempted."

(Hebrews 2:9-18)

What was special about Jesus' death? He gave up his sinless life as a willing sacrifice, thus fulfilling God's righteous requirement in condemning and destroying sin in human flesh. What happened to Jesus showed that God is just and right in His condemnation of sin. He suffered at the hands of an evil world that was bent on rebellion against the grace and truth of God revealed in Jesus and a world that preferred darkness to light. Jesus during his mortal life had the same nature as us, that is a nature that is subject to death and having a bias to temptation and sin. Yet Jesus lived a perfect life of obedience to God despite bearing our nature. So, when he was crucified sin was defeated and destroyed in him. Because Jesus was sinless, God in His righteousness raised him from the dead. And so Jesus has become the captain of our salvation. We look to him in faith and by the symbolic act of baptism we identify ourselves with what Jesus did in his life, death and resurrection and we can share in his victory over sin and death.

The significance of baptism is explained by the Apostle Paul in writing to the Romans:

"Do you not know that all of us who have been baptized into Christ Jesus were baptized into his death? We were buried therefore with him by baptism into death, in order that, just as Christ was raised from the dead by the glory of the Father, we too might walk in newness of life. For if we have been united with him in a death like his, we shall certainly be united with him in a resurrection like his. We know that our old self was crucified with him in order that the body of sin might be brought to nothing, so that we would no longer be enslaved to sin. For one who has died has been set free from sin. Now if we have died with Christ, we believe that we will also live with him. We know that Christ, being raised from the dead, will never die again; death no longer has dominion over him. For the death he died he died to sin, once for all, but the life he lives he lives to God. So you also must consider yourselves dead to sin and alive to God in Christ Jesus." (Romans 6:3-11)

Chapter 12

A final inspiration to faith

W E have endeavoured to answer the questions honestly and in a straightforward way with the revelation of the mind of God through His word as our guide. Along the way we hope to have demonstrated the brilliance of the divine mind in laying down principles suited for life, faith and worship. The Bible has emerged as a reliable and wonderful testimony concerning God and His purpose with us. The answers of scripture are so timeless; its principles so perfectly suited for human existence there can be no uncertainty regarding either scripture or the God who inspired it. But ... the absence of doubt is not the same as the presence of faith. While the case *against* doubt and uncertainty may have been supported, the case *for* faith requires some final summation before we might consider the task complete.

What can inspire us to rise above our weakness and soar to spiritual heights? What can give us such confidence in God so that we may simply and calmly say, 'God said it, I believe it – and that settles it'? Abraham had believed and obeyed (Genesis 12), he had believed in hope (Genesis 15), he learned to believe and trust that God was right (Genesis 18) and finally in Genesis 22 to believe and accept in the most demanding of tests. Abraham came to believe that whatever God did would be just and he said as much to the angel sent to destroy Sodom, "Shall not the Judge of all the earth do what is just?" (Genesis 18:25). It is no surprise that of all men he is acknowledged as the father of the faithful. Abraham was "fully convinced that God was able to do what he had promised" (Romans 4:21). How do we develop that kind of faith? Paul said simply, "faith comes from hearing, and hearing through the word of [about] Christ" (Romans 10:17). While it is, in the end, that simple, it can still be a challenge.

Ultimately the reason for faith is God. Jesus told the amazed disciples, "Have faith in God" (Mark 11:22). This is not so much an instruction to have faith but a direction in which it ought to be exercised. Human inventions may fail us, people may disappoint us, but God will not. We can have a strong faith because it is in a strong God. The strength in that equation is not our faith, but God.

Having been reminded of the obligations of forgiveness (seven times in a day) the disciples unsurprisingly asked Christ to increase their faith. The response from the Lord was probably not what they expected. We (and they) might have thought Jesus would have said, 'to get more faith you need to ...' but he did not. Instead we have the parable of the mustard seed. Jesus said:

"If you had faith like a grain of mustard seed, you could say to this mulberry tree, 'Be uprooted and planted in the sea,' and it would obey you."   (Luke 17:6)

The Lord provides inspiration for faith from the effects of faith. In effect he says that faith can do wonders and with it you will be invincible – not in a physical sense, but spiritually. The knowledge that faith can work wonders is an inspiration to further faith.

When Paul wrote that in the Gospel the righteousness of God is revealed, the purpose stated was "from faith for [KJV, to] faith" (Romans 1:17). The Greek words translated "from" and "for" refer to the starting and finishing points. That is, the Gospel of Christ is the way both to get and perfect faith. We are thus reminded of Jesus the "founder and perfecter of our faith" (Hebrews 12:2). To get greater faith requires the same thing as the origin of faith – the Gospel heard by a good and honest heart. It therefore follows that the more we think on the Gospel the stronger our faith will be. To the Corinthians Paul wrote, "We do not lose heart. Though our outer self is wasting away, our inner self is being renewed day by day" (2 Corinthians 4:16). Renewal of our inner self is only accomplished by reflection on scripture. Growth in faith is thus directly proportional to attention to the Gospel.

Clearly there are degrees of faith and we are expected to grow, but this does not make our initial faith either inferior or different in character. Of Abraham it was said, "he grew strong in his faith as he gave glory to God, fully convinced that God was able to do what he had promised" (Romans 4:20,21). He had the same faith as before but it was now impregnable and unassailable by doubt.

To the Galatians, Paul said the only thing that counts is "faith working through love" (Galatians 5:6). The thing that energises faith is love, and love produces good works. James said that separating faith from works results in a dead faith in the same way that separating breath from a person results in a dead body (see James 2:26). Works of love are intended to animate faith. If our faith does not inspire us to do anything, what is the good of it? If our good deeds are not the product of faith they are merely philanthropy, of benefit to the recipient but of no value to God.

In summary, in order to increase and strengthen our faith we need both to practise it and revisit the basis of scripture on which our faith rests on a regular basis. As we consider scripture over and over, we will reacquaint ourselves with the themes it contains. There are two essential areas that can help increase our faith.

- Consideration of events of the past.

- Prophecies of the future.

These line up broadly with the "assurance of things hoped for [future events], the conviction of things not seen [past events]" as explained in Hebrews 11:1.

The things that God has done from creation forwards, and explained to us in scripture can be very reassuring. For example, God said He created – and we see evidence of that; historians and archaeologists regularly reaffirm the authenticity of scripture, and we can learn of it and be encouraged.

Perhaps the greatest and most easily accessible testimony comes from prophecy. Unlike other prophetical writings (e.g., those of Nostradamus) the prophecies of scripture are detailed, specific and often require little interpretation (Daniel 2 is a tremendous example). This means that when the prophecy is read, we can readily gain a boost to our faith. This is exactly the sense of the words of Jesus when he explained to the disciples that he would depart into heaven, "I am going to the Father ... I have told you before it takes place, so that when it does take place you may believe" (John 14:28,29). A few verses earlier Jesus had promised, "if I go ... I will come again" (verse 3). Thus, belief is not just in the credibility of the words of Jesus regarding his departure but also of his return. There is every cause to have confidence in Jesus' return because half of the prophecy has already been fulfilled. The Apostle Peter valued this very highly and so he wrote, "we have the prophetic word more fully confirmed, to which you will do well to pay attention" (2 Peter 1:19). While it is true that some prophecies are yet to be completely realised, many have been completely fulfilled and others have seen an incipient fulfilment; these give us confidence that we are not following "cleverly devised myths" but the accurate testimony of God.

When feelings of doubt and uncertainty assault our minds we can rest confident in an eternal, unmoveable and righteous God. When we cannot make sense of our world we are comforted that He can. When the way seems dark we can trust in the light of His word. When we believe, He can help our unbelief.

Scripture index